T0329461

KINGS AND THEIR SONS

KINGS AND THEIR SONS

IN EARLY MODERN EUROPE

MARK KONNERT

Algora Publishing
New York

Library of Congress Cataloging-in-Publication Data —

Names: Konnert, Mark, 1957- author.
Title: Kings and their sons in early modern Europe / Mark Konnert.
Description: New York: Algora Publishing, 2018. | Includes bibliographical
    references and index. | Royal Families — "We Shall Find Some Other Prince
    of the Blood Who Will Serve Us Better": Louis XI and Charles VII — "Not
    as a father, but as a king": Philip II and Don Carlos — "Unworthy of the
    name of son": Peter the Great and Tsarevich Alexei — "A Monster and the
    Greatest Villain that Ever was Born": George I and George II — "Such a
    Wretch No Longer Deserves to Live": Frederick William I and Frederick the
    Great.
Identifiers: LCCN 2018035200| ISBN 9781628943573 (soft cover: alk. paper) |
    ISBN 9781628943580 (hard cover: alk. paper)
Subjects: LCSH: Europe—Kings and rulers—Family relationships—History. |
    Europe—Kings and rulers—Succession—History. | Inheritance and
    succession—Europe—History. | Princes—Crimes against—Europe—History. |
    Murder—Europe—History.
Classification: LCC D107 .K664 2018 | DDC 940.2092/2—dc23 LC record available at
https://lccn.loc.gov/2018035200

Printed in the United States

Acknowledgements

I first began to work on this book more than a decade ago. It was my aim to produce something that would be of interest to an audience broader than professional historians and university students, but I soon discovered some of the pitfalls awaiting the academic who tries to appeal to a broader public, and I am grateful to Algora Publishing for this opportunity to carry this project through. This book has its genesis in my undergraduate teaching as I recounted these stories to my students, and I am grateful to them for their responses and encouragement. Most of all, however, I am grateful to my own family: my wife, Candace, and my children Heidi and Sam. Researching the myriad ways in which family members can turn on each other has served as continual reminder of my own good fortune and reinforced my gratitude to my own parents, Bill and Ileen Konnert, to whom this book is dedicated.

Table of Contents

INTRODUCTION

Over the course of almost thirty years of teaching early modern European history (roughly 1500–1800) to university students, I was struck by how frequently I related the stories of kings and their eldest sons and heirs who did not get along, often to the point of open hostility, rebellion, warfare, imprisonment, and torture.

Several cases are relatively well known. Tsar Peter I or Peter the Great of Russia (reigned 1682–1725) had his son Alexei imprisoned and tortured before being sentenced to death. Whether Peter would actually have had his son executed remains a moot point, since Alexei died in prison before the issue came to a head. King Philip II of Spain (reigned 1556–1598), along with a group of armed companions burst into the bedchamber of his eldest son and heir Don Carlos in 1567 and had him whisked away to solitary confinement where he died a short time later under circumstances that some contemporaries found mysterious and suspicious. And in perhaps the most famous case of all, Crown Prince Frederick of Prussia (later King Frederick II or Frederick the Great, reigned 1740–1786) was physically and psychologically abused by his father, King Frederick William I (reigned 1713–1740). So distraught was the young prince that he tried to escape his brutal father's abuse by fleeing the country with his best friend, a fellow army officer. They were apprehended and tried for desertion and treason. Frederick's friend was in fact beheaded, in the presence of the young prince. (His father compelled his attendance at the grisly event, and Frederick avoided witnessing it only by falling into a dead faint.) There was a real possibility that Frederick too might follow his friend to the scaffold before his father relented.

Besides these three famous examples, there are many others. In fact, tensions between rulers and their heirs (not just sons, although that was usually the case with hereditary monarchies) were more the rule than the exception. Indeed, these famous cases really represent an extreme of the normal state of affairs, rather than extraordinary or unusual occurrences. They are different in degree, not kind. In this study, I will discuss not only these three famous cases but two others, less well known perhaps, but equally interesting and telling. As Dauphin (the heir to the French throne was known as the Dauphin), King Louis XI (reigned 1460–1483) feuded bitterly with his father, King Charles VII (reigned 1425–1460). Isolated from power, denied the traditional roles of the heir to the throne, belittled and humiliated, young Louis participated in an armed rebellion against his father, and then took refuge with his father's bitterest foe and greatest rival, the Duke of Burgundy. As Prince of Wales, the future King George II of England (reigned 1727–1760) publicly opposed the policies of his father, King George I (reigned 1714–1727), was banished from the royal court, and had his access to his own children severely restricted by his father.

In exploring this topic further, I was astonished to discover that no one had ever treated it in a systematic way. These incidents were treated as lurid episodes of political infighting and family rivalry but were then cast aside as historians got on with the real business of telling their stories. This book, then, is designed to do several things. First, I wanted to tell the stories of these sad and sometimes tragic confrontations in a comparative perspective, with an eye to outlining their similarities and differences, as well as putting them in the context of their respective times and places. History is anything but boring. That applies not only to stories about royalty, but also about leaders in politics, industry, and entertainment. I make no apologies for telling stories that I hope readers will find interesting and moving. Beyond that, however, I hope to use the stories to illuminate aspects of a past society which are not perhaps immediately apparent to us in the 21st century. What do the similarities and differences in these episodes tell us about the nature of monarchy and government in this period? About family life? About society at large?

Conflicts between rulers and their heirs were certainly not new to the early modern period, nor are they uniquely European, nor indeed have they ceased. In Old Testament Israel, Absalom launched a rebellion against his father King David, only to die in the process. In the Middle Ages, King Henry II of England feuded famously not only with his wife, the irrepressible Eleanor of Aquitaine, but with his three sons, events made famous in the play and movie *The Lion in Winter*. Why should we limit our scope to the early modern period in European history?

First, the source materials for the earlier periods are extremely scarce and limited. Illiteracy was the norm rather than the exception, even among the elites of society. The passage of time has resulted in some sources disappearing forever. For earlier periods, we are very often limited to a few scraps of gossip, hearsay at second, third, or fourth-hand. For example, we know that Tsar Ivan the Terrible of Russia (reigned 1533–1584) in a fit of rage killed his eldest son and heir Dmitri. We are, however, almost entirely ignorant of their relationship and the events that resulted in Dmitri's death. In the cases we are examining here, on the other hand, source materials are much more numerous. Government records are more plentiful and detailed, letters have survived, not only those of the principals, but of contemporary witnesses, and foreign ambassadors related their observations to their own governments. All of these source materials present their own difficulties in interpretation, but they possess the great virtue of actually being available.

Second, by the early modern period in European history, governments had amassed more control over their territories and their subjects than ever before. Though still in their infancy, bureaucratic structures were being differentiated from the person and household of the ruler. Regular and specialized institutions, staffed by trained professionals, were taking over the business of government from the handful of strongmen and cronies who surrounded the king. At the same time that governments were centralizing their power over their territories and subjects, in most countries rulers were increasingly asserting their control over their governments. This phenomenon, known as royal absolutism, was never perfected or completed, but it is undeniable that in most countries kings were asserting greater control over their governments than ever before in European history. It is, however, extremely important that we not confuse this development with twentieth or 21st century notions of totalitarianism. Everyone acknowledged (even kings and their courtiers) that there were limits to rulers' powers. They could not transgress against divine or natural law. They could not arbitrarily deprive their subjects of their lives or property. No European ruler could legitimately cry "Off with his head!" and expect his order to be obeyed. What these two developments — centralization and absolutism — mean for our purposes is that to an unprecedented degree in European history, the actions of kings and their courts affected the lives of ordinary people. Whatever happened at the courts of King David or Henry II had virtually no impact on the everyday lives of their subjects, who continued ploughing their fields, reaping their harvests, marrying and having children, and dying as they had for generations. Now, in the early modern period, however, governments were pressing in more and more on the lives of ordinary people. Primarily, this took the form of increased taxation, but it is also evident in the realms of law and justice, in economic life, and in religion too. Disorder at the top of the government in the form of discord between ruler and heir had the potential to disrupt the workings of the government and the lives of subjects as never before. (By the same token, one might observe that today there remains an abiding interest in the private lives of rulers, but as in earlier periods, this has no effect whatsoever on peoples' everyday lives and is in fact a kind of spectator sport.)

Rather than modern-day royal families whose foibles fill the tabloids, but whose real impact is negligible, the real modern parallel to these episodes of father-son hostility are to be found in the world of business. More specifically, in the world of family-owned and operated corporations we see some of the same elements at work: wealth, power, father-son relations, and the heavy burdens of expectations and the desire for independence. Accordingly, I will examine the literature on family tensions in this arena to see what light they might shed on the relations of royal fathers and royal sons.

If we are to understand these relations and these rivalries, we must also put them in the context of familial relations generally, and more specifically of relations between fathers and sons. There are two different angles to be pursued here. One is to put royal father-son relations in the context of familial relations current at the time. To what extent did the unique situation of royal families cause them to diverge from the "normal" patterns of family life of the times? The other angle is to examine what modern psychology has to say about childhood and adolescent development, and to the extent possible, to relate these insights to relations between kings and their sons in the early modern period.

It is difficult to imagine a set of circumstances better designed to produce dysfunctional families than that which pertained among the royal families of early modern Europe. Diplomacy and politics were driven largely by the interests of the ruling dynasty rather than any rational calculation of national interest. Royal princes and princesses were pawns in the strategic calculations of rulers. The heir to the throne was, from the day of his (or rarely, her) birth an important figure, and marriages were usually arranged at a very young age, sometimes even in infancy. Of course, the children did not live together as man and wife until physical maturity, often as young as fifteen or sixteen.

Because this is intended as a more popular account, rather than a purely scholarly one, I have chosen to dispense with the usual academic practice of including footnotes indicating sources. Rather, I have included a topical bibliography which indicates some of my sources for each chapter. I do not claim to have uncovered any startling new source or to have made any great discoveries about these episodes. What follows is based on published primary and secondary sources. What I do claim is that we have something to gain by re-examining these stories together, and in the light of what we currently know about family dynamics.

In the chapters that follow, I do not intend only to describe and analyze the conflicts between rulers and their sons. A certain amount of historical context is necessary to understand the complexities of these relations. So, for example, in the case of Louis XI, France was reaching the end of a disastrous period in her history, that of the Hundred Years War, when much of the kingdom was under English occupation, and the French themselves were consumed in civil war. In the case of Peter the Great, a revolutionary ruler was attempting to break with centuries of traditional beliefs and practices, and those who opposed him sought leadership in the person of his son Alexei. The Prussia of Frederick the Great was a relative newcomer to great power diplomacy and was in fact a rather fragile creation which required, and for the most part received, brilliant leadership, both militarily and politically. The stories of these kings and their sons are thus inextricably linked to their particular times and places in history.

Chapter 1: Royal Families

Happy families, as famously observed by Tolstoy, are all alike, but unhappy families are each unhappy in their own way. We shall have little to say about happy families in this book, but it will soon become apparent that the tensions in the royal families examined here share some striking similarities, Tolstoy's opinion notwithstanding. The practices common among European royalty were not only different from our norms today; they also diverged dramatically from those of their more ordinary contemporaries.

Indeed, if one set out to design a series of practices and customs to intentionally produce dysfunctional families, one would be hard pressed to surpass those of royal families in early modern Europe. There were two prevailing imperatives which lay behind most of these practices: the need to guarantee the succession, and the use of royal marriages as political and diplomatic tools.

Preserving the dynastic succession was essential; thus princes and princesses were married early and pressured to have as many children as possible as soon as possible in order to guarantee the succession to the throne. It was also important to establish that the wife was fertile, and if not, to arrange an annulment at the earliest possible date. Childbirth was also a risky business for women, so it was important that the heir start producing sons as soon as possible, in case his wife should die in childbirth.

In age where only about half of the babies born alive would survive until adulthood, you could never have too many heirs, especially if (as was the case for royal families), there were no worries about the number of mouths to feed. Even if a child survived past puberty, plague and disease struck indiscriminately at all levels of society.[1] In order to produce as many children as possible, princes and princesses were married at very young ages, most often to complete strangers, for reasons that had nothing to do with love or compatibility. The marriage of the heir to the throne was far too important to be left to the whims of romance and personal preference. Indeed, the question of the heir's marriage was often highly controversial and politically charged. Different factions at court might use it to build up their power or denigrate their opponents. When the heir was an adult, he might choose the question of his marriage to assert his independence from his father. This was an additional reason to arrange marriages at a young age: it was much easier to manipulate or intimidate a young teenager into an unwanted marriage than a mature twenty-something. Indeed, the question of whom, and when, to marry was one of the key sources of tensions between rulers and their sons. (Daughters, on the other hand, were raised from infancy with the idea that they would one day be shipped off to a foreign land to be married to a complete stranger, in order to serve as incubators for future kings.) Very often, the marriage of the heir became a political hot potato, as a court faction might curry favor with the future king by supporting his choice for a wife and opposing his father's.

We must however, distinguish between betrothal and marriage in our sense. Arrangements were often made for marriages when the principals were very young, often in infancy, but of course they would not live together as man and wife until much later, although still at ages that seem ludicrously young to us. In the cases examined here, Louis XI of France was formally married to Princess Margaret of Scotland in 1436, when he was thirteen and she eleven. His second marriage to Charlotte of Savoy took place when he was twenty-four and she was eight, although they lived apart and the marriage would not be consummated until she had reached the ripe old age of fourteen. Philip II of Spain married his cousin Maria of Portugal in 1545, when he was seventeen and she sixteen. In all the cases we will examine, the principals were married no later than their early twenties.

These considerations had a number of important consequences. First, as mentioned above, the sons of a king were usually married off at very young ages, almost never to a mate of their own choosing, since royal marriages

---

[1] The odds of survival were probably better for children born to the wealthy families of the elite, but not much. King Louis XIV of France (reigned 1643–1715) buried not only his eldest son, but also his eldest grandson, and two of his great-grandsons. Queen Anne of England (reigned 1702–14) was pregnant no fewer than eighteen times. Of these, there were twelve miscarriages or stillbirths. Of the remaining five pregnancies which resulted in live births, four children died before the age of two, while the only child to survive infancy died at the age of eleven.

were often used to seal diplomatic arrangements among rulers, or to unite territories under a single ruler. As husband and wife matured, they often found that they had little or nothing in common; indeed, they often came to despise one another, all the more so since the choice of a wife was an enduring reminder of the father's control of the son. They often maintained separate households, and frequently used their children as pawns in their conflicts.

Second, because they started having children as soon as possible, they were usually completely unprepared for the responsibilities and challenges of parenthood. This was especially true if they themselves had no positive role model as a parent. Royal children were frequently raised virtually completely apart from their parents. In some cases, the royal father may have taken a more direct interest in the raising and education of the heir. But only very rarely was the father intimately engaged with his son in ways that we would consider "normal." In the best-case scenario, the father would appear periodically in the child's life as a remote and hopefully benign authority figure.

Once married, strained relations between husband and wife were the rule rather than the exception. Of the marriages examined here, only that between George II of England and his wife Queen Caroline approached anything like domestic harmony. In these circumstances, a princess or queen often established her own household and court which could and often did serve as a focal point of opposition to a ruler's policies.

Having been married young, the couple faced intense pressure to produce children as soon as possible, while they themselves were still immature. Thus, Charlotte of Savoy, mentioned above, became a mother for the first time in 1459 at the age of sixteen. Over the next twelve years, she would bear six more children. Of these, only three survived infancy. The future George II of England was born shortly before his mother's seventeenth birthday.

In addition, royal children, especially heirs to the throne were very often established in their own household at a very young age, as was thought to befit their lofty station. Here they were surrounded by nurses, nannies, tutors, and governors. These people were appointed not necessarily in the child's best interests, but often as means of exercising control or influence over the heir, or as a means balancing noble factions, or as a reward for loyal service. Whatever the case, these children grew up apart from their parents, often in an atmosphere of fawning obeisance and perpetual intrigue and suspicion.

The dangers of childbirth and the general precariousness of life meant that royal children were often deprived of their mothers in infancy or childhood. The demands of dynastic succession compelled kings to marry again as soon as possible. The result was what we today call blended families. Even today, this is often a recipe for familial tension and hostility. With political power and social prestige at stake, these tensions were magnified among royal families, with offspring of different queens and their extended families scheming for power and influence. Maria of Portugal, the first wife of Philip II of Spain died before her eighteenth birthday, shortly after giving birth to the hapless Don Carlos. Philip would marry three more times, and outlived all his wives. Peter the Great was the offspring of his father's second marriage, and the two families feuded violently for power, not hesitating to use the children as pawns.

In short, family relations and child-rearing practices among European royalty seem custom made to produce tension and hostility. By way of contrast, the practices among more ordinary people were very different; in fact, in some ways they were superficially not that different from practices pertaining in our own world. Most people married in their mid to late twenties. Although it tended to fluctuate with economic fortunes, the average age of first marriage for men was about twenty-six, and for women, about twenty-four. Most marriages were not arranged, although the approval of parents was usually sought, as it is today. Romantic love, in our sense, was not a primary consideration, but compatibility was. Most people felt that if a match was otherwise suitable, the couple would eventually come to love each other. Most young couples established their own households, and the nuclear family household was the norm.

As among royalty, children arrived early and often, not to guarantee the succession, but because children were the only form of security for old age and survival to adulthood was so precarious. On average, a woman would become pregnant about every two years, which is about the natural rate of fertility. Of these pregnancies, of course, a certain proportion would end in miscarriages and stillbirths. Of children born alive, about 25% would die in infancy, and another 25% before puberty. Thus, if a woman married at twenty-four, and had one child every two years until menopause (at that time about the age of forty), she could expect to give birth to about six children. Of these, however, only two or three were likely to survive into adulthood. Thus, an average household would consist of husband and wife, and two or three children.

Then, as now, child-rearing practices and attitudes towards childhood and children were not monolithic. People expressed a variety of views, and it is notoriously difficult to infer attitudes from practices. For example, for the first several months of life, infants were generally tightly swaddled, which had the effect of immobilizing them. By our standards, this seems a cruel and regressive practice. Children ought to be free to move and explore. It may, however, also be seen as an expression of love and concern. Not only did it keep infants warm in houses without central heating, it also protected them in a world where mothers and older siblings had a myriad of responsibilities and could not devote their unwavering attention to supervising an infant.

It was likewise with corporal punishment. Beatings and whippings were considered a normal part of childhood. Children (along with everyone else) were assumed to have been tainted by the original sin of Adam and Eve in the Garden of Eden. (The notion that children were pure and innocent until corrupted by society was a product of the eighteenth-century Enlightenment.) Cruel though it may seem to us, it was usually well-intended. "He that spareth the rod, hateth his child," the Bible told parents. In a world dominated by authorities of various sorts, where one occupied a particular niche in society, it was important that children learn submissiveness to duly-constituted authority, whether paternal, governmental, social, or religious. Indeed, writers about child-rearing usually thought that parents were too indulgent and permissive rather than too harsh.

Children were intimately involved in all aspects of life, and there was little sense of an isolated and protected children's sphere in which they were shielded from the ugly realities of life. Some, most notably the French historian Philippe Ariès in his influential book *Centuries of Childhood*, have argued further that children were treated callously and even cruelly, as disposable little adults. This, he argued, was the inevitable result of high infant mortality. Parents simply could not afford to invest affection in babies whose odds of survival were no better than fifty-fifty. Most historians would now disagree with this assessment. Of course, one can find examples of cruelty towards children in early modern Europe, just as one can today. Imagine what a history of childhood in our times would look like if it were based only on the records of child welfare agencies. All the evidence suggests that most early modern parents loved their children deeply and mourned their deaths keenly. It is probably accurate to say that parents loved their children and wanted the best for them, but that they expressed these feelings differently than we do ours today.

It is also inaccurate to say that Europeans of this era had no conception of childhood as a separate stage of life. For example, until about the age of seven, children, both boys and girls, were dressed alike in long gowns. Most religious authorities also recognized that children were not morally accountable for their actions. Child-rearing and educational treatises alike promoted age-appropriate practices, even if they do not correspond to our norms. It is safe to say, however, that early modern childhood was not thought of as an isolated sphere, in which the child was protected from the harsh realities of life. They were usually put to work at a young age, most often at tasks appropriate to their age and strength. Their labor was often essential to the survival and prosperity of the family. In the country, this might involve tending animals or household chores. In the cities, they might sweep the shop floor or organize materials. Young girls might be sent to work as a servant or maid in another (usually wealthier) family, while boys would be sent to apprentice with a master in order to prepare for an adult career. There was, however, little naked exploitation of child labor such as would later be seen in the factories and mines of the Industrial Revolution, or in the sweatshops of the Third World today.

Among the small minority of wealthy and elite families, things were somewhat different. Marriages were often arranged according to the dictates of social or economic strategy. Children tended to be married at younger ages and were not generally put to work. Boys would be sent to school to learn Latin in preparation for university, while girls were groomed as future wives and mothers. However, except among the very high nobility, children were normally still a part of family life, experiencing regular contact with their mothers and fathers.

How might the practices of royal families have affected the development of their children, and how might these effects come into play in later years as royal sons grew to adulthood? To give us some insight into these questions, we turn first to the realms of developmental psychology and neuroscience. While the correlation is far from perfect, psychologists generally agree that early development is intimately linked to later development. To a great extent, the child really is the father of the man. Since at least the 1960s, researchers have been probing the impact of children's very earliest experiences upon their later lives. Specifically, it was posited that secure attachment to a primary caregiver forms the basis for sound relationships later on in life. By about eight months of age, in the normal course of development, an infant will have formed a secure attachment to its primary caregiver, most often its mother. Infants with secure attachment are later able to build upon this to establish other healthy relationships with other children, adults, and eventually with their own children. Children with insecure attachments as infants are at greater risk for a whole host of problems. Insecure attachment has been linked to conduct disorders, where children fail to internalize their parents' beliefs and values, obeying parents only out or coercion or fear. Insecure attachment has also been linked to anxiety disorders. Secure attachment forms a solid base from which the child can set out to explore the larger world. By about eighteen months of age, separation from the primary caregiver becomes more acceptable to the child as he or she begins to establish other relationships. Children with an insecure base of attachment are more likely to see the world as dangerous and hostile, which can later be manifested as anxiety disorders. Children with insecure attachments are also more prone to depression. If the caregiver does not reliably respond to the infant's needs, the child is likely to see him or herself as unworthy, and to view others as threatening and undependable. In addition, secure attachment may provide greater emotional stability and wherewithal to cope with life's inevitable stresses and strains.

What makes for secure attachment? The single most important factor is predictable and appropriate interaction with parents in the first months of life. A dependable response from a parent to an infant's needs creates an internal working model whereby the infant knows that parents can be relied upon for care and comfort. Therefore, parents who are absent, or unpredictable, or in extreme cases abusive, are likely to foster insecure attachments. In turn, the single most important predictor of appropriate responses from parents is the quality of their own attachment as children. There is a high level of intergenerational stability: children with secure attachment relationships are more likely to grow into young adults with secure attachment relationships, and therefore to foster secure attachment relationships in children of their own. It has often been noted that a large proportion of abusers were themselves victims of abuse. It appears that a similar, though positive sort of feedback loop is in operation in the realm of attachment.

In our own society, of course, an infant's first attachment is almost always to a parent, usually its mother. It need not be, however. From a strictly theoretical point of view, it is not the object of the attachment that is important, rather its quality. Thus, a nurse or a nanny could in theory be the object of attachment, and if it were secure, this would pose no particular problem for the forming of attachments to others later in life. On the other hand, among adolescents secure attachment *to parents* has been linked to a variety of favorable outcomes, such as higher self-esteem, closer relationships with friends and romantic partners, and greater educational and occupational achievement. To put it another way, secure attachment to and ongoing healthy relationships with the objects of secure attachments are important throughout childhood and adolescence and into adulthood. As mentioned above, the sons and daughters of European royalty were most often brought up apart from their parents, attended to by a host of servants and tutors, who generally disappeared from their lives once they had done their jobs. Although seemingly pampered, at least according to the standards of the day, caregivers of royal children often had agendas other than the well-being of the child, which could hardly result in secure attachments at all, and likely not to the mostly absent parents.

It has often been asserted that our modern Western notion of adolescence is a cultural construct. While this may be true, most cultures have constructed a stage of life between childhood and full adulthood, usually marked by marriage; that is, the period between the onset of puberty and taking one's place in the adult world of work and family. More immediately for our purposes, in early modern European society, there was a stage of life which corresponds to our notion of adolescence, even if the term itself was not used. "Youths" were a recognized component of society with their own activities, groups, practices and interests. Given the relatively late age of marriage in early modern Europe, there was a significant time span of a decade or more between the attainment of sexual maturity and marriage, which marked the passage into full adulthood.

Research has shown repeatedly that there are ongoing biological and cognitive developments which occur throughout adolescence. The pioneering developmental psychologist Jean Piaget (1896–1980) argued that children undergo universal maturational processes independent of culture. In the first two years of life, infants are in the sensorimotor stage, where they learn to coordinate the experience of the senses with their motor abilities, for example, learning to grasp a desired object such as a toy or a cookie, or learning first to crawl and then to walk. From ages two to seven, there is the preoperational stage, where children become capable of using symbolic representations, such as language, but are still limited in their ability to conduct mental operations. In a famous example, children were shown an equal amount of liquid in two containers. When the liquid from the first was poured into the taller and thinner container, the children insisted that it now contained more liquid, because its level was higher. From ages seven to eleven, there is the concrete operational stage, where children become increasingly adept at mental operations, but only in immediate and concrete situations. For example, children at this stage now understand the principle of conservation, that the amount of liquid remains constant, regardless of the shape of the container. However, they are not able to extend their mental operations into the realm of the abstract or hypothetical. They are unable, for example, to grasp a metaphor, or to distinguish sarcasm. From the age of eleven onward we have the stage of formal operations. Piaget believed that it was completed sometime between the ages of fifteen and twenty. Adolescents and adults are now capable of hypothetical and deductive reasoning and abstract thought.

Piaget's stages of development have been enormously influential and form the basis for most current thinking about developmental psychology. Subsequent research has refined and qualified his theories, but not superseded them. For example, later research has qualified his views on formal operational thinking. In adolescence, and even adulthood, there is a great deal of variation across and even within individuals. Not all adolescents or adults seem to use formal operations, and even among those who do, they are employed selectively. Piaget also underestimated or ignored the impact of culture, in particular on educational systems. Piaget's basic point, however, remains largely unchallenged: that as children mature, they not only gain in volume of knowledge, but in the sophistication with which they can manipulate and use that knowledge. Some researchers have divided Piaget's last stage, that of formal operation thought, into two stages. The first, early formal operational thought, is one in which adolescents' ability to think in hypothetical ways is unconstrained by reality and possibilities seem unlimited. In late formal operational thought, hypotheses are increasingly subject to experience. Or, in the famous words attributed to Mark Twain: "When I was a boy of 14, my father was so ignorant I could hardly stand to have the old man around. But when I got to be 21, I was astonished at how much the old man had learned in seven years."[2] The earlier stage may be thought of as marking the transition from childhood to adolescence, and the later from adolescence to adulthood.

Contemporary neuroscience also adds to our understanding of psychological development, although researchers are really only beginning to understand the very complex links between behavior and the development of the brain. One of the most significant problems which confronts researchers is the distinction between cause and correlation. Just because one thing precedes another does not mean that one causes the other. Perhaps more than anything else, scientists are in the process of discovering the extreme plasticity of the developing brain, that the brain and the environment interact in extremely complex and sometimes unpredictable ways. With these caveats in mind, however, we can at least make some tentative generalizations about behavior and the developing brain. For example, significant changes in brain-weight to body-weight ratio have been linked to Piaget's cognitive stages. There seem to be several significant growth spurts during childhood and adolescence, during which the brain grows faster than the body. (This gain in brain weight is not made of more neurons — brain cells — but rather a growth in axons, or the connections which span the gaps [or synapses]

---

[2] Although widely attributed to Mark Twain, no one has ever found these exact words in his works.

between neurons, and the greater metabolic and circulatory demands of more synaptic connections.) One of these spurts, for example, normally occurs between three and ten months, which correlates neatly with Piaget's sensorimotor stage. Others take place between the ages of two and four, between six and eight, between ten to twelve, and between fourteen and sixteen and beyond. All of these, save the last, fit rather neatly into Piaget's stages, although of course scientists are only beginning to unravel the myriad ways in which behavior and the brain are linked to each other.

More recent research has identified continued growth and development of the brain through adolescence, particularly in the prefrontal cortex. This is the area of the brain associated with higher-level thinking, planning, and self-regulation. Over the course of its development the brain will produce far more synaptic connections than are actually required. Ones that are used will become stronger and survive, while that are not will disappear, or will be "pruned" in the terminology of neuroscientists. Different areas of the brain experience this overproduction and subsequent pruning of synaptic connections at different stages of development. For example, in the visual cortex, the area of brain controlling vision, the peak of synaptic density occurs at about four months of age, while in the auditory cortex (governing hearing and language), the peak occurs somewhat later. In the case of the prefrontal cortex, adult synaptic density is not achieved until about the age of eleven.

We turn now to the theories of another very influential figure in the world of psychology, Erik Erikson (1902–1994). According to Erikson, the key feature of adolescence was a search for identity.[3] It is a time of trying on different identities, much like one might try on different clothes in order to discover which are the most comfortable and best fitting. Adolescents, according to Erikson, engage in a sort of hypothetical thinking: "If I were a movie star, or a famous athlete. . . ." "If I could marry so-and-so, we could be happy," and so on. In Piaget's terms, adolescents are in the formal operational stage, where they are mentally capable of conceiving of states which might exist, allowing them to imagine themselves in different roles. Adolescence is a period of "psychosocial moratorium" when adult roles and responsibilities are postponed while identities are sorted out. Erikson further identified three major spheres in which adolescents establish their own identity: love, or personal relationships, occupation, and ideology, or beliefs and values.

---

[3] Erikson called it an "identity crisis," but subsequent researchers have preferred the term "identity exploration."

Psychologically healthy adolescents will eventually settle on an identity, or series of identities, while others will lag in "identity confusion."[4]

Erikson famously applied his concept to historical figures, most notably Mahatma Gandhi and Martin Luther. The basis of Luther's revolt against the religious authority of the Roman Catholic Church was, according to Erikson, his troubled relationship with his father. Luther viewed his father as an unappeasable tyrant, and transposed these views onto the God of the Catholic Church, whom he tried to placate with good works. His father had intended him for a legal career, but a close call during a thunderstorm led him to become a monk instead. Even as a monk, Luther could never find the spiritual solace and assurance he was seeking, ultimately leading him to repudiate the authority of the Church, as he came to a new understanding of salvation, one in which human effort and good works played no role whatsoever. Luther's new theology, and his break from the Catholic Church, therefore had their roots in his own adolescent identity crisis.

Historians have been less than convinced by Erikson's interpretation, although this has more to do with the nature of his evidence than with the question of an identity crisis. Specifically, Erikson relied heavily on Luther's own recollections of his childhood, decades after the fact. In addition, Erikson probably overstated Luther's conflict with his father. It is true that Hans Luther was very angry with his son when he learned of the decision to become a monk. Later on, however, he expressed pride in his son and threw him a big banquet on the occasion of him conducting his first Mass. Erikson also made a great deal of Luther being beaten by his father as a child. As we have seen, however, corporal punishment was considered a normal part of childhood (as it indeed it was until very recently), and there is nothing to indicate any unusual severity in Luther's case.

Modern Western cultures tend to value independence of thought and individual choice; therefore, the psychosocial moratorium of adolescence is seen as a necessary and desirable stage of life, and in general, the choices made by adolescents are (within limits) accepted by parents and society. Indeed, it is the acceptance and support of this searching which may be the construct of modern Western culture, rather than the notion of adolescence as a distinct stage in life. Other cultures, both today and in the past, have had other values which pose different challenges for adolescents and their families. In more traditional cultures, which includes early modern Europe, parental (especially paternal) authority is highly valued, as is obedience to authority. In addition, in relatively primitive economies, there is simply not

---

[4] Erikson also maintained that identity issues are present throughout the lifespan, but that they are especially prominent in adolescence.

the same latitude in career choice. For the vast majority who were peasants living a life of subsistence agriculture, tilling the land as your father and grandfather had done was not a career choice; it was a matter of survival. For working-class and middle-class youths as well, career choices tended to be made by parents and by circumstances. In love, most people were relatively free, as we have seen, to make their own matches, although not as free as young people today. In ideology, once more, early modern European youths were not expected or encouraged to try on different belief systems. (Nor were adults, for that matter.) Of course, this is not to say that adolescents did not go through these identity explorations, but rather that their scope for doing so was much more restricted than it is now.

All of these restrictions would have been intensified among royal adolescents, especially the heir to the throne. Unlike their contemporary youths, they were denied virtually any choice regarding marriage. Certainly, for occupation, there was no choice at all: from birth, the heir to the throne was destined to be ruler.[5] It was perhaps only in the realm of ideology, or beliefs and values, that royal adolescents could pursue the exploration of identity, however limited. As we shall see, this was frequently intensified by the fact that as the heir grew to maturity, many of those opposed to the policies of the reigning king (often including the queen, the heir's mother) encouraged the heir in opposition to those principles.

Adolescence has long been seen as a time of heightened emotional turmoil. Thus, Aristotle wrote that youths "are heated by Nature as drunken men are by wine." Indeed, Anna Freud (1895–1982), daughter of the founder of psychoanalysis and an influential psychologist in her own right, theorized that adolescence was inevitably and above all a time of emotional upheaval, of storm and stress. This was a normal part of maturation and its absence was in itself abnormal. Subsequent research has largely discredited these views. Most adolescents will report good relations with their parents, and emotional disturbances are generally not so severe as to require intervention. On other hand, research *has* confirmed that adolescence is a time of heightened emotional instability and mood swings. Some of this is related to the hormonal changes of puberty, but it may also be related to Piaget's stages. For the first time, adolescents become capable of seeing things not as they are, but as they might be. This may be positive ("We can change the world!"), or negative ("What if I never find a girl/boyfriend? What if mom and dad are killed in a car accident?"), but it nevertheless marks a whole new

---

[5] This may also help to explain why younger brothers and sons of kings could cause so much trouble. They needed to be raised and educated as future rulers, given the precariousness of life, but were then denied any meaningful role or power.

stage in thinking. In addition, adolescents objectively do face a very stressful time in life, when they are confronted with decisions about education, career, love and relationships, and so on. Research, nevertheless, has shown that adolescents react to similar events with more extreme emotions than either children or adults. The highs really are higher and the lows lower.

Another relevant feature of adolescence is self-absorption, or egocentrism. Again, it will surprise no one that adolescence is a time of intense preoccupation with the self. To a greater extent than adults, adolescents feel that others are thinking about them much more than they actually are. One consequence of this fallacy is what has been termed the "personal fable." This refers to the conception that if everyone is in fact thinking about me, there must be something uniquely special about me. Thus, adolescents are inclined to think that no one has ever before felt as they do, whether it be the intensity of a first love, the pain of heartbreak, or indeed, conflict with parents. This, in turn, underlies the high-risk behavior often seen in adolescence, whether unprotected sex, or drunk or reckless driving. Pregnancy, AIDS, and car accidents are things that happen to others, not to me, simply because I am so special and unique. This may help to explain the bitterness of some of the relations between royal fathers and sons. As the son grows to maturity and seeks to establish his own identity and take his place in the world of adults, there is more or less inevitable tension with the father, whose position and power is conceivably threatened. Urged on, in many cases, by ambitious and unscrupulous courtiers, the son comes to believe that no father has ever so cruelly mistreated a son as his, that no son has ever had greater cause to resist his father's authority. The high-risk behavior resorted to is not primarily promiscuous sex (although that certainly did occur), but rather political resistance and rebellion, to the point of threatened or indeed actual civil war. This was the case in the example of Louis XI of France who fled the invading armies of his father sent to apprehend him, and took refuge with the Duke of Burgundy, his father's bitterest enemy. Philip II of Spain feared that his son Don Carlos was about to flee the kingdom and seek refuge among Philip's rebellious subjects in the Netherlands. Peter the Great of Russia feared that his son Alexei's exile in Vienna was the prelude to an invasion whose goal was the conquest of Russia and his replacement on the throne.

It will come as a surprise to no one that in our modern Western culture, adolescence is a time of heightened conflict between parents and children. This is seen as a normal part of maturation, as young people strive to establish their own independence and identities. Yet, this conflict does not seem as prominent in past societies, or in many contemporary societies. If all adolescents go through the same process of identity exploration, how is it that not all societies experience the same level of conflict between parents and their adolescent children? As mentioned above, in our society, independence and self-sufficiency are highly prized. Indeed, they are seen as essential values, necessary for participation in a pluralistic and democratic society. In the past, and in many present-day cultures, this was not the case. Obedience and respect for authority were prized values. Economic interdependency and lack of opportunity meant that adolescents did not have the same degree of latitude in charting their own course. This is not to say, of course, that there was no conflict. It is possible that socialization and cultural traits imbued in childhood had the effect of muting these conflicts.

Early modern Europe, however, was unusual among traditional societies in the predominance of nuclear family households. That is, in most traditional societies the extended multigenerational household was the norm, with more than two generations and more than one nuclear family under the same roof. European youths were therefore in a kind of no man's land: they were expected to be obedient and respectful toward authority but also to prepare themselves to one day establish themselves in an independent nuclear family household. Early modern European society was also unusual in its relatively late age of marriage. These youths were therefore confronted with a situation in which they had to delay marriage for up to a decade after they were sexually mature, but during which time they were somehow develop the skills and attitudes of independent adults.

Children of rulers, however, faced a different set of challenges than most adolescents of the time. As seen above, marriages were arranged for them, and often at very young ages. Their careers were preordained, but they could not embark on their career until the father died. In this way, an heir to the throne was confronted with a psychologically very difficult task: he was already married and usually a father, but had to wait for years, perhaps decades to perform the job for which he was born. He was expected and was taught to command, but was still required to be obedient to his father and king. In this way, conflicts during adolescence may well have been magnified by contemporary practices, all the more so, since as the prince grew into maturity, there were usually opportunistic courtiers who encouraged and enabled this conflict.

As we have seen, developmental psychology furnishes us with some useful concepts in thinking about the development of children and adolescence. There is, no doubt, a great deal which is culturally conditioned and socially constructed. But the neurological and cognitive development described above appears to be universal, although different societies have viewed these changes differently and dealt with them accordingly. On the other hand, among ordinary people in early modern Europe, family life was not so vastly different from our own that we cannot make certain extrapolations. Family life and child development among royal families thus took place in a matrix which is largely familiar to us, although as we have seen, they diverged from the norm (both in their day and ours) in very significant ways.

In early modern Europe, most work took place in the context of the family or household. That is, there was a very fuzzy distinction between the workplace and the home. For the majority who were subsistence peasant farmers, agriculture was indeed a family undertaking. Everyone's labor was necessary for survival, and the family as whole was subject to the father's authority. This was no less true among urban workers and the middle class: employees in a master's shop were in many ways considered subordinate family members rather than employees, and the boss's authority was paternal authority. An early modern monarchy was more like a family business than a government in our sense.[6] Rulers, as we shall see, made no real distinction between the interests of their families and of their kingdoms, let alone those of some abstract national entity such as England, France, or Russia. Relations among ruling dynasties determined who ruled what. (In large part this is the reason that so much care was taken in the question of royal marriages.) When early modern Europeans thought about political authority in theoretical terms, after divine right, it was the image of paternal authority that came most readily to mind. Kings ruled their subjects in the same way that fathers ruled their families. The king was the father of the kingdom. Listen to King James I of England in a speech to Parliament in 1610:

> Now a father may dispose of his inheritance to his children at his pleasure, yea even disinherit the eldest upon just occasions and prefer the youngest, according to his liking; make them beggars or rich at his pleasure; restrain or banish out of his presence, as he finds them give cause or offence, or restore them again in favor again with the penitent sinner. So may the King deal with his subjects.

In *King Lear*, Shakespeare explicitly draws the connection between biological and political paternity: Lear's failings as a father are reflected and multiplied in his failings as a king.

It may therefore be helpful to examine conflicts between royal father and sons in the context of family businesses. A whole genre of business literature has sprung up analyzing family firms and advising them on

---

[6] Indeed, this perception lingers. Senior members of the British royal family, the House of Windsor refer to the family as "The Firm," which was also the title of a recent book on the topic: *The Firm: the Troubled Life of the House of Windsor*, by Peggy Junor (St. Martin's Griffin, 2008).

how to avoid the many pitfalls that are endemic to family businesses. The travails of many prominent family businesses have been reliable fodder for business and gossip columnists alike. Many of these conflicts which plague family businesses involve siblings (most often brothers) who feud over control and the direction of the company. These examples do not much concern us here, since the rules of succession which governed the various European monarchies almost universally dictated that the eldest son inherit the throne. However, younger brothers and sons, although they could not inherit the throne, were still in a position to cause a great deal of turmoil. Much more germane for our purposes are the conflicts between fathers and their sons. Indeed, planning for and executing an orderly succession is the single biggest problem facing family firms. Studies have shown again and again that only 30% of family businesses survive the second generation and only 10% the third.

There are, of course, many examples of such familial squabbling which have received great attention. Henry Ford both foreordained his son Edsel to succeed him and undermined and belittled him into an early grave. The patriarch then clashed in a bitter and protracted power struggle with his grandson Henry Ford II for control of the company.

Less well known outside business circles is the saga of the Haft family and the Dart group. The founder of the company was Herbert Haft (1921–2004). He established a very successful chain of discount pharmacies, and later branched out into alcohol, books, auto parts, real estate, and finance. The elder of his two sons, Robert (b.1953) played an important role alongside his father in the expansion of the family's holdings, while the younger son, Ronald (b. 1959) stayed on the sidelines. Robert was extremely well-qualified and experienced, with a degree from Harvard Business School. Indeed, Crown Books, the family's successful chain of discount bookstores was Robert's project, in both conception and execution. In 1993, however, Robert made the mistake of publicly musing about the future of the company when he would eventually take the reins of power. Incensed, Herbert fired his son, ostensibly for trying to take over the company. At the same time, he ousted from the board Gloria, his wife of forty-five years. She responded by filing for divorce, citing infidelity and psychological abuse. Robert and Gloria also sued for wrongful termination. Herbert then turned to Ronald, his younger son, whom he appointed president and CEO, despite their past estrangement and a complete lack of credentials or experience. Ultimately, Herbert predictably fell out with Ronald as well. By 1998, the family's businesses were liquidated and sold.

In Canada, the Bronfman family of Seagram's fame managed to incorporate two seemingly contradictory traits across two generations. The founder and patriarch, Sam Bronfman (1889–1971), raised his son Edgar (b. 1930) to take over the company. But, like Henry Ford, he proved incapable of letting go of the reins of power. Freed by his father's death, Edgar saw the company through a significant expansion and diversification in the 1970s and 1980s. When it came time to plan for succession, he made the exact opposite mistake. He turned the company over to his thirty-one-year-old son, Edgar Bronfman Jr., despite his having no real business experience or training, with predictable consequences.

There are several areas in which family businesses tend to run into trouble which are pertinent to our inquiry. Nor are these areas self-contained. They inevitably spill over into other areas, which only intensifies the conflict. Indeed, "families are amplifiers of all emotions, positive as well as negative."[7] Planning and executing a successful succession is one of the most common problems faced by family businesses, as noted earlier. There are scores of books and journal articles dealing with such things as theoretical models for succession, practical advice to family firms, longitudinal studies of succession in family firms, and so on. It is by far the dominant topic in the literature on family businesses.

Another issue confronting family businesses is the collision of two mutually opposed systems — the family and the business: "The attributes of a healthy business system are usually at complete odds with attributes of a healthy family system."[8] The ultimate goals of the business are to make money for its owners or shareholders, and to perpetuate itself in order to continue to make more money in the future. To these ends, businesses have a well-defined and hierarchical command structure. People are employed to fill a specific role and decisions about staffing are (in theory, at any rate) arrived at through a rational cost/benefit analysis. Roles and responsibilities are clearly delineated, and continued employment is linked to performance, once again, at least in theory.

Families are very different. The goal of the family is to provide a safe and nurturing environment in which children can be raised to adulthood, eventually having children of their own, thus perpetuating the family. In evolutionary terms the family is the vehicle for the survival of our genetic material into the indefinite future. Membership is determined by birth or choice (marriage). Roles and responsibilities tend to be implicit and

---

[7] Grant Gordon and Nigel Nicholson, *Family Wars: Classic Conflicts in Family Business and How to Deal with Them* (London: Kogan Page, 2008), 166.

[8] Quentin J. Fleming, *Keep the Family Baggage out of the Family Business: Avoiding the Seven Deadly Sins that Destroy Family Businesses* (New York: Fireside, 2000), 22.

understood, rather than explicitly defined. They also change over time. Although formal authority may rest with one member (usually the father, in most societies), decisions are usually arrived at through a process of consultation and compromise. In short, the qualities that make for a successful business are largely inimical to a successful family, and vice versa.

In this regard, family businesses run into problems in two different ways: either the ethos of business is applied to the family, or the ethos of the family is applied to business. In the former case, family members are treated as employees whose job it is to do the bidding of the boss (usually the father). Performance, loyalty, and competence are enshrined as prized values. Competition among family members is encouraged. In the latter case, family members are employed in the business, regardless of competence or training. Everyone feels entitled to a say in how the business is run, and lines of authority are shifting and murky. All family businesses must negotiate these dangerous shoals, and as mentioned above, more fail at it than succeed.

Complicating the issue of succession is the long shadow cast by the founder of the family firm, the patriarch.[9] The very qualities which allowed him to succeed in business often lead to turmoil in his personal and family life. Indeed, it has been posited that successful entrepreneurs often exhibit in milder form personality disorders that in more extreme cases are labelled psychopathic. For example, many are histrionic, exhibiting a superficial charisma which masks insincerity and manipulativeness. They are often also narcissistic, concerned exclusively with themselves, lacking in empathy and exploitative in their relationships. They can also be perfectionistic, stubborn and rigid, the classic workaholic, putting work above all else. They can also exhibit anti-social tendencies in their cavalier attitude to laws and rules. None of these qualities is terribly conducive to family harmony.[10]

There are obviously a number of similarities and differences between the dynamics of family conflict in family businesses and those of royal families in early modern Europe. For example, all of the business literature regarding issues of succession in family firms advocates the desirability of long term planning and securing consensus among interested family members regarding the succession plan. Part and parcel of this is the concept that the older generation should be willing to step aside and let the younger generation take over. That is, they should avoid the experience of the Ford family, where the patriarch insisted on maintaining control at the expense of younger generations of the family. Such planning was generally not in the

---

[9] In this regard, the "founder" need not be the actual originator of the enterprise. He may be, and often is, a successor who has taken the business to new heights of success.

[10] See Belinda Jane Board and Katarina Fritzon, "Disordered personalities at work," *Psychology, Crime and Law*, 11, 2004, 17–35.

---

repertoire of royal families. There was rarely any question as to who would succeed. It was almost always the eldest surviving son. This at least had the advantage of clarity: everyone knew who the next king would be, barring unforeseen deaths. Feuding, and even civil war, among brothers certainly occurred but the lines of succession to the throne were usually very clear.

Another difference is that retirement in our sense of the word was not a normal practice. Most people, of course, had to keep working as long as they were physically able, and then rely on their children for support when they could no longer work. Certainly, retirement as a phase of life, the "golden years," was completely unknown. So it was with kings as well. They almost always ruled until their deaths. In fact, among all the rulers we will consider in this book, only one retired from government and abdicated before death. This was the father of Philip II of Spain, the Holy Roman Emperor Charles V. In 1555 and 1556, prematurely aged and exhausted, he abdicated his various titles and retired to a monastery, where he died in 1558. Since rulers and heirs married and had children at quite young ages, this meant that there was often a very long period when an adult heir was waiting for his father to die in order to assume the role to which he born, and for which he had been trained.

From one perspective, it would seem to be in the reigning king's interest to take his heir under his wing and teach him the business of governing. Yet this was often not the case. It has been widely noted in the literature on family firms that the current generation is fearful of being displaced by the younger. Thus Henry Ford demeans Edsel, and Herbert Haft assumes that Robert is out to overthrow him. Likewise, Charles VII of France is fearful of the abilities of his son Louis, and keeps him isolated from the levers of power. This tendency is reinforced when a forceful and effective ruler doubts the ability of his successor, and fears for the survival of his accomplishments and legacy.[11] So Peter the Great of Russia attempts to mould his heir Alexei into a "modern" European to ensure the durability of his policies. Frederick William of Prussia brutalizes the future Frederick the Great in an attempt to ensure the survival of his hard-won territories. Indeed, heirs, whether to a family company or a kingdom, are caught in a double bind. If they are intelligent, determined, and effective, they pose a threat to the continued power of the father. If they are not, they threaten the accomplishments and legacy of the father. They are truly in a no-win situation. This is compounded by the fact that father and son are often virtual strangers to each other. This is no less true of modern family firms than of early modern monarchies. As we have

---

[11] Sam Bronfman succinctly put his fears for the future of his family this way: "From shirtsleeves to shirtsleeves in three generations."

seen, the family practices of royal families hardly assured close emotional bonds between parents and children. Likewise, the driven workaholic father often neglects his children and is absent emotionally and often physically as well.

Another important difference between modern family firms and early modern monarchies is that in the case of the family firm, there are alternative forms of governance which can be employed to minimize tensions. Trusts can be set up to accommodate other family members. Shares can be redistributed to smooth the workings of the firm. The older generation can be given titles and board positions from which they can make their successors the beneficiaries of their accumulated wisdom and experience. Outside managers and experts can be brought in. The options for monarchs were much more limited. Almost everyone believed that monarchy, the rule of one, was the most natural and indeed the divinely sanctioned form of government. It is true, of course, that rulers had to rely on ministers and advisors, and that some rulers effectively delegated their power to others. However, there was a deeply ingrained belief that a king ought to rule as well as reign, that the man who wore the crown should actually exercise power, and be seen to exercise actual power. Anything else was considered irregular and undesirable.

Yet another important difference is that in the case of the family firm, sons (and daughters) can strike out on a career of their own. Sometimes a child is not willing to wait to take over the family firm and begins a career of his or her own. In other cases, the child finds his or her interest and inclination drawn in other directions and makes a career in another field. Edgar Bronfman Jr., for example, attempted to make a career in Hollywood as a producer of movies and music. Despite some marginal accomplishments, he never really succeeded, and, as we have seen, he ended up taking over Seagram's and tried to turn it into a multimedia conglomerate with, it must be said, disastrous results. For the sons of early modern rulers, there were really were no such options. In a system of hereditary monarchy, a prince could not escape the family business. Should the eldest son die before having a son of his own, the younger brother stepped into his place as heir or as ruler.[12] Younger sons and younger brothers of kings were in essence trapped. They could not find a niche of their own, one which suited their interests and personalities, but only in exceptional cases could they exercise the role for which they were born. It is little wonder that they were a destabilizing force in the politics of the kingdom.

---

[12] In the most dramatic case, King Henry II of France (r. 1547–59) died prematurely in a jousting accident. He was succeeded as king by three of his four sons: Francis II (1559–60), Charles IX (1560–74), and Henry III (1574–89), none of whom had legitimate male heirs of their own. The fourth son predeceased his older surviving brother in 1584.

Yet another difference between monarchies and family firms is that family firm can go out of business or be sold or taken over by a rival concern. Apart from invasion and conquest (the ultimate hostile takeover), kingdoms did not go out of business. This meant that the ultimate solution to family tensions was simply not available to royal families in early modern Europe. The kingdom and monarchy persisted, and so did the hostilities.

In the stories that follow of conflict between kings and heirs, these issues come up again and again. In the case of Louis XI of France, we will see an ambitious and determined son who arouses the hostility of his passive father. With Philip II and Don Carlos of Spain, we see an experienced and intelligent ruler who rightfully doubted the ability of his son to carry on the family business after his death. Likewise with Peter the Great of Russia. The product of his father's second marriage, the families of the two tsarinas feuded bitterly, and Peter clashed violently with his elder half-sister Sophia. Given a son, Alexei, who appeared to condemn his father's achievements and certainly lacked his energy and ability, Peter first attempted to remould his son in his own image. When that failed, Peter in the end accused his son of treason and had him imprisoned, where he died under mysterious circumstances. The German prince who became King George I of England in 1714 was the eldest son of ambitious parents, who saw in him the potential for new heights of power and prestige. He would alternately humiliate and cheat on his own wife, and when she indulged in an extramarital affair, would disavow her and have subjected to house arrest for a period of decades. Their eldest son, the future George II was denied contact with his mother, and ultimately grew to despise his father. In the case of Frederick the Great of Prussia, we see a brutal and tyrannical father determined to break the will of a son he considered weak and effeminate.

Chapter 2: "We shall find some other Prince of the Blood who will serve us better": Louis XI and Charles VII

On July 23, 1423 in the city of Bourges in central France, church bells rang out in celebration of a momentous event. King Charles VII of France announced that his queen, Marie of Anjou had given birth to a royal prince, an heir to the throne. Christened Louis, after St. Louis, King Louis IX, the pious and just Crusader king of the thirteenth century, (and also after his maternal grandfather), this future king Louis XI could hardly have been born at a less auspicious moment for a future King of France. For almost a century, successive Kings of France had fought successive Kings of England in what is known to historians (though not to contemporaries) as the Hundred Years War. Bound together in a complex bundle of feudal and dynastic relations, the two rulers had fought to clarify these reciprocal and sometimes contradictory relations. For example, the Kings of England, though sovereign in their English lands, were, or had been, also feudal lords or overlords of much of France, including the provinces of Normandy, Aquitaine, Touraine, and Anjou. When a previous King of France, Charles IV, died in 1328 without a son to succeed him, the stage was set for King Edward III of England to claim the French throne for himself, since his mother was the sister of Charles IV. For generations, Kings of England had launched campaigns in France to validate this claim, or to expand their territorial holdings, or simply to loot and plunder. Time after time, the English had vanquished the French: at Crécy in 1346, at Poitiers in 1356, and most recently at Agincourt in 1415.

On top of these seemingly interminable wars between the two kings, France had also become embroiled in a civil war. In an age of primitive communications and transportation, where information could travel no faster than a man on horseback, rulers often attempted to maintain their control of their more distant territories by ceding control of them to members of their immediate family, usually a younger brother or younger son. This practice of *appanage* also served the purpose of providing employment and income for subordinate members of the royal family, and would hopefully prevent them from meddling in the politics of the royal court. In essence, the king opened a regional branch office of the monarchy, one which typically had a fair amount of autonomy. This might work fairly well in the immediate term as the ties between father and son, or between older and younger brothers usually (though not always) brought loyalty and fidelity. By the second, third, and fourth generations, however, the ties between distant cousins (who may never have laid eyes on each other) were too weak to mean much at all.

This is precisely what happened in the case of the Duchy of Burgundy. In 1363, King John II of France made one of his younger sons Duke of Burgundy. This was Philip, subsequently known as "the Bold." Very quickly, Philip began adding to his domains, most notably in the Low Countries, where he married the daughter and heir of the Count of Flanders. He also played an important role in the French royal court. While his nephew, King Charles VI (r. 1380–1422) was a child, he acted as co-regent, along with his brothers Louis, Duke of Anjou, and Charles, Duke of Berry. Once the king attained the age of majority, but began to show signs of insanity, Philip and his brother Charles of Berry once again took up the regency. In 1402, however, the king overthrew his uncles' power, and put it into the hands of his younger brother, Louis, Duke of Orléans.

In 1407, the new Duke of Burgundy, John the Fearless (his father Philip the Bold had died in 1404) arranged for the assassination of his cousin Louis of Orléans. With a mad king, control of the government was contested between two bitterly opposed factions: Burgundian (those who supported the Duke of Burgundy), and Armagnacs (those who supported the new Duke of Orléans, Charles, son of the murdered duke).[13] The government over which they were fighting was nominally headed by the eldest surviving son of the mad Charles VI, a fifteen-year-old boy who had become heir to the throne, or Dauphin, upon the deaths of his two older brothers.

In 1415, English forces under King Henry V (immortalized by Shakespeare) once again thrashed the French at the Battle of Agincourt.

---

[13] The Orléans faction is more often known as the Armagnacs, because Charles had married the daughter of the Count of Armagnac, who led the opposition to the Duke of Burgundy after the assassination of Louis of Orléans.

Unlike previous English kings, Henry aimed at conquest of the entire French kingdom, rather than mere occupation of provinces. English armies went from victory to victory, supported by their ally the John the Fearless, Duke of Burgundy, conquering the wealthy and populous province of Normandy. In May of 1418, the gates of Paris were opened to the English and Burgundians. There ensued a general slaughter of Armagnacs and the flight of the Dauphin and his supporters from the capital.

In an effort to end the fratricidal violence, the Dauphin arranged for a meeting with Duke John the Fearless, in hopes of ending the Burgundian-Armagnac civil war. In September 1419, the two men met in the town of Montereau. Not only did they fail to reconcile, however, but angry words were exchanged, whereupon a member of the Dauphin's entourage killed the Duke. This murder cemented as nothing else could the alliance between England and Burgundy and its new duke Philip the Good (r. 1419–67). The united forces of England and Burgundy were too strong to be resisted. They seized the person of the mad Charles VI and dictated the terms of the humiliating Treaty of Troyes of 1420.

The Dauphin (later King Charles VII and father of the future Louis XI) was declared illegitimate and was disinherited. (His mother, Isabeau of Bavaria, cheerfully admitted that he was the product of an adulterous affair, and given her sexual escapades, no one had any trouble believing it.) Henry V of England was to marry the daughter of Charles VI, and he or his heir were declared heir to the throne of France. However, Henry V predeceased Charles VI by two months in 1422, and when the King of France died, the infant son of Henry V became King of both England and France. The disinherited son of the late king, known to historians still as the Dauphin, claimed to be the rightful king of France as Charles VII, retreated south of the River Loire to the town of Bourges, abandoning Northern France to the English under the Duke of Bedford, uncle of and regent for the infant King Henry VI. It was in these perilous times that the future Louis XI made his appearance into the world in 1423.

Given these dire circumstances, one could hardly blame the Dauphin Charles for succumbing to depression and lassitude. Not yet twenty years of age (he was born in 1403), he had been called a bastard by his mother, disinherited by his insane father, forced out of Paris into exile in the provincial town of Bourges, and set upon by England and Burgundy. His household and court at Bourges was a rather shabby and pathetic affair. He was surrounded and manipulated by men far more politically adept than he and who seemed content to dominate the constantly shrinking domain of the Dauphin. It must have seemed to Charles that the English were destined for ultimate victory, and that the best he could hope for was to delay the inevitable. The dismal decade of the 1420s has led many historians to dismiss his qualities of leadership throughout his reign, even to question his mental stability. It is probably more accurate to see this period as a reasonable response on the part of an inexperienced youth to a very difficult and disheartening situation.

The Dauphin's fortunes began to take a turn for the better in 1429, when he was roused to greater action by an uneducated young peasant girl from eastern France. Young Joan of Arc had become convinced of her divine mission to expel the English from France. Arriving in the town of Chinon in February of 1429, she announced to the astonished Dauphin that he was the true heir of France, that he must be crowned in the traditional manner in the city of Reims, as French kings had been for centuries, that the English must be expelled, and that she, Joan, was to be the divine instrument of these goals. She very quickly managed to relieve the English siege of the strategic city of Orléans. (Had Orléans fallen to the English, all of central and southern France lay open to the invaders.) She fought her way to Reims, deep in English-held territory, where on July 17, 1429, Dauphin Charles underwent the ceremony of coronation and became more widely recognized as King Charles VII.[14] Joan led Charles's armies in several more campaigns before being captured by Burgundian forces at Compiègne in May of 1430. She was sold to the English, tried as a witch and burned at the stake in Rouen on May 27, 1431. Charles VII and his advisors did not lift a finger to help her. Indeed, she was now something of an embarrassment, and the evidence suggests that Charles and his advisors were glad to be rid of her.

Be that as it may, Joan's campaigns and their effect on the King turned the tide. Roused into action, Charles VII threw off his earlier torpor and became a relatively effective ruler. No one has ever accused him of great personal courage or integrity, but his cautious methods seemed ideally suited for the times and the task at hand. By 1453, the English had been virtually expelled from France, earning Charles the nickname, "the Victorious."[15] In these latter stages of the Hundred Years War, the French cause was aided by several other factors. In 1435, the English governor of France, the Duke of Bedford, died. He was a younger brother of Henry V and acted as regent in France

---

[14] The ritual of coronation was much more than political theatre. It was a religious consecration of the king, an idea better conveyed by its name in French, the *sacre*. Indeed, it was a widely-held belief that the ceremony made the king, rather than simply acknowledging the wearer of the crown. That is, the king was not really king until he had been crowned at Reims. Following the *sacre*, the king became the only lay person in France to receive both the bread and wine during the sacrament of Mass, and was believed to possess miraculous powers of healing.

[15] I say "virtually" because the English did hold on to the Channel port of Calais for another century.

for his young nephew, Henry VI. With his death, the English lost their most effective leader and general. In 1435 as well, Duke Philip the Good of Burgundy abandoned the traditional Burgundian alliance with England, and henceforth Burgundy's substantial power and resources were either neutral or allied with France.[16]

While the birth of the future Louis XI in 1423 elicited demonstrations of joy among the towns still loyal to the Dauphin, the "King of Bourges" could not afford the luxury of extended celebrations. Barely a week after Louis' birth, on July 31, English and Burgundian forces crushed the Dauphin's army at Cravant and proceeded to threaten Bourges itself. Information regarding Louis' infancy and youth is sparse, and out of necessity much of what follows is surmise and informed speculation.

As was customary among families of the elite, care of the infant was assumed by nurses rather than the mother. Louis' mother, the Queen of France, was Marie d'Anjou, who from all accounts was a pious and gentle soul, but who played virtually no part in raising the heir to the throne. We do know that his mother and father were away from Bourges quite a lot, and that the young prince saw little of either parent. He was cared for in infancy by his nurses, who were ordinary women, not of the elite of society.

By the age of two, a separate household had been established for young Louis and he had been removed from Bourges to the isolated fortress of Loches in the province of Touraine. Here, cared for by his nurses, he apparently grew up in humble circumstances, at least considering his exalted status as heir to the French throne. His governess, in charge of the young prince's household, was his godmother, Catherine de l'Isle-Bouchard. She was a spectacularly ambitious and ruthless political animal. She was married first to the Count of Giac, one of Charles VII's chief advisors, in the bleak period of the mid 1420s. She persuaded her husband to disinherit in her favor his children from a previous marriage. In 1427 she conspired with an ambitious and equally unscrupulous nobleman, Georges de la Trémoïlle, to murder her husband. Shortly thereafter she and la Trémoïlle were married.

It is speculation, but it is certainly possible that in these circumstances, Louis failed to form a secure attachment to a caregiver. Lending plausibility is the fact that throughout his life, Louis seemed to have few if any close relationships. He feuded bitterly with his father and completely ignored his mother. He was married twice, first to Princess of Margaret of Scotland,

---

[16] The price that Charles VII paid for this was the wealthy and populous province of Picardy, which adjoined the Duke of Burgundy's lands in the Low Countries. This added significantly to the Duke's wealth and power, which set the stage for a protracted conflict between the grown king Louis XI and Philip's successor as Duke later in the fifteenth century.

and second to Charlotte, daughter of the Duke of Savoy. The first, he actively disliked, and the second he largely ignored, apart for the conjugal relations unfortunately necessary to produce heirs. As a grown man, Louis kept his own son and heir (later King Charles VIII, b. 1470, r. 1483–98) in relative isolation, much as he himself had been, confiding his care to others. Although he kept himself well-informed as to the health and education of his son, this seems to have been more out of concern for the future of the kingdom than out of affection or emotional attachment. The elder of his two daughters, Anne (b. 1460), he would respect for her intelligence, calling her "the least stupid woman in France." Louis married her to the son of the powerful Duke of Bourbon, and after Louis' death, Anne and her husband acted as regents for her under-aged brother. It is however, in his treatment of his younger daughter Jeanne (b. 1464), that we see the real consequences of Louis XI's emotionally stunted childhood. Pious and gentle, Jeanne suffered however from some physical deformities, the severity of which varied according to different observers. Certainly, one shoulder was higher than another, although it is debatable whether or not she should be considered a hunchback, and one leg was shorter than the other. It was also widely believed that she was incapable of having children. From the age of five, she was confined in a country château, where her caregivers were granted a tiny budget. Louis, in fact, did not lay eyes upon his daughter until 1475. Upon seeing her for the first time (from a distance), he remarked, "I didn't believe she was so ugly!" In 1473, she was betrothed to the young Louis, Duke of Orléans (b. 1462), at the insistence of her father, who hoped thereby eventually to incorporate the extensive holdings of the dukes of Orléans into the royal domain. Jeanne herself wanted nothing more than to live a quiet life of piety and contemplation, and the young duke certainly wanted nothing to do with Jeanne. Orléan's mother was threatened with exile, and the duke himself with confinement to a monastery. The marriage itself took place in 1476 when the groom was fourteen. Even then, young Orléans had to be threatened with death before going through with the wedding. The king then brutally ensured that the marriage was physically consummated in order to deny grounds for an annulment.[17]

---

[17] Louis of Orléans would later become King Louis XII (r. 1498–1515), when Charles VIII died without male heirs. When diplomacy dictated a marriage to the previous king's widow, Anne of Brittany, Louis XII launched annulment proceedings against Jeanne in order to hold on to the province of Brittany. In a very ugly case, he claimed (without proof or witnesses) that the marriage had never been consummated, that in fact, Jeanne's physical deformities precluded sexual relations. Jeanne consistently maintained that the marriage had been consummated, producing witnesses who testified that Louis had once boasted of having "mounted my wife three or four times in the night." Despite the weakness of Louis XII's case, Pope Alexander V granted the annulment for political

The future Louis XI likely grew up playing with the boys of the surrounding villages, and certainly later in his life showed little patience with the nobility's need for ostentatious display of wealth and status. Indeed, even as king, he was often mistaken for a gardener or a workman, due to his ordinary clothes and humble appearance. It also seems that it was during his childhood at Loches that he acquired his love of the outdoors, and of animals and hunting. Again, as king, he was an avid collector of natural curiosities, amassing a menagerie which included an elephant, camels, leopards, and ostriches, among more ordinary sorts of animals.

Although he did not frequently see his parents, care was taken to educate him in a manner befitting a future king of France. His tutor was Jean Majoris, a well-respected clergyman and friend and student of Jean Gerson. Gerson was rector of the University of Paris, and an administrator and theologian of European importance. It was Gerson who designed the curriculum for the education of the young prince. He was taught to read and write both French and Latin, although Majoris was instructed to conduct his education mostly in French. He was to be verbally reprimanded rather than subjected to corporal punishment. Above all, he was to be taught piety and compassion, remembering that all are equal in God's eyes, and that all, regardless of earthly rank, will be judged by God's standards. Little Louis seems to have been especially fond of history, and of the lives of the saints, which were at the time the most popular form of religious literature, indeed the means by which literate people received most of their religious knowledge. Once more we see that the child was the father of the man. For his whole life, Louis remained very devout, at least according to the standards of the day. To our minds, his religious faith appears somewhat superstitious and childish, for he was extremely devoted to physical relics of the saints and their supposed wonder-working powers.

Actual historical records which mention the prince in his childhood are rare. In 1429, a young nobleman named Guy de Laval, having stopped by Loches on his way to join Joan of Arc's army, wrote to his mother: "After vespers . . . I went to the castle to see Monseigneur the Dauphin, who is a very handsome and graceful lord. He must be about seven years old." According to a German chronicle, at about the same time, he was seen by Joan of Arc herself, who prophesied great things for the young prince. When he was about ten, Jouvenel des Ursins, an important bishop, historian and statesman, wrote that Louis was "good and well brought-up."

reasons. Jeanne was granted the title Duchess of Berry, and lived in solitude until her death in 1505. She founded an order of nuns, and was canonized in 1950 by Pope Pius XII.

Louis's circumstances changed dramatically in 1433, due to a palace coup at his father's court. Georges de la Trémoïlle, who had dominated the king since about 1427, was forced from power by a coalition of powerful nobles that included the younger brother of Marie of Anjou, Queen of France, and the mother of young prince Louis. Louis was taken from the isolation of Loches and at the age of ten joined his mother's household in the picturesque château at Amboise, on the bluffs overlooking the River Loire. From now on, he appears much more prominently and regularly in the historical record. His father also began to show more interest in his eldest son and heir. In 1434, father and son visited the important city of Tours, where they were greeted with adulation. For two years, Louis remained in Tours while his father directed the war against the English.

In 1436 and 1437, Louis passed the threshold from childhood to adolescence. First came his marriage, at the age of thirteen. In the summer of 1436 in the Cathedral at Tours, he was married to Princess Margaret, eldest daughter of King James I of Scotland. Scotland and France were traditional allies against their common English enemy, and diplomatic marriages were a key element in solidifying such alliances. There can be no question that Louis had no choice in the matter. As royal marriages went, this was a decidedly low-key affair. The father of the groom did not bother to greet his future daughter-in-law before the day of the wedding, and he was noticeably parsimonious in his treatment of his visitors from Scotland. He did not provide the usual games and jousts which accompanied a royal wedding, instead putting on only a relatively modest banquet. He arrived in Tours only the morning of the wedding and attended the ceremony still in his riding clothes, not even bothering to remove his spurs. It was agreed by all concerned that given their tender ages, they should not live together as man and wife. What Louis thought of his bride is not known, although we are certainly justified in supposing no great emotional attachment. They proved to be completely different in character: Louis grew into manhood as a pragmatic and realistic politician, while Margaret devoted herself to poetry and court life. Even when they were of an appropriate age, they hardly lived as man and wife, and they had no children together. She died in 1445 at the age of 21, likely of pneumonia.

In 1436 as well, a household of his own was established for the Dauphin. That is, he was no longer formally attached to his mother's household, and now entered the world of men much more fully than before. The governor appointed for him was Bernard d'Armagnac, Count of La Marche, a nobleman notable for his piety, severity, and ascetic lifestyle. His tutor, Jean Majoris, now became his confessor, or personal priest. The Dauphin's household was provided with a relatively modest annual income of 10,500 *livres* to meet his expenses.[18]

In the years after his marriage, Louis' father began the process of his political apprenticeship. It was also in this period that the first hostility appeared between father and son. No doubt the two are related. We see here the conundrum that confronted royal fathers. They understood that the heir needed training in governing to ensure an orderly succession and a stable kingdom. On the other hand, they were acutely conscious that they were training their own replacements, and that the heir might not wait until his father's death to flex his political muscle. Indeed, many kings must have remembered their tense relations with their own fathers.

Many historians have tried to determine and analyze the causes of the rift between Charles VII and the Dauphin, reading into events interpretations which have no sound basis in evidence. On the other hand, a good deal of a historian's work is to speculate on causes for which there is no direct written record. What seems to have happened is this: as young Louis grew to manhood, he began to show signs of determination and ability which his father lacked. For his whole life, Charles VII had had his fate determined by others: his mother, who disowned him; an insane father; a circle of ambitious nobles who saw domination of the king as their path to power and wealth; and an illiterate peasant girl who led his armies to victory when no one else could. It seems very likely that Charles began to resent and fear the abilities he saw developing in his son. Sharing only their genetic material, there was no emotional or affective tie to bind them together. Like Henry Ford, Charles both groomed his heir for power, and at the same time rarely passed up an opportunity to humiliate him, to remind him of who was still boss.

In 1436, father and son embarked on a tour of several parts of the kingdom. (Royal tours such as this were a common method of expressing and enhancing royal authority in the absence of a large bureaucracy and modern communications. They were also used to extract tax revenue from subjects in whose lives the royal government was normally a very distant force.) They toured southern and southeastern France, areas in which royal power was often more theoretical than real. Basically still strangers to each other, throughout the tour father and son maintained separate households,

---

[18] Monetary values are a minefield, given the varieties of coins in circulation. The *livre* was a fictitious "money of account." That is, it did not correspond to an actual coin; rather, the various coins in circulation were assigned a value in *livres* for accounting purposes. By way of comparison, the household of Louis' mother, Marie of Anjou, spent over 14,000 livres between November 1422 and June 1423. Even this was considered frugal, especially when compared with the expenses of the previous queen, the infamous Isabeau of Bavaria, whose household spent 26,700 *livres* from January to June of 1402, and 30,000 from January to June of 1404.

and were rarely in the same place at the same time. Louis visited the province of Dauphiné, which he looked forward to one day governing as a sort of apprenticeship before assuming the government of the entire kingdom.[19] He also visited the wealthy trade and banking center of Lyons, where he was very much impressed by the possibilities of commerce and finance. Indeed, when he became king, he was very solicitous of the needs of middle class businessmen. This concern served to further distance him from the concerns and preoccupations of the nobles, who held such occupations in utter contempt. In the southern provinces of Auvergne and Languedoc, Louis was confronted by the grievances of his subjects. In particular, these regions were subjected to the predations of *écorcheurs*, or bandits. The violence and disorders of the Hundred Years War allowed free reign to groups of deserted soldiers, criminals, and lawless nobles who preyed on local populations. The royal government seemed powerless to stop the violence, which must have impressed on young Louis just how ineffectual his father's government was.

In the summer of 1437, fourteen-year-old Louis saw his first military action. Charles had laid siege to the town of Château-Landon, then held by the English. Louis was given command of a force which assaulted and captured the town. Showing an uncharacteristic fierceness, he had the English defenders beheaded and their French allies hanged. It seemed as well that the son's success goaded his father into greater action, as the king embarked on an uncharacteristic and concentrated spurt of military activity. In the fall of 1437, Charles and Louis made their formal entry into Paris, which had been in English or Burgundian hands for decades.

In early 1439, father and son once again took to the road, this time through the provinces of Limousin, Auvergne, and Languedoc. Their chief objective was to gain their assent to tax revenue in order to prosecute the war against the English and to rid the countryside of *écorcheurs*. Indeed, it was the province of Languedoc which posed the greatest problems on both these scores. It was potentially a wealthy and important province, but one beset by bandits, noble feuds, and lawlessness. It also adjoined English-held Guyenne, and was therefore strategically important in the struggle to evict the English from France. In the spring, king and dauphin appeared before the assembly, or Estates, of Languedoc to gain their consent to taxation. The assembled delegates granted a substantial sum, but in turn requested greater government action against the *écorcheurs* and lawless nobles who were sapping the wealth of the people. Charles acceded to this request by

---

[19] In the fourteenth century, the last independent ruler of the region sold his lands to the King of France. Thereafter, the title of Dauphin was granted to the heir to throne, and when he came of age, he was given the province to govern.

appointing his fifteen-year-old son as lieutenant-general in Languedoc, essentially granting him vice-regal powers in the province.

Thus, at an age when today boys are eagerly anticipating obtaining their driver's license, young Louis was given command of an important province faced with serious and numerous problems. Could it be that Charles was attempting to humiliate his son by giving him an impossible task? There is nothing in the historical record to support such a supposition, but it is surely at least conceivable. It would certainly fit the king's accustomed *modus operandi*, and we do know that it was shortly afterwards that the first open breach occurred between the two. In addition, Charles had left Louis with a very difficult task, but provided no money and no men with which to accomplish it.

Whatever his father's expectations, Louis threw himself wholeheartedly into the job, and was, in fact, a spectacular success in his first real political role. He travelled from town to town, consulting with city governments and with merchants. He gained their assent to grants of funds, and demonstrated to them that they were spent in a good cause. Rather than confront the *écorcheurs* from a position of weakness, he bribed their leaders to leave Languedoc and assuaged public opinion by executing the worst offenders among their followers. Both of these features would be hallmarks of his later government of France. He had little patience with the arrogance and ostentation of the great lords who dominated the royal court, with their finely-honed sense of honor and conspicuous consumption. He courted, and relied upon, men of humbler origins: the lawyers, merchants, and businessmen who were the backbone of the kingdom. He was careful to consult them and include them in his decision-making process, much to the contempt of the great lords, who looked down upon these people as lesser sorts of beings. He was always acutely aware of the importance of finances, not because he was miserly, but because he understood that a prosperous kingdom was a powerful kingdom. He also became a master manipulator of people, in ways both positive and negative. In Languedoc, as later in his career, his actions demonstrated to ordinary people that their tax money brought tangible benefits in the form of order and security, rather than simply disappearing into the pockets of greedy courtiers. As his treatment of the *écorcheurs* attests, he was not above striking a deal with unpalatable features, but very few got the better of him in the long run. He would eventually become known as the "universal spider" for his ability to weave webs of intrigue and manipulation in which he ensnared his foes.

At the same time he was dealing with the *écorcheurs* and coaxing funds from the people, he also attempted to bring peace to feuding nobles, although in practice there was often precious little to distinguish them from the *écorcheurs*. The most egregious case concerned Mathieu de Foix and the Count of Armagnac, who had been conducting their very own private war for a decade. Armagnac's mother, the countess of Comminges, already a widow twice over, at the age of fifty-six married de Foix, her thirty-two-year-old cousin. Foix then proceeded to imprison his new wife while he pillaged her lands, which were now under his control. Understandably, Armagnac resented this treatment of his mother, all the more since he felt he had a greater right to these lands than a trumped-up gigolo like de Foix. Forces loyal to the two lords laid waste to the lands in question and the violence spread throughout the countryside. No one, neither priest, noble, nor judge, was able to convince them to put down their arms. No one, that is, until the Dauphin Louis. Summoning them to appear before him, Louis persuaded the two to accept a truce, during which their lawyers would attempt to arrive at a solution acceptable to both parties. Once again, we see Louis adopting a tactic which he would later follow as king. Whenever possible, he opted for compromise, negotiations, and manipulation, rather than war. Once again, this was counter to the prevailing noble ethos of the day, where war was a glorious endeavor. Only in combat were the qualities inherent in gentlemen of true quality clearly revealed. The medieval and early modern nobleman was above all a warrior, and deprived of an actual war in which to fight, he was just as likely to manufacture the pretext for one. It is perhaps overly speculative to suggest, but it certainly seems likely that Louis' earliest years, spent in humble circumstances at Loches, far from the royal court and its pomp and ritual (such as it was for the "King of Bourges") imbued in him a fundamental antipathy for the pretensions of his noble subjects.

Having brought order to chaotic Languedoc, Louis was on the verge of attacking the English in Guyenne when he was abruptly ordered by his father to return to the royal court. The reasons for this are unclear, although some historians have speculated that Charles was jealous of his son's success:

> Shrewd beyond his years though Louis was, he would never understand that his father meant, consciously or unconsciously, to revenge himself for his weakness by thwarting a son who was anything but weak.[20]

Although plausible, we lack "smoking gun" evidence for this interpretation, and in particular, it may suffer from historical hindsight. That is, we know that father son did become bitter enemies, and we see all previous events in light of this. There is an additional factor to consider here.

---

[20] Paul Murray Kendall, *Louis XI* (New York: Norton, 1971), 47.

Charles VII was beginning the process of transforming his military forces. Throughout the middle ages, kings had relied for their armies on the feudal levy. That is, the nobles of France were the king's vassals, bound to him by a personal and voluntary feudal contract. As part of this contract, vassals were obligated, when called upon, to furnish their lord (in this case the king) with a specific number of soldiers for a specified period of time, often forty days a year. This was a terribly unwieldy and inefficient way to fight a war. Soldiers tended to be more loyal to their immediate noble commanders than to the king, and when their specified period service was up, they went home, regardless of the tactical or strategic situation. Noble commanders were motivated not by the king's strategic aims, but by their desire for military glory and plunder. Most of the battles of the Hundred Years were fought by armies of this type (supplemented most often by mercenary forces who were even more unreliable), with disastrous results for the French. Although there had been earlier attempts, in the 1440s Charles VII brought into being the first permanent royal army in European history, one which was paid for by the royal government, and commanded directly by the king or his delegates. This was created by a royal ordinance of 1445, and the units created by it were known as the *compagnies d'ordonnance*. However, in 1439, the king took the necessary preliminary step of forbidding nobles to raise their own military forces. This was very controversial, since it seemed to undermine the nobles' *raison d'être*, and they saw it, not unreasonably, as an assault on their power and prestige. The discontent produced by this measure, which the king must have anticipated, seems to be behind his recall of his son from Languedoc. This was either because he wanted his very able son at his side in difficult circumstances, or because he feared (as eventually happened) that his resentful nobles would attempt to enlist his son in their plots against him. Indeed, a handful of powerful nobles were conspiring to assert their dominance over the king: the Duke of Bourbon, the Duke of Alençon, the so-called "Bastard of Orléans" (an illegitimate son of the Duke of Orléans), and Georges de la Trémoïlle.

Frustrated though he was, Louis reluctantly obeyed his father and returned to court, where he chafed under his father's domination. He felt that he should be invested with the traditional territory of Dauphiné. After all, his father had taken possession of it when he was fourteen. Louis was now seventeen and already an accomplished administrator. He lacked any revenue of his own, and the grants he received from the king were inadequate to maintain an appropriate household establishment. His wife, Margaret of Scotland had become a favorite of the king and queen, and they refused Louis' requests that she join him in an independent household. He had the same governor at seventeen that he had had at ten. In short, Louis felt that his father was still treating him as a child, rather than the competent adult he had become.

Shortly afterwards (December 1439), Louis was once again sent by father to subdue a disorderly region, namely the western provinces of Poitou, Aunis, and Saintonge, which had fallen prey to the same plagues as Languedoc. Once again, Louis accomplished his task with aplomb. At the same time, however, the rebellious nobles made contact with the young Dauphin to enlist him in their schemes. The chief noble schemer was Charles, Duke of Bourbon, a wealthy and powerful noble, according to a contemporary "the best athlete in France and the most persuasive man of his time . . . an Absolam, another Trojan Paris." It is possible that the king sent Louis into the western provinces precisely to remove him from the machinations of Bourbon. If so, the gambit failed spectacularly. By early 1440, Louis, Bourbon and the other noble rebels had agreed on a plan. The king was to be captured and control of the government was to be seized by the Dauphin. (The rebellious nobles no doubt intended that they were to be the powers behind the throne.) Louis met with Alençon in the latter's town of Niort in February of 1440. Following this meeting Louis purged his household of his father's appointees including his governor, Bernard d'Armagnac, whom he suspected of spying on behalf of his father.

This noble rebellion of 1440 became known as the Praguerie, because it reminded contemporaries of a recent revolt in Bohemia. Its ostensible cause was noble dissatisfaction with the conduct of the war. (In time-honored fashion, the rebels protested that they would of course *never* rebel against the king; rather, they were attempting to liberate him from the influence of his evil advisor, in this case Duke Charles of Maine, brother of Queen Marie.) Although the nobles phrased their discontent in terms of the public welfare, this was simply a smokescreen for their own political ambitions. As mentioned above, they feared the impact that military reforms would have on their own power. They had a fundamentally different, and backward-looking view of France as a kind of noble republic rather than a centralized kingdom. They saw the king not as their sovereign lord, but as first among equals. They were the king's natural partners in governing France. They owed the king loyalty and obedience when he was right, but when he was wrong, they had the right, even the duty, to rebel against him. The Dauphin Louis and the rebel nobles each had their reasons to rebel, and they needed each other if they were to have any chance of success. The nobles needed the legitimacy that the heir to the throne brought to the cause, and Louis needed the men and money that the nobles commanded. Each thought they could use the other to attain their goals. (It is ironic that when he became king, Louis himself faced a similar revolt with his younger brother as the figurehead, and that throughout his reign Louis would suppress the pretensions of the nobles much more effectively than his father had ever done.)

But Charles VII was no longer the inexperienced and depressed youth of the 1420s. The royal army moved quickly against the rebels, who found little support for their cause among ordinary people. In the wake of military defeat, Alençon and Bourbon quickly abandoned the rebel cause, leaving Louis isolated.[21] As a condition of peace with the rebels, Charles demanded they turn his son over to him. Louis responded with terms of his own:

> In order that the said Lord Dauphin may maintain his estate, may the King be pleased to grant him possession of the province of Dauphiné, since it appears to him unjust that the province has been so far withheld from him, though past Dauphins received it before they arrived at the present Dauphin's age.

Since the revenues from Dauphiné were insufficient to support his household, Louis further demanded that he be appointed governor of either the provinces of Languedoc, Guyenne, Gascony, or the Ile de France, the region around Paris. His followers were to be granted amnesty for their actions during the rebellion. These demands, especially the additional governorships, were very likely intended to be unacceptable to the king, since they would place a large part of the kingdom under Louis' control. And indeed, Charles responded in a noncommittal manner:

> when the Lord Dauphin presents himself at court with due humility the King will treat him as his son and provide for his estate as well as for that of Madame la Dauphine [Louis' wife, Margaret of Scotland] in such manner as shall content him. The requests made in his letter, touching the associates of the Lord Dauphin, will be met to his satisfaction.

Still, Louis resisted. He responded with two suggestions of his own. First, his father the king could mount an all-out war against the English, which Louis would command. Second, Louis was willing to submit his cause to the judgement of the Estates-General, a national representative

---

[21] We need not think of the Praguerie as a war to the death. Such noble revolts were relatively common and followed a familiar pattern. Dissatisfied nobles would publish a manifesto of their grievances, call their supporters to arms, and assert their control over towns in their territories. The king and his supporters would march against them. A few skirmishes would ensue, whereupon the rebels would announce their submission and the king would meet their demands halfway, allowing both sides to save face. This was the way that the game was played.

body which met infrequently, normally only at times of great crisis. Either choice would entail the suggestion that Charles had lost control of both his son and his kingdom. Military operations resumed, with the rebel cause losing strength day by day. Finally, by July, Bourbon had convinced Louis to reconcile with his father. Even then, however, Louis felt he had reason to mistrust Charles. As Bourbon and Louis approached the town where Charles was staying, a delegation from the king informed Louis that three of his most ardent supporters would not be amnestied. Louis wished to turn around and resume the rebellion, but Bourbon pointed out to that they were, in fact, trapped.

Louis knelt before his father and asked forgiveness, both for himself and his followers. The king replied that Louis himself was welcome and forgiven, but not his three followers. Louis continued to argue the case: "What, sire? You would have me break my pledged word to these gentlemen?" To which the king responded:

> Louis, all doors are open to you. If they are not wide enough, I will make a breach in the wall, so that you can leave whenever you wish. You are my son, and you may not grant favors to anyone without my permission. If it pleases you to leave, then with God's blessing we shall find some other prince of the blood who will serve us better in maintaining our honor and sovereignty than you have done.

With no real alternatives, Louis had no choice but submit. Charles made a public show of punishing his disobedient son. His entire household was dismissed, except for his cook and his confessor. Louis was made to accompany his father on a triumphal parade of defeated towns which had shortly before supported the Dauphin and the rebels. So much for the stick; Louis also got the carrot, for by the end of July 1440, Charles granted possession of Dauphiné to his son along with a substantial monthly stipend. On the surface, at least, the reconciliation between father and son appeared complete.

From his experience in the Praguerie, Louis likely learned several lessons that he would recall when he became king. First, the great nobles of France cared fundamentally only about themselves and their power and prestige. This was a double-edged sword. It meant that they were tremendous obstacles to the expansion of royal power in France. On the other hand, because they were concerned with their own narrow self-interest, they were susceptible to tactics of divide and conquer. He also likely learned that he could trust no one but himself, and those who depended on him and him alone. He felt betrayed by the nobles who had led him into the Praguerie, and then abandoned him when it suited their interests.

For the next several years, relations between father and son seemed to be on the mend. Louis was increasingly used as a military commander and continued to meet with notable success in battles against the English and the *écorcheurs*. Most notably, in 1443 he commanded the army which raised the English siege of the important Channel seaport of Dieppe. By 1444, the English were seeking peace with France. Ultimately, only a two-year long truce emerged from these negotiations, but once again Louis played an important role. The problem was that peace between kings did not always bring peace to the kingdom. Disbanded and deserted soldiers, lawless nobles, and other assorted bandits and *écorcheurs* would continue to plague towns and countryside alike. The best way to get rid of these problems was to provide soldierly employment for them, preferably outside the kingdom.

As it happened, Frederick III, the Holy Roman Emperor was looking for allies in helping to subdue his rebellious subjects in Switzerland. It seemed to Charles VII a heaven-sent opportunity to kill at least two birds with one stone: he could assist an ally while ridding France of the *écorcheurs*, and at the same time establish French power further to the east, hemming in his rival the Duke of Burgundy. Louis, just having turned twenty-one, was given command of this army of brigands and cutthroats. In August of 1444, a motley horde of some 25,000 *écorcheurs* assembled near the city of Langres in eastern France, not far from the border with Burgundy. They made their way through Burgundy, laying waste the countryside and threatening the towns, much to the annoyance of Duke Philip the Good. Louis' forces encountered the Swiss near the town of Basel. In a hard fought and bloody battle, Louis' forces prevailed, with significant casualties on both sides. One of the consequences of this battle was that Louis and the Swiss acquired a healthy respect for each other. Louis was impressed by the fierceness of the Swiss soldiers, and the Swiss liked what they saw in Louis as a commander. In the aftermath of this victory, he moved forces to the north into Alsace. (Alsace was at that time a patchwork of towns and small territories and noble holdings. German in culture and language, it was in theory ruled by the Holy Roman Empire, but in actual fact, the towns and nobles were virtually independent.) His goal was twofold: he needed quarters and supplies for army through the winter, and second, he seems to have been enhancing his own political and military power. In short, he was beginning to act as an independent political player, backed by his army of cutthroats and fortified by his victory over the Swiss. From his headquarters in the town of Ensisheim, he sent for his wife in order to establish his own court.

Once again, we may speculate that Charles VII was goaded into activity by the military accomplishments of his son. He launched an ill-thought-out and ultimately futile assault on the heavily fortified city of Metz. He also ordered Louis to cease his operations in Alsace. He may have felt that his son's successes showed him up, or perhaps that Louis was making French relations with other rulers more complicated, particularly those with the Duke of Burgundy and the Holy Roman Emperor. He may also have been motivated by his genuine concern for his son, for Louis had suffered a serious wound to his knee. Certainly, this was the pretext given for the orders to quit Alsace. Whatever the case, Louis once again reluctantly and belatedly obeyed his father and in January 1445 joined his father's court in the city of Nancy in Lorraine. Lorraine was in the fifteenth century an independent duchy on France's eastern boundary with the Holy Roman Empire. The duke at the time was the renowned poet and bon vivant René of Anjou, brother of Queen Marie and therefore the brother-in-law of Charles VII. As the name implies, he was also Duke of Anjou, and in addition to that, he was Count of Provence, and claimed to be the rightful king of the Italian Kingdom of Naples and Sicily, although he never exercised actual power there. René was a much better poet than ruler and was very much dependent on the goodwill of Charles VII and France. He was also one of the political powers in the court of Charles VII and tried to use his influence with the king to enhance his own wealth and power.

For the next two years, Louis remained at the royal court, first in Nancy, and then as it travelled around France. It was a miserable period for the Dauphin, one in which the breach with his father became irreparable, and which would end with his expulsion from the royal court. In Nancy, the court was completely preoccupied with an impending marriage. Margaret of Anjou, the beautiful and accomplished daughter of "King" René, and niece of the king and queen was to be married to King Henry VI of England. In typical fashion, the event was celebrated by an extended period of festivities, balls, banquets, and jousts. Still hobbled by his knee injury, Louis took little part in these celebrations, which were in any case not much to his liking.

It was also a time of significant stress in Louis' own marriage. He and Margaret had proved to be completely incompatible, although it is certainly debatable whether Louis would have found acceptable any wife of his father's choosing. Unlike her husband, Margaret revelled in court life. She was devoted to the latest fashions and surrounded herself with like-minded young women. Like her father, King James I of Scotland, she fancied herself a poet, though none of her compositions has survived. Not only was she a wife of the king's choosing, she had endeared herself to the king and queen, which could only further disparage her in her husband's mind. She prided herself on her fashionably slim figure, and to maintain it consumed a weird diet made up of vinegar and green apples. Most important of all, she had not given birth to an heir and seemed to show no interest in doing so.

Louis, already an accomplished soldier and administrator, struggled to find a suitable role during this period. His father once again both made use of his talents, and at the same time endeavored to demonstrate that he was still the boss. For example, Louis was put in charge of negotiating a number of jurisdictional disputes with the Duchess of Burgundy. He made good progress, but refused to press a side issue. This was a substantial debt owed to the Duke of Burgundy by René of Anjou. When Louis refused to negotiate the cancellation of the debt, his father ended his diplomatic mission. To add insult to injury, Charles then made a number of concessions to Burgundy in exchange for the cancellation of his brother-in-law's debt. The Milanese ambassador reported to his government:

> There are in the bosom of the House of France bitter jealousies and red-hot factional strife. There could not be more violent hostility than that which reigns between the illustrious Lord Dauphin [Louis] and the King of Sicily [René]. This comes from the fact that the King of Sicily is the one who runs everything in the realm.

It must sometimes have seemed to Louis that his father went out of his way to humiliate him. For example, Charles kept his son on a humiliatingly short financial leash. He had to borrow 5,500 *livres* (a substantial sum) from one of his friends just to pay his household expenses. The most that the king would do for his son's finances was to give him permission to ask a number of towns for grants of revenue. At the same time, the king gave the Dauphine Margaret 2,000 *livres* to buy silks and furs.

Charles also made a point of snubbing Louis' associates, one of whom was an accomplished soldier named Antoine de Chabannes, Count of Dammartin. He had been at Louis' side for a number of years, mostly recently during the campaigns in Switzerland. As mentioned above, in 1445, Charles VII established the first standing royal army in French history, the *compagnies d'ordonnance*. Chabannes was pointedly passed over for a command.

Without a meaningful task to occupy him, Louis became involved in the plotting and factional infighting which dominated the royal court of Charles VII. For his entire reign, Charles was dominated by a series of ambitious nobles and courtiers, some more capable than others. No doubt this predisposed Louis against such practices. When he finally became king, not only did he not rely for counsel on prominent nobles as his father had done, he was always at pains to be seen to govern as well as to reign. Although he was ably assisted by ministers and counsellors, there was never any hint that he was captive to noble factionalism, as his father had been.

During this period at his father's court, Louis also became a widower. Margaret of Scotland, never very robust, succumbed probably to pneumonia in August of 1445. Contemporaries attributed her death in large part to vicious rumors about her conduct circulating at court. Some historians have seen the hand of her husband behind these rumors, but on very slender evidence. Whatever the case, her death caused more grief for her father-in-law than her husband.

At this time in 1440s, René of Anjou and his brother Charles, Count of Maine had the ear of their royal brother-in-law. By the mid 1440s, however, their influence with the king was on the wane. The new forces at court were Pierre de Brézé and especially the king's new mistress Agnès Sorel. De Brézé was from a minor noble family, and first became prominent in the service of the Anjou family. By 1443, he had established himself as Charles VII's preeminent counsellor, surpassing even the influence of his former patron, Charles, Count of Maine. At roughly the same time, the beautiful young noblewoman Agnès Sorel caught the attention of the middle-aged king. Over the next several years (she died in 1450 of complications from a miscarriage), she would bear him three illegitimate daughters.[22] Charles VII showered her and her family with money and gifts, and she exercised enormous influence in the royal court. She was granted the estate of Beauté and was known appropriately as the *dame de Beauté* (the lady of Beauty). The exact relationship between de Brézé and Sorel is unclear, although they were certainly political allies. Contemporaries gossiped that she was or had been de Brézé's lover, and that he procured her services for the king. Other gossip had it that she was also Louis' lover, and that she was the cause of the estrangement between father and son. This seems unlikely, but at the very least we can imagine that Louis felt it was inappropriate for his forty-something father to be so infatuated with a woman twenty years younger, that is, of Louis' own age.

Louis certainly attempted to play the game of noble factionalism at the royal court, although somewhat half-heartedly and without much success. He sent de Brézé a large quantity of fine Rhine wine, and the evidence suggests that Louis was attempting to exercise influence on the king through de Brézé. He also seemed, at least at first, to be on reasonably good terms with Agnès Sorel, even if they were not lovers. He sent her a set of costly tapestries as a gift. By late 1446, however, the Dauphin was clearly at odds with his father's most intimate counsellors. In all likelihood, everyone

---

[22] Illegitimate births among royalty and the nobility were not the scandal that one might suspect. Given the realities of arranged marriages, people sought romantic attachments and found sexual attraction outside of marriage. Many illegitimate children were well-provided for and played prominent roles in social and political life.

concerned felt that the royal court was simply not big enough for all of them, that Louis could expand his influence only at the expense of Agnès and de Brézé, and *vice versa*. Stories circulated of a physical confrontation between Louis and Agnes, although observers differed on the details.

At this point, in the fall of 1446, Antoine de Chabannes, Louis' comrade-in-arms came forward with details of Louis' plotting against his father. According to Chabannes, and his testimony must be taken with more than a grain of salt, in the spring of 1446, Louis approached him with a scheme to overthrow the influence of de Brézé and Agnes, to suborn or overcome the king's Scottish bodyguards, and seize the person of the king. Louis would then exercise power in France. The only evidence for this plot is Chabanne's own deposition, and Louis vehemently denied the accusations. Nevertheless, the king clearly believed Chabannes, as well as additional evidence adduced by de Brézé. Louis was clearly a destabilizing influence and needed to be put into a position where he could not meddle in the politics of the royal court. The king therefore sent him into a kind of exile for four months, during which time he was to go to Dauphiné and receive the allegiance of the inhabitants as Dauphin. It is hard to imagine that Louis saw this "punishment" as anything but a liberation from the factional infighting and gossip-mongering of the royal court. Besides, this was exactly what Louis had been after for years: a chance to play a meaningful political role, out of his father's shadow, while he waited for his turn on the throne.

On January 1, 1447, Louis set off for Dauphiné. What was supposed to be a four-month exile from the royal court in fact lasted for a decade and a half. Louis never saw his father again, although Charles lived until 1461. Several days before his departure, his mother, Queen Marie, gave birth to a baby boy. Named Charles after his father, his birth meant Louis' position as heir to the throne was not as secure as it had been. Remember the king's words to Louis in the aftermath of the Praguerie: "If it pleases you to leave, then with God's blessing we shall find some other prince of the blood who will serve us better in maintaining our honor and sovereignty than you have done."

The region of Dauphiné was in an anomalous political situation, even by the chaotic standards of the time. Technically, it was not part of the Kingdom of France, but rather part of the Holy Roman Empire. In actual fact, its ruler, who carried the title of Dauphin, was virtually independent of outside control. In 1349, the Dauphin sold his political rights in the region to the current King of France, with the understanding that several conditions be observed. The province was to be governed by the king's eldest son and heir, henceforth known as the Dauphin, who was to govern it as an *appanage*. It was never to be formally incorporated into the Kingdom of France, and it is inhabitants were to enjoy in perpetuity exemption from many taxes assessed in France proper. Although not wealthy or populous — it had only two largish towns, Grenoble and Valence — it was strategically important in several different ways. To the west it bordered the commercially vital Rhône River. To the east it adjoined the territories of the independent Duke of Savoy, which straddled the Alps and extended into northwest Italy. Italy was the most prosperous region in Europe, and in the fifteenth century was undergoing the cultural and literary revival of the Renaissance. It was, however, politically disunited and vulnerable, presenting a tempting target to European rulers. If the King of France wanted to participate in the diplomatic affairs of Italy, Dauphiné and Savoy were crucial linchpins. To the north lay the lands of the Duke of Burgundy, who was once again emerging as the French king's greatest rival and threat.

Of all the Dauphins in French history, from the fourteenth century through the French Revolution, only Louis XI lived in the region for any period of time and governed it at first hand. As he had done on previous occasions when given a political task, Louis threw himself into the job. Indeed, his career and achievements in Dauphiné may be seen as template for what he would do when he eventually ascended the French throne. Although in theory a unified territory, Dauphiné, like France itself, was in fact a hodgepodge of overlapping, competing, and contradictory jurisdictions. Its bishops claimed political jurisdiction over large areas, and its nobles conducted themselves as independent potentates.

Administratively, Louis revolutionized the government of Dauphiné. He persuaded the bishops, through a variety of means, to abandon their claims to political jurisdiction. He outlawed private war between nobles, and compelled the nobles to personally do homage and swear allegiance to him. He further required them to furnish him with armed men at their expense, providing himself with an army. He met frequently with assemblies of his subjects, from whom he was able to coax greater tax revenues. He eliminated many of the overlapping and frequently conflicting feudal jurisdictions that had hampered both the judicial system and the economy. He set up a *parlement*, or supreme court, in his capital of Grenoble, to oversee the administration of justice. In 1452, he founded a university at Valence to compete with much older and more established institutions at Montpellier, Toulouse, and Orléans.

As he would throughout his life, Louis took an avid interest in commerce and industry, highly unusual for rulers at the time, who generally concerned themselves only with court politics, warfare, diplomacy, hunting, and women. To encourage grain production, he imposed a tariff on imported grain in times of plentiful harvests, but also subsidized imports in times of poor harvests. He encouraged and subsidized enterprising merchants, and attracted foreign merchants and craftsmen to immigrate. He exempted Jewish financiers from the restrictions that had hampered their activities.

Not only was he happy in his work, but personally as well he seems to have found some contentment at last. For the first and really the only time in his life, he discovered the joys of feminine companionship. Normally indifferent to women, he enjoyed the attention of two mistresses in these years. With one of them, he fathered three daughters, for whom he made generous provision and arranged prestigious marriages.

He also spent a good deal of time indulging his one true passion, outside of governing and politics, that of hunting. In the foothills of the Alps, Dauphiné was a rugged land and teemed with game. Hunting was considered a traditional royal pastime, as it was seen as a preparation for war, and in some ways a substitute for it. Unlike many other rulers, however, for Louis the hunt was not a ceremonial display for the court. He was a true outdoorsman who enjoyed roughing it.

No one, however, least of all Louis or his father, could forget that one day he would be King of France. Father and son continued to correspond, and their letters were reasonably cordial, although somewhat formulaic. Each had agents and spies at the other's court, and each attempted to meddle in and manipulate the other's affairs. Ambitious courtiers sought to advance their fortunes by manipulating these tensions. One of the spectacular cases was that of a man named Guillaume Mariette. He had accompanied Louis to Dauphiné in 1447, and was shortly afterwards sent on a mission to the royal court. He attempted to ingratiate himself with de Brézé and the king by informing them that Louis was actively plotting against his father. Imprisoned on account of unrelated offenses, including forging documents, he managed to escape from prison and returned to Dauphiné, where he attempted to turn double agent. He informed Louis that the whole thing had been de Brézé's idea, an attempt to poison the king against his son and enhance de Brézé's power. In the end, Louis sent him back to France where he was eventually beheaded. In the meantime, Louis' supporters at the French court launched proceedings against de Brézé for attempting to turn the king against his son. De Brézé admitted having met with Mariette, but Charles pardoned him, stating that the offense was a minor one, more than outweighed by his services to the kingdom. As always, Charles was prepared to believe the worst about Louis, while condoning similar, or worse, conduct among his favorites.

The event which brought tensions to a head was Louis' proposed marriage. A widower in his mid-twenties, Louis was still childless. He had on several occasions requested his father's assistance in making a suitable match, but nothing ever came of them. In 1450, Louis requested Charles's permission to marry eleven-year-old Charlotte, the daughter of his neighboring ruler, the Duke of Savoy. Louis' goal was undoubtedly to combine the forces of Dauphiné and Savoy in pursuing conquests in Italy. Charles refused to give his permission, as he saw the match as unsuitable. It was clearly more in Louis' interest as the ruler of Dauphiné to establish a marriage alliance with his neighbor than it was in the interest of the King of France, as France was already allied with Savoy. Charles likely feared anything that would strengthen his son, while at the same time he sought to reassert his paternal control. He flatly forbade the marriage and ordered Louis to the royal court. Louis' answer was to proceed with preparations for the wedding as if nothing had changed. He was clearly no longer a youth who could be pressured into obeying his father. He was by now an experienced soldier and ruler who knew his own mind and was prepared to pursue his own course of action.

Charles sent an envoy to Savoy to prevent the marriage, who arrived just in time to be greeted with a *fait accompli*: on March 9, 1451, the twenty-seven-year-old Dauphin married twelve-year-old Charlotte of Savoy. Charles was furious, of course, but there was not much that he could do. He continued, on the one hand, to threaten his son, and on the other, to entice him back to the royal court. In his more heated moments, Charles VII mused about disinheriting Louis in favor of his much younger brother Charles. For his part, Louis wrote to his father that he wanted nothing more than to be reconciled, but on two conditions: first, that he not be required to return to the royal court, and second, that he not be forced to abandon his friends and supporters. In the summer of 1452, Charles mounted a military expedition against Savoy in order to separate its duke from the Dauphin. Louis greatly feared that its real objective was Dauphiné and himself. A stalemate had been reached. Both father and son professed a desire for reconciliation, but each put conditions on their desire that made it impossible for the other to accept.

Charles VII, meanwhile, was occupied with the war against the English. In 1452, the English once again invaded the southwestern province of Guyenne, seizing control of the city of Bordeaux. The following year, French forces once again expelled the English, bringing to an end the Hundred Years War, although no one at the time could have known it. With the defeat of the English, Charles once again turned his attention to his wayward son.

Negotiations continued, letters were dispatched back and forth, but reconciliation proved impossible in the end. Louis mistrusted his father, and Charles insisted that Louis first submit himself to his authority, and then they could talk about the future. Throughout the spring and summer of 1456, Louis desperately sent envoy after envoy to the royal court, to no avail. Charles continued to insist that Louis submit himself unconditionally, while Louis refused to budge on his two conditions. Finally, Charles had had enough, and in August put together an army to march on Dauphiné to bring his son back by force. This army was commanded by Louis' former comrade in arms, Antoine de Chabannes. Louis was in fear of his life, perhaps not so much from his father, but from his advisors, who had reason to fear their fates when Louis would become king. Their best chance, it might seem to them, was to have Louis disposed of in favor of his younger brother.

For some time, Louis had been contemplating several escape strategies. He made it known that he was thinking of visiting England. He had maintained his contacts in Switzerland and sent an emissary there. He mused about joining a Crusade against the Muslim Turks proposed by the Duke of Burgundy. In the end, he decided for Burgundy, since this option at least allowed him to maintain the pretense that he was not fleeing his father, but rather enlisting in a Crusade. On August 30, Louis and a small group of friends fled Dauphiné, arriving in the town of Louvain several weeks later.

Despite the crusading pretext, it is difficult to see Louis' decision to seek refuge with the Duke of Burgundy as anything other than a deliberate insult to his father, for Duke Philip the Good of Burgundy was Charles's strongest rival and greatest threat. As we have seen, in the later fourteenth centuries, the Dukes of Burgundy had become an important political force. Although theoretically subordinate to the king of France, successive dukes had established virtual independence. From this position they allied with the English, and schemed to dominate the government of the mad king Charles VI of France. At the same time, they increased their landholdings, primarily in the wealthy and populous Low Countries. Duke Philip the Bold (r. 1363–1404) had acquired the neighboring Free County of Burgundy (Franche-Comté), technically part of the Holy Roman Empire, and the counties of Artois, Flanders, Nevers, and Rethel. His grandson, Philip the Good (r. 1419–67), further expanded his holdings in the Low Countries, acquiring the provinces of Namur, Hainault, Holland, Frisia, Zeeland, Brabant, and Luxembourg. Although we call him the Duke of Burgundy, his real wealth and power came from his lands in the Low Countries.

As we have seen, in 1435 Philip abandoned his alliance with England, and from then on was either allied with France or neutral. In exchange he acquired the wealthy province of Picardy, which adjoined his Dutch territories. In the mid-fifteenth century, Philip the Good was the most powerful ruler in Europe, despite his lack of a royal title and his theoretical subservience to the King of France. His court was a focal point of art and culture, and Philip himself was an extravagant patron. He established the Order of Golden Fleece, a chivalric order which quickly became the most prestigious in Europe, as its membership was limited to twenty-four. It was based on the legends of King Arthur and the Knights of the Round Table. Strategically, Philip aimed at linking up his territories in Burgundy with those in the Low Countries, which could only threaten France's eastern frontier. So, in taking refuge with Philip, Louis was delivering to his father a deliberate slap in the face.

On the other hand, Louis' uninvited presence presented Philip with a dilemma. He was, after all, technically a subject and vassal of the King of France, and Charles VII's demands to return his prodigal son put him in a very awkward position. At the same time, as Charles's rival and the most powerful ruler in Europe, Louis presence provided him with a significant benefit. For the five years that Louis remained in Philip's lands, the duke would play the part of the benevolent "uncle" (his first wife was Louis' aunt), who wanted nothing more than to reconcile the feuding father and son. At the same time, however, such a reconciliation was the last thing he really wanted. Nor could he ever forget that his guest would one day be King of France.

Louis also had his own tightrope to walk. Basically a penniless refugee, he depended utterly on Philip's goodwill. As Dauphin, however, he was superior in rank to the duke. Philip always made a great show of observing such distinctions, while Louis went out of his to diminish them. This cautious posturing was fortunately well-suited to the temperament of each man. For Philip was the epitome of the glorious feudal prince. Devoted to the ideals of chivalry (as witnessed by his founding of the Order of the Golden Fleece), he played the part of the generous patron and noble to perfection. The Burgundian court was held up as the ideal. Philip sponsored vast banquets and tournaments, maintained a huge and costly household, and had at least thirty mistresses by whom he produced no fewer than seventeen acknowledged bastards. Louis, on the other hand, as we have seen, had little inclination towards or patience with such grandiose posturing, preferring simplicity in dress, food, and lifestyle.

For five years Louis remained under the protection of Philip the Good. Philip gave to Louis an estate and château for his use at Genappe, in the countryside near Brussels, and substantial annual grant of 36,000 *livres*. In doing so, of course, he not only intended to arouse Louis' gratitude, but also to contrast his benevolence with the stinginess of Charles VII. At Genappe,

Louis was able to lead a life very much to his liking: comfortable but not luxurious or ostentatious, with plenty of hunting, surrounded by several dozen of his closest supporters. Despite his pension from Philip, Louis was continually short of cash, not because he spent liberally on himself, but because he insisted on paying his servants and advisors generously. His only personal indulgence was on animals, especially those used in hunting, such as horses and dogs. He borrowed money from his supporters, and in addition, Philip was glad to recommend Louis to his own bankers. Most notable in this respect was the Italian financier Giovanni Arnolfini, whose wedding was immortalized in oil by the Philip's court painter Jan van Eyck.

Charles VII, meanwhile, had followed through with the invasion of Dauphiné that had led to his son's flight, depriving Louis of much needed revenue. Correspondence between father and son was correct, if formulaic. Louis continued to insist that he wished nothing more than to be reconciled with Charles and be welcomed back to France, but that first Dauphiné be restored to his control. In addition, he demanded that Charles promise not to act against Philip the Good for giving him refuge. As he had before, Charles responded repeatedly that Louis must submit himself without conditions, and that he could trust in his father's benevolence. In his more panicked moments, Louis feared for his life, and there were certainly rumors that he would be disinherited and his younger brother Charles named heir to the throne.

Charles VII had by this time more or less given up governing personally, preferring instead to surround himself with beautiful young women and his favorite noblemen. Pierre de Brézé effectively governed France, but the royal court was as divided and faction-ridden as ever. It was, indeed, the king's relationship with his elder son that was one of the crucial cleavages in these intrigues. A number of courtiers clearly had one eye on the not very distant future, when Louis would be king.

There is one incident that is particularly instructive both of the intricate plotting of the royal court, and of Louis' accustomed method of operation. This concerns Antoine de Chabannes, Louis' former comrade, who had gone to Charles VII and implicated Louis in a plot to overthrow his father. Chabannes would later command the army that Charles sent to Dauphiné to apprehend his son. From his exile, Louis wrote a letter to one of his agents in his father's court, who also happened to be Charles's mistress at the moment. The letter Louis wrote was clearly designed to arouse Charles's suspicions of Chabannes:

> Mademoiselle, I have read the letter you have written me. And I appreciate the news you have given me in your letters, and be assured

that . . . one day I will reward you. I have likewise had letters from the Count of Dammartin [Chabannes], whom I pretend to hate, which are like yours. I beg you, tell him that I hold him always in high favor, as I have informed you.

The letter fell into the hands of someone who passed it on the king, whether by design it is impossible to say, and for a time Chabannes was expelled from the court.

Louis also became caught up in the intrigues of the Burgundian court. Strangely enough, these centered around the strained relations between Philip the Good and his son Charles, Count of Charolais, later Duke Charles the Bold. Unlike his pleasure-loving and sensual father, Charolais was moody and humorless, a strict and ascetic figure. Philip clearly feared the growing power and influence of his son. He was determined not to relax his grip on power, and relied increasingly for advice and counsel on the brothers Antoine and Jean de Croy, whom Charolais detested. At one point, Philip lost his temper with his son, and threatened him with a knife. He relented only with the intervention of his duchess and of Louis himself. Louis once again had to walk a tightrope, trying to stay good terms with both the current and future duke. He stayed on good terms with Charolais, despite their very different temperaments. The one interest they did have in common was hunting, which they enjoyed together frequently. Louis served as godfather to Charolais' daughter Marie, born in 1457.[23]

It was also during his exile that Louis first lived as man and wife with young Charlotte of Savoy. She was summoned by Louis from Dauphiné in 1457, and joined her husband in the Low Countries. Their first child, a boy they named Joachim, was born in 1459, with Philip the Good as godfather, and Charolais' wife as godmother. The baby died, however, when he was four months old. Their second child, a girl they named Anne, was born in 1461. The names are significant, as Joachim and Anne were, according to Church tradition, the father and mother of the Virgin Mary. His whole life long, Louis was ardently devoted to the Virgin.

In July of 1461, Louis received word that his father was deathly ill. He ordered his household to prepare to return to France. Indeed, his succession to the throne was not a foregone conclusion. There were certainly men around Charles VII who feared for their own positions and even their lives should Louis become king. It was not implausible that they might try to

---

[23] In a strange twist of fate, after Louis became King of France, he and Charolais, who had since become Duke of Burgundy, were bitter enemies. In 1477, Charles was killed in battle against Louis' Swiss allies. Louis then seized by force the Duchy of Burgundy and the province of Picardy from Marie, her father's only heir.

place on the throne Louis' younger brother Charles. Louis' apprehensions are revealed in his correspondence with Philip the Good: "If it happens that you hear that he [Charles VII] has died, I beg you and your people to ride immediately for the vicinity of Reims, where we will meet you." In case of a disputed succession, it was imperative to be crowned in Reims as quickly as possible.

Charles VII died on July 22, 1461, after an extended period of poor health. Father and son were never reconciled. On his death bed, he charged Antoine de Chabannes to watch over his younger son Charles, seeing that he was not a bad son, like his older brother. The news reached Louis several days later on July 25. He ordered a requiem Mass said for his father, but later that day went hunting, and forbade his followers to wear clothes of mourning. He and his household departed for Reims within a day or two. At the age of thirty-eight, he was now King Louis XI of France.

Judgements of Louis XI as a man and as a ruler have varied widely, from his time to ours. Philippe de Commines, possibly the greatest historian of the fifteenth century, was glowing in his praise:

> God had granted him one particular favor for he had endowed him with more sagacity, liberality and virtue in all matters than any other prince who ruled at the same time as he did, whether they were his enemies or neighbors, and as he had surpassed them in all achievements so he exceeded them in length of life, although not by very much. . . . But without any exaggeration it may be said he possessed more of the qualities needed to be a king or a prince than any of the others. I have seen almost all of them and knew their abilities so I am not guessing.

Commines was the son of a Flemish nobleman, and grew up at the court of Duke Charles the Bold and became an important counsellor of the duke. He was so impressed, however, by Louis XI, that in 1472, he left Burgundy to enter the service of the French king. He became a very close friend and advisor of Louis XI, and towards the end of his life wrote his famous *Memoirs*. As much as he admired the king, he was not blind to Louis' flaws, but maintained that more good could be said of him than evil.

Other contemporaries were not nearly so positive in their assessments. Thomas Basin was a Norman bishop who had originally been a supporter of Louis XI. During a rebellion against Louis, the League of the Public Weal, Basin turned his city of Lisieux over to the rebels. Louis never forgave him, and banished him from France. Basin got his revenge in his *History of King Louis XI and his Times*:

> Louis XI . . . deprived clergymen of their offices, oppressed the nobles, subjected the people to taxes. . . confirmed the suspicions which surrounded the death of Charles VII by the little affection he showed him . . . took pleasure in destituting the servants of his father. . . submitted France by terror to his arbitrary fiscal policies . . . plotting the death of the Duke of Burgundy . . . corrupted two of his servants to poison his brother.

Other contemporary sources of information are two Burgundian chroniclers, Georges Chastellain and Olivier de la Marche. Unlike Louis, the Dukes of Burgundy, first Philip the Good, and then his son Charles the Bold, cared a great deal about public relations, and paid writers for good publicity. Heavily influenced by the tradition of chivalry, and much enamored of the trappings of the Burgundian court, they were generally critical of Louis, though not as toxic as Basin. What particularly galled them was Louis' unkingly bearing, especially when compared to those paragons of medieval knight-errantry, Philip the Good and Charles the Bold. They were particularly disturbed by what they saw as Louis' betrayal of the dukes, after Philip had given him refuge from his father.

It is this negative view of Louis XI that has lived on in popular literature and culture. In *Quentin Durward* (1823), Sir Walter Scott portrays the king as a cruelly paranoid tyrant:

> That Sovereign [Louis XI] was of a character so purely selfish — so guiltless of entertaining any purpose unconnected with his ambition, covetousness, and desire of selfish enjoyment, that he almost seems an incarnation of the devil himself, permitted to do his utmost to corrupt our ideas of honor in its very source. Nor is it to be forgotten that Louis possessed to a great extent that caustic wit which can turn into ridicule all that a man does for any other person's advantage but his own, and was, therefore, peculiarly qualified to play the part of a cold-hearted and sneering fiend. . . . The cruelties, the perjuries, the suspicions of this prince, were rendered more detestable, rather than amended, by the gross and debasing superstition which he constantly practised. The devotion to the heavenly saints, of which he made such a parade, was upon the miserable principle of some petty deputy in office, who endeavors to hide or atone for the malversations of which he is conscious, by liberal gifts to those whose duty it is to observe his conduct, and endeavors to support a system of fraud, by an attempt to corrupt the incorruptible.

In *Notre-Dame de Paris* (1831), Victor Hugo likewise portrayed Louis XI as reclusive and paranoid miser, who carefully went over expenses with a fine-tooth comb. The only expenses of which he really approved were a new axe for the royal executioner, and an elaborate iron cage in which he could allow prisoners to languish for decades. He was positively jubilant at the prospect of violently suppressing a rebellion whose aftermath would allow him to amass even more power and wealth.

Both Scott and Hugo were much influenced by the Romantic movement and especially with its tendency to romanticize and idealize the chivalric middle ages. From their perspective, Louis was the negation of these lofty ideals of sacrifice, honor, and chivalry. He was miserable and miserly bean-counter, who isolated himself behind the walls of his castles. He saw plots and conspiracies everywhere, and subjected his victims to the cruellest tortures, delighting in their screams of anguish.

Modern historical assessments of Louis as a ruler are much more positive, although no one claims that he was an especially likeable figure. Indeed, as Niccolò Machiavelli pointed out several decades after Louis' death, the qualities that make for a likeable man are likely to lead a ruler to ruin. Especially towards the end of his life, he did become reclusive and more suspicious, fearing especially noble plots to seize him and put power in the hands of his young son Charles, just as he had attempted to do his own father twenty-five years earlier. According to Commines: "never was there a man who feared death so much nor did so much in an attempt to prevent it." As his health declined, he sought all sorts of talismans and relics which he thought would relieve his suffering. He donated vast sums to various churches and shrines all over Europe. From Rome, he received from the Pope the linen cloth over which St. Peter was supposed to have said Mass. He sent one of his sea captains to the Cape Verde Islands to acquire the blood of sea turtles, which was reputed to have healing properties. He sought the counsel of hermits and holy men, such as Francis of Paola, who travelled from Naples to console the ailing king.

As a ruler, Louis' accomplishments were many, and his legacy impressive. Indeed, it was during his reign that we see the changes taking shape that would transform France from a decentralized feudal kingdom into something approaching a centralized state. He was concerned to eliminate or reduce the power of the most important nobles to act independently in their own lands, and to meddle in the politics of the royal court. His policies provoked a very serious noble rebellion in 1465, known as the League of the Public Weal (*Ligue du Bien Public*). As in the Praguerie of 1440, a handful of great nobles clothed their political ambitions in the public good, and sought to supplant Louis with his younger brother, Charles Duke of Berry. Charles was almost exactly the same age as Louis had been when involved in the

Praguerie. In some ways, Charles was more like a son than a brother, at least in terms of the twenty-four-year difference in their ages. Among the plotters was Louis' former hunting companion, Charles of Charolais, soon to become Duke Charles the Bold of Burgundy, as well as the Duke of Bourbon, Antoine de Chabannes, and Duke Francis II of Brittany. (Like Burgundy, Brittany was a semi-independent enclave, theoretically part of France, but under the effective power of a virtually independent duke.) Charles of Berry was dissatisfied with his *appanage* of Berry, and was vulnerable to manipulation by older and more experienced men such as Charolais and Bourbon. Each of the plotters had their own specific grievances, but as a group they felt that Louis XI had cut them out of the political power and influence that they had enjoyed under Charles VII. There was, indeed, a lot of truth to this, as Louis had decided to be his own man as king, not to rely on factions of self-interested nobles, as we have seen.

The revolt was very serious, much more serious in fact than the Praguerie. Louis had to make serious concessions to the rebels. However, he was aided by the fact that the towns and the middle classes who paid royal taxes, came to his support. In the end, Louis was able to employ strategies of divide and conquer, as the nobles were essentially self-interested. Bit by bit, over the subsequent years he was able to reverse the concessions he had been forced to grant.

Probably the most important achievement of Louis's reign was the defeat of the threat from the Dukes of Burgundy. Philip the Good died in 1467 and was succeeded by his son who now became Duke Charles the Bold.[24] Louis understood that he could not afford an open confrontation and so embarked on a diplomatic offensive. He patiently cultivated alliances with Charles's other enemies, primarily the Swiss and the Duke of Lorraine, on whose lands Charles had designs. Charles's ultimate goal, as had been that of his predecessors, was to use his holdings in Burgundy and the Netherlands as the core of a powerful state between France and Germany. Louis had kept in touch with the Swiss since his time there commanding his army of *écorcheurs* in the 1440s, and they had a mutual respect. In 1477, Charles the Bold was killed in battle against the Swiss. He left behind only his nineteen-year-old daughter Marie.

Louis seized the opportunity presented by Charles's death, despite the fact that he was Marie's godfather. He had designs on all of her lands, and indeed tried to secure her hand in marriage for his young son Charles

---

[24] The French word usually translated as "bold" in this context is *téméraire*, which carries connotations of rashness or foolhardiness. Charles the Bold is therefore sometimes called Charles the Rash.

(later King Charles VIII). Marie, however, was able to resist with the aid of other European rulers, and in the end, Louis managed to wrest away from only the Duchy of Burgundy and the provinces of Artois and Picardy.[25] It was also during Louis' reign that the territories of the House of Anjou were definitively incorporated into the Kingdom. "King" René died in 1480, having been predeceased by his son and grandson. He bequeathed to Louis XI and France his family's *appanages* of Anjou and Maine as well as the County of Provence in the south.

Prior to the reign of Louis XI, France was largely a collection of semi-independent nobles and cities that owed theoretical allegiance to the king, but which were inclined to go their own ways. The Dukes of Burgundy were the extreme exemplars of this tendency, but they were not alone. As king, Louis XI took many of the early steps which would eventually remake France into a more centralized and effectively governed kingdom. Here, his experience in Dauphiné provided a template for France as a whole.

As king, Louis was very attentive to the needs and desires of the wealthy middle class. He consulted with their representatives frequently, and enacted policies designed to enhance their wealth, for he understood that a prosperous kingdom meant more tax revenue for the royal treasury. He greatly expanded both the fiscal bureaucracy and the amount collected in taxes. At the beginning of the reign, the annual revenue of the crown was about 1.8 million *livres*, and by the end it was about 4.8 million. He sponsored commercial fairs at Lyons and elsewhere, which were designed to bring more wealth into the kingdom. His government subsidized infant silk industries in Tours and Lyons. The acquisition of Provence brought with it the great seaport of Marseilles, and Louis fostered grand ambitions — largely unrealized — to make France into a naval and commercial power in the Mediterranean. As he had done in Dauphiné, he established an efficient postal system for the kingdom, so efficient that in 1477, word of Charles the Bold's death reached Louis before it reached Charles's court.

From neglected child to ambitious and impatient teenager to penniless exile, and finally to adult king, Louis XI's life and career were shaped by his childhood and stormy relationship with his father. His father's life and conduct of the government provided him with a template of what not to do. In almost every way, Louis was determined to do things exactly opposite to the way his father had.

---

[25] Because of her wealthy inheritance, Marie was most sought-after princess in Europe. In the end, she married Maximilian of Habsburg, the heir of the Holy Roman Empire. The Burgundian inheritance would catapult the Habsburg dynasty into European prominence for centuries thereafter. By 1493, Louis was unable to hold on to Artois, which reverted to the rule of Maximilian.

CHAPTER 3: "NOT AS A FATHER, BUT AS A KING": PHILIP II AND DON CARLOS

In the case of Charles VII and Louis XI, we saw a son who was much more effective and determined than his father. To return to the analogy of family businesses, the son had big plans for the family firm, and could hardly wait to take the reins of power from the old man in order to restore it to its former glory. The case of Philip II of Spain (r. 1556-98) and his son Don Carlos (1547-68) presents us with the opposite scenario: an experienced and powerful ruler who has inherited vast territories and power, but who has very serious misgivings about the abilities of his heir. In a family business this no doubt presents many difficulties, but there are ways around it. Control of the family firm can be vested in another child. Outside experts can be brought in while the heir is given a decorative but powerless role. In a system of hereditary monarchy, these options were not available, at least not without the dangers of rebellion and civil war. In this case, the contrast between father and son was all the more evident because of the nature of the relationship between Philip and his own father. In addition, the difficulties were complicated by a family history of mental illness compounded by a family tradition of marrying cousins. Philip's relationship with his own father was about as healthy as could be expected, and it is entirely reasonable to assume that relations between Philip and Don Carlos would have unfolded similarly, if not for the mental illness of the heir.

Philip's father was Holy Roman Emperor Charles V (1500-58) of the Habsburg dynasty, a grandson of Marie of Burgundy, a portion of whose lands Louis XI had managed to seize following the death of her father, Duke of Charles the Bold.[26] Through a series of dynastic marriages and unforeseen deaths and accidents of inheritance, Charles V came to control a worldwide empire.[27] His father was Philip, known as "the Handsome," the eldest son of Emperor Maximilian of Habsburg and Marie. He had been married to Juana, or Joanna, a daughter of King Ferdinand of Aragon and Queen Isabella of Castile. Philip, however, died prematurely in 1506, and his death drove the emotionally unstable Juana into more or less permanent mental illness giving her the nickname Juana *la Loca* (Joanna the Mad). When Philip died in 1506, the young prince Charles became Duke of Burgundy and ruler of the various provinces of the Netherlands. In 1516 his maternal grandfather Ferdinand of Aragon died, and Charles became king of both the Spanish kingdoms of Castile and Aragon as well as the Kingdom of Naples in Italy and of Castile's possessions in the New World.[28] When Charles's paternal grandfather, Holy Roman Emperor Maximilian I died in 1519, Charles inherited his hereditary lands in Austria, and was subsequently elected Holy Roman Emperor.[29]

It is important to emphasize that Charles's lands formed a purely personal and dynastic empire. They came into his hands not by any forethought or planning, but through accidents of marriage, death, and inheritance. They had no unity apart from the fact that the same man happened to rule all the various territories. There was no common government or administration, no uniform system of laws or judicial system, no common currency or army. Even in the Iberian peninsula, Charles was not King of "Spain," but rather King of Castile and King Aragon, two separate entities each with its own laws, institutions, customs, culture and language.[30] As Duke of Burgundy, Charles acquired the various provinces of the Netherlands, but he was not

---

[26] See above, p. 86.

[27] The Habsburg dynasty's knack for contracting advantageous marriages was expressed in a much-quoted line of Latin poetry: "Bella gerant alii, tu felix Austria nube!" ("Let others wage war, while you, happy Austria, marry!").

[28] Queen Isabella of Castile had died in 1504, whereupon her son-in-law Philip was recognized as King Philip I of Castile. Upon the death of Philip in 1506, Ferdinand became regent for his daughter Juana in Castile, and effective ruler of the country. Charles was technically co-ruler of Castile along with his mother Juana until her death in 1555. In actual fact, Juana was locked up in an isolated castle and Charles acted alone as king. As king of Spain, he was King Charles I, but he is commonly known as Charles V according to his more exalted title of Emperor.

[29] In 1521 Charles would cede control of the Austrian lands to his younger brother Ferdinand. Although he was elected Holy Roman Emperor in 1519, he would not be formally crowned by the Pope until 1530, the last Emperor to be so crowned. From 1519 to 1530, therefore, his title was technically "King of the Romans," the title accorded to the Emperor-elect. For the sake of simplicity, we shall refer to him as Holy Roman Emperor, even during the period that he was formally King of the Romans. (The title was purely honorific and conferred no power in Rome itself.)

[30] Although he was and is often referred to as King of Spain, this is simply a term of convenience.

ruler of the "Netherlands" per se, but rather of its individual provinces: Count of Flanders, Duke of Brabant, Count of Holland, and so on.[31] In 1519 his various dignities and titles were expressed thus:

> Roman King, future Emperor, semper augustus, King of Spain, Sicily, Jerusalem, the Balearic Islands, the Canary Islands, the Indies and the mainland on the far side of the Atlantic, Archduke of Austria, Duke of Burgundy, Brabant, Styria, Carinthia, Carniola, Luxemburg, Limburg, Athens and Patras, Count of Hapsburg, Pfirt, Roussillon, Landgrave of Alsace, Count of Swabia, Lord of Asia and Africa.

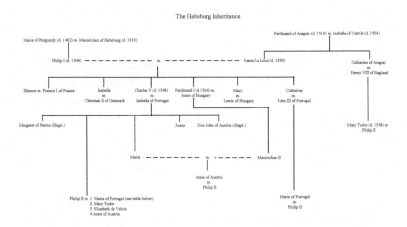

The Habsburg Inheritance

Governing such a far-flung and diverse empire in age of primitive communications would be extremely challenging in any circumstances, but Charles was faced with a number of difficulties on several different fronts. In Spain, for example, he was a foreigner, having been born and raised in Flanders. When he became king in 1516, he had never been to Spain and did not speak the language. In 1520 and 1521, his government was faced with a very serious revolt in Castile, that of the Communeros who objected to heavy taxation and Charles's appointment of Flemings to positions in Castile and America. Eventually, however, Charles suppressed the revolt and reconciled with his Castilian subjects and Castile became the core of his empire.[32] He was also faced with a dual threat from the Muslim Ottoman Empire, which controlled the Middle East, the eastern Mediterranean, and large parts of

---

[31] To the vast lands he inherited Charles added others: in the Netherlands the provinces of Tournai, Artois, Utrecht, Groningen and Guelders, and in Italy the wealthy and strategic Duchy of Milan.

[32] This reconciliation is reflected in Charles V's often quoted words: "I speak Spanish to God, Italian to women, French to men and German to my horse."

southeastern Europe. His lands in Austria and Germany were on the front lines in the land campaigns against the Ottomans, while his lands in Italy and Aragon were threatened by Turkish naval dominance in the Mediterranean. For example, in 1526 the Turkish army invaded up the Danube valley and defeated and killed in battle the King of Hungary and Bohemia. In 1529 they laid siege to Vienna, and in 1532 invaded once again.[33]

As Holy Roman Emperor, Charles V sought to restore real power to the imperial title.[34] In this task he was faced with several very serious obstacles. First, by the sixteenth century, real power in Germany was exercised by a series of territorial princes such as the Elector of Saxony, the Duke of Bavaria, the Landgrave of Hesse and so on, and by about 150 self-governing Imperial cities. None of these powers was happy to see an ambitious emperor who brought to his plans vast revenues and resources. In addition, in the early sixteenth century the Protestant Reformation shattered the religious unity of Western Europe under the auspices of the Roman Catholic Church. The concept of a Christian Holy Roman Empire was inextricably linked with the religious unity of the Roman Catholic Church. ("Catholic" means "universal.") The end of this religious unity dealt a fatal blow to Charles's imperial ambitions, as many German rulers adopted the new religion as a means of further enhancing their independence of and resistance to the Holy Roman Emperor.

In addition to all these obstacles, Charles faced determined opposition from the kings of France, the successors of Louis XI, most especially from his contemporary Francis I (r. 1515–47) and his son Henry II (r. 1547–59). Everywhere the king of France looked, he was surrounded by territories belonging to the Habsburg dynasty: to the south in Spain, to the southeast in Italy, to the east in Germany, and in the northeast in the Low Countries. From the early sixteenth century until the later seventeenth, the primary diplomatic imperative of French kings was to break the threat of encirclement by the Habsburg dynasty. To achieve this aim, they entered into alliances with Charles's enemies: the Ottoman Turks, German Protestant princes, and Italian rulers who resented and feared Charles's power, including several

---

[33] King Louis of Hungary was married to Charles's younger sister Mary, while Charles's younger brother Ferdinand was married to Louis' sister Anne. Upon Louis' death in 1526, Ferdinand was elected King of Hungary and Bohemia, further adding to the Habsburg dynastic empire.

[34] The Holy Roman Emperor as the theoretical successor of the Roman Emperors of the ancient world occupied a rank superior to all other European rulers. Even at the height of their power earlier in the Middle Ages, however, the Emperors had never clearly exercised such supreme power. Over the course of the middle ages, their power had become limited essentially to what is now Germany, giving rise to the formulation "Holy Roman Empire of the German Nation." By the sixteenth century, even effective control over Germany had been lost.

popes. In all, Charles V fought five separate wars against France, and even when they were not technically at war, the two sides were continually plotting and scheming for the next war.

The Family of Philip II

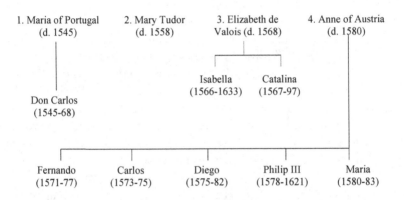

Charles V attempted to personally govern with this far-flung and diverse empire by constantly travelling throughout his dominions, by seeing and being seen by as many of his subjects as possible, and establishing personal relationships with noble elites. He was seldom in one place for very long. It has been estimated that in the forty years of his reign, he spent one day in four travelling, and slept in about 3,200 different beds. He was born and raised in Flanders, and travelled to Spain for the first time in 1517. In 1520 he departed for the Low Countries and Germany, returning to Spain in 1522. He would remain in Spain until 1529, when he departed for Italy and eventually Germany, where he needed to deal with the Protestant Reformation. From 1529 until his retirement in 1556, he would return to Spain only four times, never for longer than two years at a time. In 1543, he saw Spain for the last time for fourteen years, until his return in 1556 as a prematurely worn-out retiree.

It was during Charles's longest sojourn in Spain that his wife, Empress Isabella of Portugal gave birth to their eldest son, Prince Philip, on May 21, 1527. The happy event took place in the city of Valladolid, the customary residence of the Castilian kings.[35] Unusually for rulers at the time, Charles was actually present for the birth and greeted his son's arrival with great joy and celebration. Indeed, it is not too much to say that by the standards of royal families the relationship that emerged between father and son was probably the best that could be expected. Although Charles was absent for much of Philip's childhood and youth, and although his mother died when he was twelve, Philip admired and attempted to emulate his father. It must also be said, however, that for him Charles was a remote authority figure rather than a flesh and blood presence in his life. For his part, not only did Charles stay by his wife's side during thirteen hours of labor, and not only did he greet the birth of his son with genuine joy, he actively supervised (from a distance) his son's education and upbringing, and at the appropriate time provided Philip with an excellent apprenticeship in the craft of monarchy.

As a young child, Philip lived in the household of his mother, the imperious and reserved Empress Isabella of Portugal. Although the marriage of Charles and Isabella was an arranged one, the two came to love each other deeply, and when Charles was absent from Spain, Isabella acted as his regent. The Empress Isabella played a very large part in the care and raising of the young prince. Her circle of friends and advisors was largely Portuguese, imparting to Philip an enduring affinity for all things Portuguese.[36] Indeed, his governess as a young child was a Portuguese woman named Leonor Mascarhenas. So close to her was Philip that when Don Carlos was born in 1545, Philip would appoint her as governess to his own son. Great care was taken to inform Charles V of the health and upbringing of his heir. In 1531, for example, the absent Emperor was informed that "he is so mischievous that sometimes Her Majesty [Isabella] gets really angry; she spanks him, and the women weep to see such severity." It is apparent that Philip had none of the attachment issues that we saw in the case of Louis XI. Although death deprived him of his mother when he was twelve, Philip was very close to his two younger sisters, Maria (born 1528) and Juana (born 1535).

Having left Spain in 1529 when Philip was still an infant, Charles returned in 1533 to a young boy. Philip was now given a household of his own, removed from the company of women and introduced to the world of men. He was given a tutor, Juan Martínez de Siliceo, and a governor, Don Juan de Zúñiga. Zúñiga's wife Estefania served as a sort of surrogate mother for Philip after

---

[35] Madrid would be established as the royal capital only during Philip's reign later in the sixteenth century. Valladolid was only one of a number of royal residences, but the royal court spent more time there than anywhere else.

[36] In the wake of a succession crisis in Portugal, in 1580 Philip would successfully lay claim to the Portuguese throne, based on the extensive ties between the royal families of Castile and Portugal.

the death of his own, and Zuñiga's son, Don Luis de Requesens, was one of Philip's closest boyhood friends and as an adult one of his closest confidants. Despite a reputation for coldness, Philip was obviously capable of real affection, but it was reserved for very few. In this he seems to resemble his mother rather more than his father, for Charles V was extremely gregarious and a renowned *bon vivant*.

In most ways, Philip seems to have been a normal boy. He occasionally neglected his studies, and far preferred hunting and playing with his friends. He was a good enough student, and especially liked mathematics, history and geography. Unlike his multilingual father, however, he showed little aptitude for languages. Completely fluent only in Castilian Spanish, he had a rudimentary knowledge of Portuguese. Like all aristocratic boys, he was given a thorough education in Latin, which he could read and speak with relative ease, while his Greek remained very elementary. He was able to understand some French, but not to speak it very well at all. Combined with his perceived aloofness, this lack of linguistic ability would cause him trouble in later years, as many of subjects (especially in the Netherlands) came to view him with suspicion. He was also well-versed in the traditional aristocratic pastimes of riding, fencing, hunting, and jousting, which were all seen as training for war.

If education did not make a scholar out of Philip, he did become an important connoisseur and collector. He was especially enamored of architecture, painting and music. Later in his life, he always found time to closely supervise the construction and renovation of royal palaces, paying special attention to landscaping. This was especially true of El Escorial, the palace, monastery and royal mausoleum he built just northwest of Madrid. He himself painted, and patronized important artists and collected their works. He was also devoted to music and dancing, and played the guitar himself. Eventually he would amass a vast library at El Escorial, and was an important patron of writers and scholars.

On May 1, 1539 young Philip's world changed dramatically when his mother, Isabella of Portugal died of complications from a miscarriage at the age of thirty-five. Almost twelve years old, Philip felt the loss deeply. Among the Portuguese who had come to Spain with Isabella was a young noblewoman whose son, Ruy Gomez da Silva (1516-73), was one of the young nobles who was educated alongside Philip. Philip and Ruy formed a very close friendship and Philip would come to rely on his advice and friendship for years afterwards. Philip's devotion and loyalty to Gomez was at least in part because he represented a link to his mother. Charles too mourned deeply the loss of his only wife. The Emperor secluded himself in a monastery for seven weeks. He never remarried, and wore mourning clothes of black for the rest of his life.

In the years that followed his mother's death, Philip underwent the transition from childhood to young adulthood. At the age of fourteen, in 1541, he took his first communion. In late 1541 Charles returned once more to Spain, and in 1542 began Philip's political apprenticeship. They set out on a royal progress through the component districts of the Kingdom of Aragon: Catalonia, Valencia, and Aragon proper. In each, Philip was recognized as heir to his father, and in turn he swore to observe the historic rights and liberties of his subjects.[37] In May of 1543, Charles once again left Spain, this time for his longest absence of all, fourteen years. He appointed sixteen-year-old Philip as his regent, surrounding him with able advisors. Father and son would not see each other again for six years.

It is apparent, therefore, that unlike Charles VII of France, Emperor Charles V took great pains to give his heir the proper training to be a successful king, and within the customs of the time and many distractions of a vast empire, to provide him with as stable an emotional life as was feasible. We see this especially upon Charles's departure from Spain in 1543. He entrusted his young son with the regency, and surrounded him with able and trusted advisors. There was Francisco de los Cobos, Charles V's principal secretary of state, and the closest thing there was to a prime minister. There was also Philip's governor, Don Juan de Zúñiga, as well as Fernando Álvarez de Toledo, Duke of Alba, one of the most powerful nobles in Castile, and an experienced general. Philip's inner circle was completed by Juan de Tavera, Cardinal-Archbishop of Toledo and Inquisitor-General.

Charles also left for his son two long letters of advice and instructions, one dated May 4, 1543 and the other May 6. The first was labelled "confidential" and was to be read to Philip by Zúñiga, who as his governor was still responsible for Philip's conduct. First, Charles thanked God for giving him "such a son." He must "keep God always in mind" and "never allow heresies to enter your realm." He must dispense justice impartially, and be vigilant for corruption among his officials. He was to listen to all opinions, and take good advice from his counsellors. Personally, Charles now counselled his son to assume the role of a grown man, in view of his regency and his impending marriage. He must not neglect his further education. He must partake of the pleasures of the conjugal bed with moderation, because excess in this

---

[37] Royal power in Aragon was much more circumscribed than in Castile. The assemblies or *Cortes* of the three districts guarded their privileges zealously, as reflected in the famous coronation oath sworn by the subjects of each new king: "We who are as good as you swear to you who are no better than we, to accept you as our king and sovereign lord, provided you observe all our liberties and laws; but if not, not."

"besides being harmful to bodily growth and strength, often it impairs the capacity to have children and can kill." He should therefore keep away from his wife "as much as possible," and be with her only briefly.[38]

The second letter, that of May 6, was labelled "Secret," and Philip was instructed to share its contents with no one, not even his wife. In it, he advised Philip not to become beholden to any one advisor or any one faction. Make use of all, but be dependent on none. He was to rely on los Cobos, but not exclusively, for he was greedy and had many enemies. The Duke of Alba should be listened to, especially on military matters, "because he is the best that we have," but he was proud and ambitious, and would always treat Philip as a child. On no account was Philip to "let him or the other grandees get a firm footing in government, or you will regret it afterwards."

Philip took his father's advice very seriously for the rest of his life; indeed, often too seriously. He proved utterly inflexible on religion (less flexible even than his father), which provoked a great deal of unrest and dissent in the Netherlands, the loss of which was the greatest blemish on his reign. He applied himself diligently to the business of government, going over reports and letters from all his realms with a fine-tooth comb. He took great pains to ensure that he was the only one who had the whole picture, and the final decision rested always with him. Combined with distance and rudimentary communications, funnelling all correspondence and orders through the king produced enormous backlogs. As Cardinal Granvelle, Philip's chief advisor in the Netherlands, said: "If death came from Spain, I should be immortal." It is no wonder that Philip often felt overwhelmed by mountains of paper. On one day, he would later report, he had read and signed 400 separate documents. Although he often complained of the workload, he seemed constitutionally incapable of delegating authority:

> I have just been given this other packet of papers from you. I have neither the time nor the strength to look at it, and so I will not open it until tomorrow. It is already past ten o'clock and I have not yet dined. My table is full of papers for tomorrow because I cannot cope with any more now.

From 1543 on, Philip was in fact, if not in title, the actual ruler of Spain. Under the supervision of his advisors he began to play a larger and larger role in government. Looking back at his career thirty years later, he wrote, "I

---

[38] Here Charles was likely thinking of his own life and sexual exploits, and counselling Philip to do as he said, and not as he did. He already had one illegitimate child, Margaret of Parma, and in 1547 had a son with an eighteen-year-old German girl, Barbara Blomberg. This was Don John (don Juan) of Austria, who would later play a prominent role in Philip's reign.

began to govern in the year 1543." He and his advisors kept Charles informed of events, and solicited his advice, but increasingly Philip was willing to strike out on his own, to disagree with his father, and to pursue his own policies.

Philip also in this period crossed another threshold into adulthood when he married. Negotiations had been underway for some time, and it was formally concluded in early 1543 that he would marry his cousin, Princess Maria of Portugal, six months his junior.[39] On November 12, 1543, the young couple — he was seventeen and she just shy of her seventeenth birthday — were married in Salamanca. Charles, however, was not present for the occasion, having left Spain earlier that year to deal with pressing issues in Germany and the Netherlands. It appears that in the following months Philip and Maria experienced some of the tensions common to newlyweds, especially, one might surmise, to teenagers who had never met before their wedding. The emperor wrote to Zúñiga that he had heard "of the coldness the prince adopts to his wife in public, which distresses me very much." On the other hand, los Cobos reported that Philip and Maria "get on together very well," and that Philip was following his father's instructions regarding sexual activity. None of this would appear out of the ordinary, given the circumstances of their marriage. It is entirely reasonable to suppose, given Philip's relationships with his subsequent wives, that eventually they might have become affectionate companions. They were, however, not to be afforded this opportunity.

Maria became pregnant within a year of their marriage, and on July 8, 1545 gave birth to a son. Named Carlos (Charles) after his grandfather, he was born after a very long and difficult labor. Princess Maria died of a haemorrhage four days later, at the age of eighteen. The loss shook Philip. He isolated himself in a monastery for three weeks, and los Cobos wrote that "the prince felt the loss deeply, which shows that he loved her." At the age of twelve, Philip had buried his mother. Now, at eighteen, he was a widower with an infant son, as well as regent of Spain for his absent father. Truly, his transition into the adult world was swift and brutal.

Work, however, would not wait for Philip's grief, and shortly afterwards he was back in harness. In short order, death or absence deprived him of the circle of advisors his father had placed around him. Cardinal Tavera died in 1545, Zúñiga in 1546, and los Cobos in 1547, while Alba was with Charles in northern Europe. Their replacements, able men all, found themselves more

---

[39] Actually, Philip and Maria were cousins twice over. Her father, King John III of Portugal, was the brother of Philip's mother Isabella. In addition, her mother Catherine was a sister of Philip's father, Charles V.

in the role of servants and advisors to the young prince, rather than that of mentors. Indeed, Philip was increasingly surefooted in his conduct of the government, to the point of openly disagreeing with his father about what courses to take on several important issues.

Meanwhile, the Emperor found that his affairs in northern Europe were prospering. In 1547 at the Battle of Mühlberg, his army crushed the forces of the German Protestant princes. In that year as well, two of his rival rulers died: Henry VIII of England, and his bitterest foe, Francis I of France. In 1548, he was able to impose a compromise religious settlement on the Protestants in Germany. It was time, he felt, that Philip was introduced to his non-Spanish realms and subjects to prepare him for the role he would eventually play as the most powerful monarch in Europe. In early 1548 Charles sent Alba back to Spain with instructions that Philip was to join his father in the Netherlands.

That September, Philip's cousin Maximilian (the son of Charles's brother Ferdinand) arrived in Spain and was married to Philip's sister Maria. He spoke perfect Spanish — his father had been raised in Spain — and he and Maria were named regents during Philip's absence. Philip departed from the port of Rosas, near Barcelona, on November 2, 1548 for the Italian city of Genoa. For the next three years, Philip made a grand tour of Italy, Germany, and Netherlands. Everywhere he went he was welcomed with banquets, tournaments, and processions. Accounts of his demeanor and behavior varied, with some finding him cold and distant. The majority, however, especially the ladies, found him perfectly charming. It is probably accurate to say that given Philip's exalted position he was bound to disappoint some people. He simply could not please everyone. It took six months for Philip to travel to Brussels where, on April 1, 1549 he was reunited with his tearful father. They had not seen each other for six years.

From July to October, Philip accompanied Charles on a tour of the seventeen provinces that made up the Netherlands. In each, he was received with due pomp and ceremony and was duly recognized as his father's heir. Charles had already decided that the Netherlands would form part of Philip's inheritance, and to that end, he had formally severed their connections to the Holy Roman Empire. There were, indeed, sound reasons for doing so. The economic ties between the Low Countries and Spain were strong, as Spanish wool was woven into cloth in the great industrial cities of Flanders such as Ghent, Bruges, and Antwerp. A Spanish connection to the Netherlands also served a strategic purpose in conflicts with France, as Paris was only eighty miles from the frontier. No one, of course, could have known that the

Netherlands would pose Philip's greatest challenge and that ultimately he would lose control of seven of the seventeen provinces.

Especially notable among the festivals which greeted Philip was that staged at Binche by his aunt Mary of Hungary. Since the death of her husband in 1526, Mary had acted as Charles's regent in the Netherlands. For a whole week in August 1549 Philip and the lords and ladies of the court took part in dramatic re-enactment of *Amadis of Gaul*, a classic work of chivalric romance, and one of Philip's favorite books. So successful was the party that it became proverbial: "More splendid than the festival at Binche!" There is no doubt that Philip enjoyed all these festivities immensely, taking part in jousts, dancing with the pretty young women of the court, and generally enjoying life to the full. Hostile historians (and some contemporaries) have used this to portray him as a debauched libertine, without morals or restraint. Rather, it was typical letting loose of a young aristocrat confronted with all the pleasures his age and status presented.

Philip and his entourage were very much impressed by the wealth and culture of the Netherlands. They were especially struck by the wealth of the large and prosperous city of Antwerp, "the very richest of cities," and "the marketplace of the world." When he returned to Spain, Philip brought back a taste for Flemish painting, architecture and music. Not only that, Philip became acquainted with his future noble subjects in the Low Countries. Among them were William of Nassau, Prince of Orange, Lamoral, Count of Egmont, and Philippe de Montmorency, Count of Hornes. Philip got on well with his young contemporaries; no one could suspect that within twenty years they would find themselves on opposite sides of a religious and political chasm, and that two of them (Egmont and Hornes) would be beheaded at Philip's command, and that Orange would flee to exile in Germany.

Departing the Netherlands in June 1550, Charles and Philip travelled to Germany, where Philip assisted his father at the Imperial assembly (the *Reichstag*, or Diet) in Augsburg. Charles, prematurely aged and infirm, was looking towards the future and making arrangements for his succession. He assured German Protestants that he would respect the liberties and privileges that they had been granted. Philip, despite his later rigidity when it came to religion, displayed no dissent. Indeed, he had for several years been in close contact with Protestants in Germany and the Netherlands, and had visited lands inhabited by Protestants. We must remember, however, that he was still very young — in 1550 he celebrated his twenty-third birthday — and his views on many subjects were still being formed.

Charles's succession plans did however cause some acrimony within the Habsburg family. In 1521, Charles had given the Austrian lands to his brother

Ferdinand, who ruled them as archduke. In 1526 Ferdinand was elected King of Hungary and Bohemia in succession to his dead brother-in-law. In addition, in 1531 he was elected King of Romans, an honorific title granted to the Emperor-elect. For twenty years, therefore, it had been established that Ferdinand would succeed Charles as Holy Roman Emperor. Charles wanted very much for Philip to succeed Ferdinand as Emperor, which Philip also desired. Ferdinand also had a son, however (Maximilian, who was currently regent in Spain), and they both believed that Maximilian should succeed his father. It was a very contentious issue. Their sister Mary of Hungary acted as a mediator, but for a time the two brothers refused to speak to each other. In the end, they agreed that Philip would succeed Ferdinand, and that Maximilian or his heir would succeed Philip, establishing the principal that the imperial dignity would alternate between the Spanish and German branches of the dynasty. In the end, however, Maximilian succeeded Ferdinand and for 250 years the title remained in the German branch of the family.

Finally, after an absence of two and a half years, Philip returned to Spain in July 1551. His chief business turned out to be the raising of money for Charles's renewed wars, for the Emperor was caught completely unaware by his enemies. In late 1551, the Turks captured the North African port of Tripoli, from which they threatened Spanish and Italian shipping in the western Mediterranean. At the same time, the German Protestant princes struck an alliance with Henry II of France and attacked the Emperor's forces. Charles himself barely escaped a humiliating capture at Innsbruck in May 1552 only by fleeing across the Alps in a litter during a blinding snowstorm.

The other important issue that occupied Philip at this time was his remarriage. He had an heir, Don Carlos, but as we have seen, one could never have too many heirs, and Don Carlos was sickly besides. Negotiations were well-advanced for Philip's marriage to yet another Portuguese princess, when a more intriguing possibility opened up. In July 1553, young King Edward VI of England died at the age of fifteen. The heir to throne was his older half-sister, Princess Mary. Mary was the daughter of King Henry VIII and his first wife, Catharine of Aragon. (Catharine was the daughter of Ferdinand and Isabella, and thus an aunt of Charles V and Philip and Mary were therefore first cousins.) A marriage to Queen Mary made sense from many different angles. It could be an important building block in the revival of the old alliance between Burgundy and England against France. Perhaps more importantly, Mary was a Catholic, unlike her brother Edward and younger half-sister Elizabeth, and her fondest wish was to restore England to the Roman Catholic Church. A marriage with Mary therefore presented the possibility of a Catholic heir to the throne and a Catholic England into the indefinite future.[40]

Faced with the prospect of marrying Philip, eleven years her junior, Mary responded with glee. At the age of thirty-seven, her child-bearing years were quickly approaching their end, and a quick marriage with the most eligible prince in Europe suited her perfectly. Philip's response was more dutiful. He lacked any real enthusiasm for the match but accepted it as a political move and as his filial duty. Sensitive to English opinion against their queen marrying a foreigner, Charles negotiated on behalf of his son a series of restrictions on Philip's power as prospective King of England. He was to share power with Mary, observe English laws and customs, and not appoint foreigners to positions in England. England was not to be dragged into the wars of Philip's other realms, militarily or financially. Philip's power in England would cease with Mary's death. Any heir would become ruler of England, the Netherlands, and the Free County (Franche-Comté) of Burgundy, while Don Carlos or his heirs would inherit the Spanish kingdoms. Should Don Carlos die childless, the heirs of Philip and Mary would then inherit the Spanish kingdoms. (No one could have known at this point that eight-year-old Don Carlos would indeed die childless and predecease his father.)

Philip and a very large entourage of about 4,000 left for England in July 1554. He left as his regent in Spain his sister Juana. (Juana had been married to the King of Portugal, and had recently been widowed and returned to Spain.). Charles had turned over to Philip the Kingdom of Naples, so that the marriage between Philip and Mary was one of equals, and the wedding took place on July 25 in Winchester Cathedral.

Both parties entered this marriage with their eyes wide open. This was a diplomatic arrangement and love was certainly not expected to play any part. Philip, in fact, before leaving Spain signed a secret document which stated that he was only submitting under duress. Quite unexpectedly, however, Mary fell very much in love with her new husband. For his part, Philip acted correctly and was always courteous toward and solicitous of his new wife, even if Mary's passion was not returned. Spanish opinion of Mary was quite unflattering. Ruy Gomez described her as "old and flabby."

---

[40] Henry VIII had established an independent Church of England in order to obtain an annulment of his marriage to Catharine of Aragon who, despite a number of pregnancies, had only one child who survived: Princess Mary. Under Henry, the Church of England remained essentially Catholic in doctrine and practice, though independent of Rome. Under Henry's son Edward VI (r. 1547–53), the Church of England became Protestant in doctrine and practice. Historians debate the religious orientation of the English people at this time. It is probably most accurate to say that the religious opinions of most English people were still rather malleable. Government policy was therefore paramount in charting England's future religious course.

Another observer wrote: "the queen is in no way beautiful; she is short, frail rather than fat, and very white and fair-haired; she has no eyebrows; she is a saint; she dresses very badly."

Philip reported that the English received him very well, but his Spanish followers despised their hosts:

> We are in an excellent land, but among the worst people in the world. These English are very unfriendly to the Spanish nation. This has been seen very from the many incidents, some of them important, that have taken place between them and us.

The Venetian ambassador would report that Philip was not only respected by his new subjects, but loved, and would be even more popular without the Spaniards who surrounded him.

Mary's chief goal, of course, was the restoration of England to the Roman Catholic Church, which she accomplished with little fuss, by repealing her father's legislation which had severed the ties between England and Rome. At first, Mary was inclined to be quite lenient to those who did not re-embrace the Church. Eventually, however, she and her advisors decided that a harsher policy was needed, and beginning in 1555, some 280 Protestants were burned at the stake for heresy. This, of course, is what has earned her the nickname "Bloody Mary," unfair though it may be. By contemporary standards, this persecution was relatively mild. Mary's main problem was her devotion to principle. But the winners, of course, get to write the history books. Mary's treatment at the hands of posterity would have been very different had she burned fewer heretics and hanged more traitors, as indeed her sister Elizabeth would do in her reign.

There can be no doubt that Philip heartily approved of England's return to the Catholic Church. However, he was determined not to meddle in English affairs and played little or no role in the persecution. He did not object in principle to burning heretics: in fact he wrote to Juana that "things have been going from good to better and some heretics have been punished." On the other hand, he certainly recognized that making martyrs was not conducive to reconciling the English with Rome. His personal chaplain delivered a sermon in which he "did earnestly inveigh against the bishops for burning of men, saying plainly that they learned it not in scripture to burn any for conscience sake; but the contrary, that they should live and be converted." Certainly, his exposure to Protestants in Germany and the Netherlands had shown that he was able to subordinate religious purity to political necessity if required.

By early 1555, it was widely rumored that Queen Mary was pregnant, which, after all was the whole point of the marriage in the first place: to produce a Catholic heir to ensure that England would remain Catholic into the indefinite future. Had this been true, English and European history would have turned out very differently. The queen was not, in fact, pregnant. Most likely, she was already suffering from the uterine cancer which would eventually kill her. But at the time everyone, including Philip, believed that she was. As the months wore on, however, it became increasingly evident that Mary was not pregnant, and Philip began preparations to leave England, after a stay of a little more than a year, for he had been summoned to the Netherlands by his father.

Prematurely aged at 55, worn out from long years of travel and warfare, sick from a lifetime of over-indulgence in food and drink, and depressed over the failure of his grand ambitions, Charles V was preparing to abdicate his titles and retire to a Spanish monastery to await his imminent death. On October 25, 1555 seated between his son Philip and his sister Mary, Charles addressed the assembled nobility of the Low Countries and his other realms:

> I have been nine times to Germany, six times to Spain, and seven to Italy; I have come here to Flanders ten times, and have been four times to France in war and peace, twice to England, and twice to Africa . . . without mentioning other lesser journeys. I have made eight voyages in the Mediterranean and three in the seas of Spain, and soon I shall make the fourth voyage when I return there to be buried.

There was not a dry eye in the house, and overcome with emotion, Charles too broke down and wept. Philip knelt before his father who embraced him and blessed him with his hands on his head. Philip then accepted the responsibilities his father entrusted to him. He spoke a few words in halting French, and explained that since he could not speak the language well, Cardinal Granvelle would speak for him. Philip was now the new ruler of the provinces which made up the Netherlands. In January 1556, Charles formally passed to his son the Spanish kingdoms, and in February, the Free County (Franche-Comté) of Burgundy.[41] He would not formally abdicate the Imperial Crown in favor of his brother Ferdinand until 1558. In September 1556, he made his last voyage, from the Netherlands to Spain. Accompanied by his sisters Mary and Eleanor, he took up residence in the monastery at Yuste, where he died in August 1558, clutching to his breast the same crucifix which his wife Isabella had held when she died almost two decades earlier.

* * *

---

[41] Charles's mother Juana *la Loca*, had finally died in May 1555, which freed Charles to abdicate in favour of Philip without abrogating the status of his mother.

Philip's relationship with his father was obviously complex. Although absent for most of Philip's childhood and youth, Charles attempted — largely successfully — to provide his son with as stable and "normal" an upbringing as possible, at least within the norms of European ruling dynasties.

Charles V did provide Philip with excellent training in the art of ruling. Philip was introduced to power at a young age, at least by our standards, and was surrounded with advisors who were neither docile yes-men nor overbearing control freaks. As we have seen, on his departure from Spain, Charles left for Philip two detailed letters of advice and instruction, which Philip took very seriously for the rest of his life. Indeed, as we have seen, in some respects he took his father's advice too seriously. Philip obviously had great respect for his father, and loved him in his way, but it cannot be said that they had a very intimate or affectionate relationship. Likewise, Charles loved his son and appreciated his abilities, and did provide him with a model political apprenticeship. On the other hand, Philip did depart, consciously or not, from his father's example in several important ways. As we have seen, Philip was more introverted than his father, to the point where people often found him cold. Certainly, he did like to spend time alone, and although he was no recluse, he lacked the ease with which Charles related to others. In addition, whereas Charles, as we have seen, spent large parts of his reign travelling among his realms, Philip was very much a homebody. After his return to Spain in 1559, he never again left the Iberian peninsula, and his only departure from Castile and Aragon was a two year stint in Portugal after he took over that kingdom in 1580.

As a young child, Philip was close to his mother, and for his whole life was very close to his sisters Juana and Maria. His first marriage, to Maria of Portugal was cut short by her death before they could form an emotionally stable relationship. Certainly his marriage to Mary Tudor lacked passion from his perspective, although he was not as cruelly callous as he has often been portrayed by his enemies and by hostile historians. He was extremely fond of his third wife Elizabeth de Valois, and treasured their two daughters. He would marry a fourth time, in 1570. He was not keen on remarriage, but with Don Carlos having died in 1568, he had only two surviving children, both daughters. He accepted the need to remarry for the sake of the dynasty's future. His fourth wife was Anna of Austria. She was the daughter of his cousin Maximilian and his sister Maria, and had been born in 1549 when her parents were Philip's regents in Spain during his travels to northern Europe. Even by the standards of the Habsburg dynasty, this was an unusually inbred match, as twenty-one-year-old Anna was both cousin and niece to forty-three-year-old Philip. It is impossible to say for certain, but it is certainly likely that genetic weaknesses played a role in their sad reproductive history.[42] They had five children together, but only one, Philip, survived to adulthood, succeeding his father on the Spanish throne as King Philip III (r. 1598–1621). Quite unexpectedly, Philip fell deeply in love with his new young wife and found a level of companionship with her that he had found with none of his other wives, or indeed with any other woman. She was shy and retiring, rather than lively and vivacious as Elizabeth de Valois had been, and she was the perfect companion for the middle-aged Philip. When she died in 1580 during an influenza epidemic, Philip was distraught. He felt that his own death was sure to follow, and re-examined his will, "in case I should go." He would not marry again.

Philip seems therefore to have developed secure attachments and was certainly capable of affectionate and fulfilling relationships. On the other hand, outside a very small circle of family and friends, he was perceived as cold and detached, although this is perhaps understandable given the loss of his mother and first wife at a young age, as well perhaps as an innate trait of personality inherited from his mother.

* * *

Philip remained in the Netherlands until March 1557, when he returned to England, much to Mary's delight. He remained in England just long enough to arrange English support for a declaration of war against France. In July he left England for the last time, leaving behind a terminally ill and childless queen. He returned to Brussels from where he supervised the war effort which resulted in a crushing victory over the French at St. Quentin (August 10, 1557). Ruy Gomez commented that God Himself must have granted Philip victory, since the battle was won "without experience, without troops, and without money." Indeed, a lack of money prevented Philip from following up this victory by marching on Paris, only 40 kilometers away. English participation in the war ended disastrously with the loss in 1558 of Calais, England's only remaining continental possession from the era of the Hundred Years War. St. Quentin was Philip's first and only experience of actual combat. Unlike his father, who had been present at and directed many battles, Philip was a strategist rather than a general.

Within three weeks in November 1558, Philip learned of the deaths of his father and his wife. Mary had died on November 17, making Philip once again a widower. With her death, Philip's power in England ceased, although he

---

[42] Over the history of the Spanish Habsburg dynasty (1516–1700), their rates of infant and child mortality were in fact substantially higher than the rates recorded from Spanish villages. See Alvarez G, Ceballos FC, Quinteiro C, 2009, *The Role of Inbreeding in the Extinction of a European Royal Dynasty*. PLoS ONE 4(4): e5174. doi:10.1371/journal. pone.0005174.

sounded out her half-sister and successor Elizabeth about the prospects of a marriage between them. Elizabeth herself gave the idea serious consideration before rejecting it.

Peace was made between the combatants by the Treaty of Cateau-Cambrésis of April 3, 1559. France would keep Calais, but give up any claim to lands in Italy, sealing Spanish domination of the peninsula for a century and a half. To seal the new-found amity, it was arranged for Philip to marry Elizabeth de Valois, eldest daughter of King Henry II of France. There had been some discussion that she might marry Philip's son, Don Carlos, who was the same age as Elizabeth. In the end, however, Philip decided to have her as his own wife. Some have speculated that there were already severe misgivings as to Don Carlos's suitability as heir, and that this was what prompted Philip to marry her, instead of having her marry his son. In June, Philip's emissaries Orange, Alba, and Egmont arrived in Paris, and a magnificent proxy wedding was held in Notre Dame, with Alba standing in for his absent king.

Part of any respectable royal wedding, besides the festivals and banquets, was a tournament. The bride's father, Henry II, was then forty years old and an accomplished athlete and warrior. Against the wishes of his wife and advisors, he took part in a joust on June 30 1559. His opponent's lance splintered, and a portion of it penetrated the king's visor, and went through his eye and lodged in his brain. He fell into a coma and died ten days later. He left behind an Italian widow, Catherine de Medici, three daughters, and four young sons. The three elder sons would each reign as king, but none had legitimate heirs, while the fourth predeceased his elder brother. The death of Henry II and the resulting political instability would combine with religious upheaval to produce thirty-five years of bitter and brutal civil war in France.

Philip sailed from the Netherlands for Spain in August of 1559, leaving his older half-sister Margaret of Parma as his regent in the Netherlands. In early September, he arrived back in Spain after an absence of eight years. His new wife, Elizabeth de Valois joined her husband in Spain in December and in January 1560 they were formally married in person. She was fourteen years old, while Philip at thirty-two was already a widower twice over. Although she was not conventionally beautiful, Philip was captivated by her vivaciousness, as was the entire court. She became especially close to her sister-in-law Juana, who took the young princess under her wing. Philip conducted several affairs early in their marriage, but gradually settled into a routine of marital fidelity, especially after Elizabeth began her periods in August 1561. In 1566 she gave birth to a girl, Isabella, who would become Philip's favorite child. In 1567 she bore another daughter, Catalina Micaela.

In 1568 she became pregnant again. In October, however, she prematurely delivered a still-born girl and died several hours later, after apologizing to Philip for not having given him a son.

Having returned to Spain after a lengthy absence, Philip was confronted by a number of different problems throughout his vast realms. One was money, or rather the lack of money. His diplomatic and military commitments continually overwhelmed even the vast revenues available to him. Already in 1557 he had suspended payments to his creditors, effectively declaring bankruptcy, which he was to do on two further occasions. There was the ever-present threat from Turkish naval dominance in the Mediterranean, which was compounded by the presence in Spain of a minority discontented and rebellious Muslims, the *Moriscos*, who it was feared might make common cause with the Turks.[43]

Philip was also very concerned to preserve religious unity within his realms, no doubt remembering his father's advice to "never allow heresies to enter your realm." Philip was a steadfast supporter of the Inquisition and attended a number of *autos-da-fé* at which recalcitrant heretics were burnt at the stake. He was especially concerned with the encroachment of Protestantism in its Calvinist form into the Netherlands. He, his sister Margaret, and Cardinal Granvelle came up with a plan to reorganize the Catholic Church in the Netherlands in order to more effectively combat heresy. These plans not only alienated the Protestants, but also many Catholic nobles who felt that they had not been consulted, and that they violated their historic and customary rights and privileges. Ultimately, Philip's policies provoked a series of rebellions which required forceful repression. His absolute refusal to compromise one iota when it came to religion doomed any hope of reconciliation. In the end the seven northern provinces would depose Philip as their ruler and establish their own independent Protestant state, the United Provinces or the Dutch Republic, under the leadership of William of Orange.

How are we to square this intransigence with Philip's earlier seeming tolerance of religious dissension in Germany and his attempted moderation of Mary's persecution in England? Basically, in those lands religious diversity was already an established fact, and restoration of unity was politically unpragmatic and would cause more problems than it solved. This was

---

[43] Philip's great-grandparents Ferdinand and Isabella had in 1492 conquered Granada, the last outpost of Muslim power in Spain. All Muslims were ordered to convert to Christianity, and the practice of Islam was forbidden. Practical necessity, however, had delayed enforcement of these policies until the 1560s, when the government insisted on enforcing these rules. The result was a serious and bloody uprising in the mountainous region of the Alpujarras.

what Mary, in her stubborn devotion to principle, failed to grasp. As he would show on a number of occasions, Philip was nothing if not pragmatic, eventually becoming known as *el Prudente*, the Prudent One. In Spain and the Low Countries, however, he was dealing with his own lands and his own subjects, and he was determined to prevent heresy from gaining a foothold there. The best way to prevent religious dissent was to nip it in the bud.

Among the other problems which confronted Philip upon his return to Spain was that of his son and heir, Don Carlos. The difficulties between father and son were not the result of family dysfunction or stunted emotional lives. As we have seen, Philip's family relationships were relatively normal, given the standards of his time and social class. Philip's relationship with his own father, while not close or affectionate by our standards, was certainly not such that it would have poisoned Philip's relations with his own son. Indeed, everything suggests that Philip intended that Don Carlos be brought up and educated in much the same way he himself had been.

In later years, when Don Carlos's problems became evident to all, stories circulated about an unusual birth. For example, the Venetian reported that he had been born with three teeth, and bit his wet nurse so hard that she almost died, and that he did not speak until the age of three. This report, however, was written in 1563, when Don Carlos was already seventeen years old. There is no contemporary evidence of any such problems. We must also remember that in the sixteenth century, people were fascinated by stories of unusual or "monstrous" births, whether human or animal. They were breathlessly recounted in cheap publications and were seen as portents of future catastrophes. It is therefore hardly surprising that people would retrospectively look for such omens in the sad case of Don Carlos.

Deprived of his mother just days after his birth, Don Carlos was placed in the household of his aunts Juana and Maria in the town of Alcala de Henares, northeast of Madrid. He lived here until 1548, when they were brought to Valladolid in preparation for Philip's voyage to the Netherlands to meet his father. As Maria and her new husband Maximilian were named regents during Philip's absence, Juana was given special responsibility for Don Carlos. During Philip's absence, his son resided in Juana's household in the town of Toro. In 1552, however, Juana left Spain to marry the heir to the Portuguese throne. Deprived of his mother through death, his father through absence, Carlos now lost his primary caregiver as well.

The observation that Philip intended that his son be brought up in the same way that he himself had been is borne out in several ways. As mentioned above, he appointed as his son's governess Leonor de Mascareñas, the Portuguese noblewoman who had been his. When Don Carlos was seven, and the time came to appoint a tutor, the man Philip chose was Honorato Juan, who had been one of his own teachers. As his own father had been, Philip was mostly absent during Don Carlos's childhood and youth. As we have seen, Philip was gone from Spain from November 1548 until July 1551, and again from July 1554 until August 1559.

In 1553 Don Carlos was granted his own household, with Antonio Rojas as his governor and Honorato Juan as his tutor. Both his father and grandfather were kept apprised of his education. At this point, there was still no hint of the problems which would later become apparent. Juan reported to Philip that the prince was eager to learn and applied himself well to his lessons. There were, however, some physical issues. Don Carlos was small for his age and frail. One shoulder was higher than the other, and one leg longer than the other. Observers reported that he had an unusually large head.

As we have seen, in 1556 Charles V returned to Spain to retire in a monastery, having abdicated his titles. Young Don Carlos was thrilled at the prospect of meeting his grandfather for the first time. For two weeks the elderly emperor and his namesake grandson visited in Valladolid before he travelled to his retreat at Yuste. There are conflicting reports on the emperor's impression of his grandson. One observer reported that he was so impressed that he would have liked Don Carlos in his council to discuss affairs. On the other hand, he is reported to have said to his sister Eleanor: "He [Don Carlos] seems very boisterous to me; his manners and humor do not please me much; I do not know what will become of him." He was also reportedly displeased with Don Carlos's lack of respect for his aunt Juana. It is, however, important to remember that the prince was at this point twelve years old, still a child. We must resist the temptation to view history backwards, to seize on any hint of problems in the light of what we know would later happen. There is nothing to indicate anything beyond normal childhood and adolescent mood swings.

It was shortly after, however, that we do begin to see evidence that contemporaries were growing increasingly concerned about the heir to the throne. His governor Don Garcia de Toledo (Antonio de Rojas had recently died) would write to Charles V:

> [R]egarding his studies, he is not very advanced, because he studies only with ill grace. It is the same when it comes to exercise and fencing. In everything he requires the incentive of a reward. Sometimes he goes riding, but I do not let him do it often, because he is so careless and absentminded that it is dangerous.

In a later letter, he suggested to the Emperor that a visit to his grandfather at Yuste might help to straighten out the prince. Princess Juana suggested the same to her father. But Charles would not disturb his repose with the presence of a rambunctious child. Honorato Juan, Don Carlos's tutor would write at about the same time to Philip, who was then in the Netherlands:

> His Highness [Don Carlos] is well, thanks be to God! When it comes to his studies, I have done all that I can, and more, more perhaps than any other tutor could do. I regret that I have not succeeded as I would have wished. . . . It gives me great pain to see that the fruit of His Highness's lessons does not correspond to what it had been at the beginning and for several years afterwards, as everyone can see and as Your Majesty has been informed. . . . I beg Your Majesty to pardon the boldness that I have permitted myself in this letter, and to destroy it, since my intention is that it be read by Your Majesty alone.

Philip responded by reassuring his old teacher that he knew he had the prince's best interests at heart and that he was blameless for Don Carlos's scholarly deficiencies. At the same time, Philip wrote Garcia de Toledo to keep a close eye on the boy's application to his studies.

Beyond his education, troubling reports began to circulate about Don Carlos's behavior. In 1557, the Venetian ambassador reported that the prince would roast rabbits alive, and when a pet snake bit his finger, he bit off its head.

> Everything about him suggests that he will be proud without equal: for he cannot be long in the presence of either his father or his grandfather, hat in hand. He is as angry as a young man can be, and obstinate in his opinions. . . . [he] only wants to talk about war and to read books about war.

Certainly genetics explains a great deal about Don Carlos's condition. First, there was a significant family history of mental illness. His grandmother Juana *la Loca*, as we have seen, spent nearly fifty years in isolation due to mental illness, likely schizophrenia. Her son, Charles V, although he escaped the severity of his mother's afflictions, was prone to bouts of depression and melancholy. One of his great-great-grandmothers (and grandmother of Juana *la Loca*), Isabella of Portugal, Queen of Castile (1428–1496), also suffered from severe mental illness.[44] Not only was there a family history of mental illness, but it was concentrated by generations of inbreeding. Don Carlos had only four great-grandparents, instead of the normal eight, and only six great-great-grandparents rather than the normal sixteen. His mother and his father were not only first cousins, but shared the same degree of consanguity

---

[44] She should not be confused with her more famous daughter, also named Isabella, mother of Juana, whose marriage to Ferdinand of Aragon united the two Spanish kingdoms.

as if they were half-siblings. The wonder is not that Don Carlos suffered from significant physical and mental disabilities, but that his father was as normal as he was.

It is also probable that disease played a role in Don Carlos's problems, as he suffered from malaria, with its alternating bouts of fevers and chills. This may also explain his small stature and frailness, as well as his failure to progress academically after a promising start. Malaria in children can lead to increased intercranial pressure and cognitive impairment, as well as anemia during a period of rapid brain development.

Some of Don Carlos's physical and mental problems were thus becoming apparent by the time that Philip II returned to Spain in 1559. Nevertheless, the king, no doubt recalling his political education under his father, attempted to do the same for Don Carlos. In late 1559, the prince attended a meeting of the Cortes of Castile, along with his father, at which he was recognized as Philip's heir as king. He was, however, suffering from malaria, which prevented him from taking part in the festivities which marked the marriage of Philip and Elizabeth de Valois. As a result of his illness, he was relocated to the town of Alcala, which was believed to have a healthier climate. In addition, Alcala was home to a famous university, and Philip believed that attending classes there might have a beneficial effect on his son. This demonstrates that while Philip may have been aware of Don Carlos's problems, they were not seen as insurmountable. Philip had not written off his son.

In Alcala, Don Carlos was accompanied by two other young men of the royal court. Philip may have had in mind his own youth and fast friendships with Ruy Gomez da Silva and Don Luis de Requesens. Carlos's companions were his uncle Don John, and his cousin Alexander Farnese. Don John of Austria, as he was known, was an illegitimate son of Emperor Charles V. Born in 1547, he was therefore actually younger than his nephew Don Carlos. Raised in Spain from a young age, he endeared himself to Philip who treated him as a son, although he was careful to preserve the distinction between royal and non-royal children. Don John was a dashing and romantic figure, handsome and athletic. He would later play an important role in Philip's reign: as the suppressor of the revolt in the Alpujarras, as the commander of the great naval victory over the Turks at Lepanto in 1571, and as Philip's governor-general in the Netherlands. Alexander Farnese (1545–92) was the son of Margaret of Parma (1522–86), another illegitimate child of Charles V and therefore a half-sister of Philip II. She had been married first to the Duke of Florence and then to the Duke of Parma. As a young boy Alexander had lived in the Netherlands, but accompanied Philip on his voyage to Spain in 1559 where he was raised and educated alongside Don Carlos and Don John.

He would eventually succeed Don John as Philip's governor-general in the Netherlands and would prove to be the most brilliant general of the later sixteenth century.

While at Alcala, Don Carlos suffered a serious accident which had the effect of worsening his mental health. In April 1562, while trying to see a young woman, he fell down a flight of stairs and hit his head, knocking himself unconscious. As soon as he heard about the incident, Philip rushed to Alcala to be with his son, bringing with him his own physician, the great Flemish anatomist Andreas Vesalius. In May, Don Carlos fell into a coma and appeared near death, despite — or more probably because of — the attention of physicians. Prayers for his health were conducted throughout the kingdom, and Philip spent many tearful hours by his bedside. Finally, on Vesalius's advice, the prince's skull was trepanned. In addition, the remains of a local holy man, Brother Diego of Alcala were brought to his bedside. For whatever reason, Carlos responded and by the end of May was out of danger. Philip attributed his son's recovery to the remains of Brother Diego and would later have the Pope canonize him.

Many people attributed Don Carlos's problems to his brain injury; however, it is clear that many of his problems preceded his fall. On the other hand, brain trauma can of course have a severe effect on behavior, as it seems to have done in this case. Although a definitive diagnosis is of course impossible, Don Carlos displayed many symptoms of what psychologists today call Conduct Disorder. These include cruelty to animals or other people. Even before his accident, we have seen reports of his cruelty to animals. On one occasion he maimed twenty horses in the royal stables, and on another he so mistreated one of his father's horses that it died. He was also capable of violence toward people. When a bootmaker presented him with boots that were too tight, he made the craftsman eat them. When one of his servants came too slowly when summoned, he attempted to throw him out of a window. On one occasion when several drops of water fell on him while he was passing a house, he ordered its inhabitants killed and the house destroyed. Fortunately, his companions were able to assuage his rage. When he learned that the Duke of Alba was being sent to the Netherlands as governor-general, a position he wanted for himself, Don Carlos ordered the duke not to accept and attempted to stab him.

Conduct Disorder may also involve sexual deviance. It was widely rumored that Don Carlos was impotent, rumors which he attempted to deny in very graphic ways. He would accost women in the streets of Madrid and forcefully embrace them while degrading them with crude insults. There are reports that he would go into brothels and chase out patrons who seemed to be more able with the ladies than he. On one occasion, he had three physicians administer an aphrodisiac and then tested its results with a compliant prostitute. So pleased was he with the result that he related the episode to the imperial ambassador as proof of his virility. He gave the physicians an annual pension of a thousand ducats, and the prostitute a gift of 12,000 ducats, as well as a house for her and her mother.

It has been noted that Conduct Disorder has a distinct genetic component. In particular, a family history of schizophrenia and/or mood disorder heightens the risk for Conduct Disorders. As we have seen, Don Carlos's family tree is replete with such mental illnesses, reinforced and enhanced by generations of inbreeding.

Besides his mental disorders and frequent malaria-induced fevers and his slight but apparent physical deformities, Don Carlos also suffered from other conditions. Like his grandfather Charles V, only even more so, he was a renowned glutton. The Imperial ambassador related in 1564:

> the prince eats so much and with such avidity that it can hardly be described; and he has barely finished before he is ready to begin again. . . . Many believe that if he continues in this way he will not live for long.

In 1565 William of Orange wrote from Madrid to his brother that Don Carlos had recently eaten sixteen pounds of fruit and four pounds of grapes. Even allowing for hyperbole and gossip-mongering, there are enough and consistent enough reports to conclude that Don Carlos had a severe eating disorder. Nor was his intake always limited to food. On one occasion, the Venetian ambassador reported, Don Carlos's jeweller showed him an exceptionally fine pearl. The prince pried it from its mounting with his teeth and swallowed it. Fortunately for the jeweller, it was returned to him three days later when Don Carlos's digestive system had finished with it. According to the French ambassador, the prince "has strength only in his teeth."

Philip was obviously aware of his son's problems, but still he hoped that they could be rectified or at least compensated for. Within the limits of the prince's capabilities, Philip sought to involve his son in the government in much the same way that his own father had done. In 1564 he appointed the prince to the Council of State and encouraged his involvement in affairs. His participation was irregular and infrequent until the following year when Philip also appointed Don John to the council. In Philip's system of government, however, the Council of State was largely ceremonial, while the real decisions were made by Philip in concert with a handful of relevant advisors, depending on the business at hand.

Don Carlos, however, was beginning to chafe at his lack of influence and power. He turned twenty years old in 1565, and his father had yet to entrust him with any real responsibilities. Philip, on the other hand, had served as regent for his father at the age of sixteen. He believed especially that he ought to be named governor of the Netherlands. Indeed, on his departure from the Low Countries in 1559, Philip had promised to send his son as governor, plans that were put into abeyance by the prince's illness and accident, as well as by Philip's growing doubts about his suitability to govern. In 1564, Philip wrote the Duke of Alba that "in intelligence and personality as well as in judgement, [the prince] lags far behind what is normal at his age."

Then there was the question of Don Carlos's marriage. Philip, it will be remembered had been married at seventeen, and then a father and widower at eighteen. As we have seen, for the ruling dynasties of Europe, it was imperative that heirs to the throne marry as soon as possible, in order to start producing future heirs as soon as possible. On paper, Don Carlos was the most eligible royal bachelor in Europe. And indeed, there was hardly a princess who was not proposed as a bride at one time or another. In fact, Elizabeth de Valois, Philip's third wife, had originally been proposed as a bride for Don Carlos. Her mother, Catherine de Medici, proposed Elizabeth's younger sister Marguerite. Other possible candidates were Mary Stuart (Mary Queen of Scots), Queen of Scotland in her own right, and widow of King Francis II of France, who died in 1560, and Queen Elizabeth of England, who had succeeded to the English throne upon the death of her half-sister Mary (Philip's second wife) in 1558. The most unusual suggestion, and one that Philip was partial to, was that Don Carlos marry his aunt Juana (Philip's sister), who had cared for him as a young boy. Despite the fact that she was ten years older than her nephew, Juana was in favor of the match, but Don Carlos refused absolutely to contemplate it.

Of all the candidates, the one that Don Carlos preferred was his cousin Anne of Austria, the daughter of Maximilian and Philip's sister Maria. In fact, Anne had been born in Spain when her parents were Philip's regents in Spain. Although he had never met her, Don Carlos had seen a portrait (and everyone agreed that she was very attractive), and convinced himself that he loved her passionately. The match was pressed urgently first by Emperor Ferdinand I (Anne's grandfather and Philip's uncle) and after his death in 1564 by the new Emperor Maximilian II (Anne's father). Philip delayed committing to the match, at first due to his son's fragile health, but then, after he recovered from his fall, because he was coming increasingly to doubt his son's suitability as his heir. In 1564 Philip instructed his ambassador to inform the Emperor that

> I had already informed him that my son was not in a physical situation which allowed him to marry; I am now forced with great regret to repeat to him the same thing; that, although my son is nineteen years old and although there are other delayed young people, God has willed that he be more delayed than any other . . . we must be patient and put off this affair until the marriage may take place; because if it takes place any earlier, the evil that would result would affect both our families. . .

Don Carlos also resented his father's continued control over his household. In 1564, Philip named his close advisor and childhood friend Ruy Gomez da Silva as head of Don Carlos's household. The prince rightly suspected that Gomez was put in this position as Philip's eyes and ears.

Faced with all these resentments, Don Carlos found a friend in the queen, Elizabeth de Valois. From her arrival in Spain, the young queen had cultivated the friendship of the prince. This was at least partly due to political calculation: as the future king (as far as anyone knew), Don Carlos would be an important figure in her life and the lives of her future children. Don Carlos was also the same age as she, and it was to be expected that she might have more in common with him with than her husband, who was eighteen years older. She probably also felt sorry for him. Don Carlos returned the affection. He gave her costly presents, and when she fell ill in 1564, he was continually at her side. This puppyish devotion gave rise to rumors of an affair between them. Certainly Don Carlos may have felt that she should have been his wife, rather than his father's. It is also clear, however, that however much Elizabeth valued him as a friend, there was nothing more between them.

So, by the mid 1560s, Don Carlos and his father were clearly on a collision course. Philip was increasingly coming to the realization that his son was very poorly suited for the role to which he had been born. Some have speculated that Philip may have even been planning to have Don John succeed him. There was clearly precedent for something like this in the case of Juana *la Loca*, where first her father and then her son ruled in her name. In a system of hereditary monarchy, family tragedies are necessarily transformed into political crises. In this case, however, events were given a special urgency by developments in the Netherlands.

When Philip left the Netherlands for Spain in 1559, he left behind his elder half-sister Margaret of Parma as his regent there. She was to be advised by council made up of the most important nobles, including Egmont, Hornes, and William of Orange, all of whom Philip had gotten to know during his time there. The leading figure in the government was, however, Antoine de Perrenot, Bishop of Arras and Cardinal Granvelle. As we have seen, Philip was greatly disturbed by the incursions into the Low Countries of Protestantism in its relatively new Calvinist form. In order to combat this, keeping always his father's advice in mind, Margaret, Philip and Granvelle came up with a plan to reorganize the Catholic Church in the Netherlands to make it more efficient and responsive in the fight against heresy.

These plans aroused great opposition among Protestants, as one might expect. They were, however, relatively powerless to resist. More importantly, these plans earned the opposition of many Catholic nobles, who objected on political rather than religious grounds. These plans had been drawn up and put into effect without their consultation and consent. They therefore violated the nobles' rights and privileges. The nobles further resented Granvelle's influence with Margaret and Philip. In March 1563, three leading nobles, Egmont, Hornes, and William of Orange demanded Granvelle's resignation, informing Philip that they were leaving the council until Granvelle resigned. The major issue at stake was the enforcement of the very strict laws against heresy which Philip wanted to implement. Nobles objected not so much out of religious sympathy for Protestants, but rather because they believed that they could use this issue to leverage concessions from Philip.

Faced with widespread opposition to his policies among the political elite, Philip dismissed Granvelle in early 1564 at Margaret's request. The dissatisfied nobles sent Egmont to Spain in early 1565 to gain Philip's consent to moderation of his religious policies. Philip was noncommittal and Egmont returned home to announce that the king agreed to moderate his policies, a complete misstatement of Philip's policy, one which, however, was understandable given Philip's vagueness. Egmont's views were contradicted, however, by letters from which arrived shortly afterwards announcing that persecution was to continue unabated. A general protest ensued, in which about 400 nobles signed an agreement called the "Compromise of the Nobility," which called for religious toleration and the suspension of the heresy laws. Faced with the opposition of the social and political elite of the Netherlands, and without help from Philip, Margaret had no choice but to back down. (Philip was occupied with naval affairs in the Mediterranean where the Turkish navy had laid siege to Malta.) The council of state sent to Spain one of their number to impress upon Philip the gravity of the situation in the Low Countries and the need for moderation and consultation. This was Floris de Montmorency, baron de Montigny, brother of the Count of Hornes, who arrived in Spain in June 1566. As Egmont had in the previous year,

Montigny also seemed to have secured Philip's agreement to moderation. Hardly had the documents been drawn up, however, when Philip in a secret legal ceremony signed a retraction of his concessions, claiming that they had been extorted under duress.[45]

This tense situation was made worse in the summer of 1566 when Calvinist preachers attracted vast crowds to open-air sermons outside major towns. Some of these crowds became violent, harassing Catholic priests, breaking into churches and destroying the images they found there. When Philip learned of these disorders in September, he felt that he had to act decisively. He simply could not tolerate such overt challenges to his authority. (Nor could any ruler, for that matter.) In 1567, he sent the Duke of Alva to Netherlands with an army of 10,000 to restore order by imposing a kind of martial law. Alva's preferred solution to any problem was the immediate application of maximum military force, and this time Philip agreed. Egmont and Hornes were arrested and executed, and William of Orange escaped the same fate only by seeking exile in Germany. In the end, Philip's rigidity and Alva's repression backfired. They set off a much more serious revolt which would result in the seven northern provinces of the Netherlands deposing Philip as their ruler and establishing an independent state known as the United Provinces or the Dutch Republic.[46]

Don Carlos, as we have seen, believed that the government of Netherlands was his by right, and resented his father for not allowing him to take his rightful place. This is superficially similar to Charles VII denying his son the government of Dauphiné. However, in that case, Charles feared that the ability of his son would underscore his own shortcomings. In the case of Don Carlos, Philip clearly understood that his son was not capable of handling such a delicate and complex situation. This did not prevent Don Carlos from trying, however. He may have met with Montigny and certainly attempted to enlist support from the Netherlands as a way of enhancing his position. A contemporary biographer of Philip II states that Montigny sought out Don Carlos's support, inviting him to come to the Netherlands as their ruler instead of his father. This is exceedingly unlikely, as it would present the appearance of treason which Montigny and the other Dutch nobles were

---

[45] Montigny was denied permission to leave Spain and was eventually imprisoned. After an attempted escape he was sentenced to death. He was strangled in secret in 1570.

[46] The split between an independent and largely Protestant north and a Catholic and Spanish-ruled south was dictated by military events rather than any pre-existing or inherent division. Philip and his successors continued to try to reconquer the northern provinces for decades, while the northern provinces attempted to "liberate" the south. Spain would not formally recognize the independence of the United Provinces until 1648.

desperate to avoid. In addition, they can hardly have been unaware of Don Carlos's physical and mental handicaps.

What is clear, however, is that Don Carlos contemplated something of the sort, and that Philip had to take it seriously. He never forgot his father's experience during the revolt of the Communeros in the 1520s. The Communeros had rebelled against a foreign king in the name of his mother, Juana *la Loca*. That Juana was insane and incapable of governing in no way diminished the threat to Charles. Likewise, in this case, Philip could not be sure that his opponents would not attempt to use Don Carlos in their resistance to him, an impression which the prince went out of his way to reinforce.

Indeed, Don Carlos's behavior speaks of increasing paranoia and hatred of his father. What seems to have tipped the balance was the cancellation of a proposed visit to the Netherlands. For some time, Philip had contemplated returning to Low Countries in order restore order personally. The latest proposed visit had been announced to the Cortes of Castile at the end of 1566. Philip further announced that Don Carlos would accompany him, much to the displeasure of the assembled delegates who no doubt remembered the long absences of Charles V from Spain. When they asked that Don Carlos remain as Philip's regent, the prince exploded in anger and threatened to strip the delegates of "all their power" if they continued to meddle in his affairs. It seems that to Don Carlos, the proposed visit to the Netherlands was a sort of panacea for his problems. Contemporaries and historians are disagreed about whether or not Philip actually intended to undertake this journey, or whether it was simply a smokescreen to allow Alva to impose order when he would arrive in the summer of 1567. When Alva reported that the situation was unstable and it was dangerous for Philip to come to the Netherlands, the king cancelled preparations. By late 1567, bitter and frustrated in his ambitions, Don Carlos began to actively plot his escape from the watchful eye of his father.

The way in which he did this, however, speaks of a childish naïveté. He had no money. Indeed, despite a substantial income from his father, he still had to borrow money to maintain his lavish lifestyle, loans which he had trouble repaying. Unable to borrow any more from the usual sources, he sent servants throughout Spain to solicit loans on his behalf. He pawned his jewellery to raise ready cash. He wrote letters to a number of important nobles inviting them to accompany him on an important voyage he was about to undertake. Several of these nobles passed his letters along to the king. He also wrote letters outlining his grievances against his father to other rulers, claiming that he was forced into such desperate actions by Philip's cruelty. In sum, it was impossible for Philip not to know what his son was up to. Don Carlos was also showing signs of paranoia. He began to sleep with weapons under his bed, and had a locksmith fashion a device with which he could lock and unlock his door from his bed.

Don Carlos also attempted to enlist Don John in his plans, whom he considered his best friend in the world. Don John's cooperation was essential because Philip had just named him Captain-General of the Sea, giving him supreme command of Philip's Mediterranean fleet. Don Carlos required his uncle's ships to take him to Italy, on the first leg of his escape. In return, he promised Don John control of Naples or Milan. Don John attempted to dissuade Don Carlos without success. Finally, he informed Philip of the prince's plans.

In late December, Don Carlos informed his confessor that he had conceived a mortal hatred towards someone and intended to kill him. His confessor replied that he could not absolve him unless he renounced his hatred. Upon further questioning, he revealed that the man in question was his father. Philip was now in a position where he had to act. Should Don Carlos somehow find his way to the Netherlands, he could be a potent symbol of resistance to his father. Nor could he leave Don Carlos in Spain to govern in his absence. More than that, perhaps, Don Carlos had shown himself by this point irrefutably to be mentally unbalanced, so that even his father could no longer make excuses for him.

Having spent Christmas at his palace at El Escorial, Philip returned to Madrid on January 17, 1568, and immediately convened a meeting of his closest advisors to discuss the problem of the prince. Philip and Don Carlos attended Mass together on January 18, in what turned out to be the prince's last public appearance. Later that day, when Philip requested that his son come see him, Don Carlos pleaded illness.

Shortly after midnight on January 19, Philip, dressed in full armor and a helmet and armed with a sword, accompanied by four members of the Council of State including Ruy Gomez and four aides, broke into Don Carlos's bedchamber and seized all the weapons before waking the prince. "Does Your Majesty wish to kill me?" asked Don Carlos. Philip reassured his son that he wished him no harm, and had only ever wanted what was best for him. The prince threw himself at his father's feet, begging him to kill him, or he would kill himself. That would be the act of madman, responded Philip. He was not mad, Don Carlos said, but rather desperate. When Don Carlos gave way to his anger and blamed Philip for his harshness, the king replied that from now on, he would treat him not as a father, but as a king.

The king then ordered the windows and doors of his son's room boarded up, and all dangerous items removed. He seized all of Don Carlos's papers, including lists of those whom he considered his enemies and his friends. At the top of the list of enemies was Philip himself, followed by Ruy Gomez, while the queen topped his list of friends, followed by Don John. A round-the-clock guard was place on Don Carlos.

The following day Philip cut off all communication between Madrid and the outside world and began to send out letters to selected recipients informing them of what had transpired: the Imperial ambassador, selected nobles, the bishops and representatives of the towns of Castile:

> Having enclosed the most serene prince Don Carlos, our very dear and well-loved son in our palace, and having established in his household, service, and treatment a very different order than had been observed until this time, the importance of this change has led us to inform you of it. The determination that we made is based on a foundation so just, and reasons so essential and urgent that we could not neglect them and still fulfill our obligations. . . . We believe that our course of action is the most suitable for the service of God and the public advantage. . .

He wrote in similar terms to the governments of his other realms and his viceroys there, to his aunt Catherine, dowager queen of Portugal and other members of his family, including the Holy Roman Emperor Maximilian II and his sister, Empress Maria. In all these letters Philip justified his actions by pointing out how "disordered" and "excessive" Don Carlos's conduct had been, without going into particulars. When Philip informed his wife, she burst into tears, and the French ambassador reported home that she "has not stopped crying for two days."

Philip wrote to Pope Pius V in his own hand:

> It is well that Your Holiness learns that in the education of the prince, since childhood, in the service, company, and counsel given to him, we have given great care and attention, as we ought to have, to the preparation of a prince, heir to so many kingdoms and states; we have employed all appropriate means to repress certain excesses which proceeded from his nature and character, and to reform his tendencies; that, during so many years, up to his present age, we have tried everything, and nothing has worked; that things have finally gone so far that in order to accomplish what I owe to the service of God and to the good of my kingdoms and states, I have been absolutely forced, with what pain and regret Your Holiness will understand, since it concerns my eldest and only son, to make this

change regarding his person, and to take such a resolution founded on such serious and just causes.

Philip issued orders that Don Carlos was to be kept in strict isolation in the royal palace. Even the queen and Juana were denied permission to see him. Philip also disabused anyone of the notion that the prince's imprisonment was to be temporary. Orders were given to repair the castle at Arevalo, where Don Carlos's great-great-grandmother Isabella of Portugal had been held in isolation, and arrangements were made to put in charge of the prince's supervision the same man who had guarded his grandmother Juana *la Loca*.

Don Carlos was understandably thrown into despair. At first, he resolved to kill himself, but left without weapons, he embarked on a hunger strike. When informed of his son's efforts to starve himself to death, Philip responded simply, "He'll eat when he's hungry enough." And so he did, going to the opposite extreme and gorging himself. Acting on a common belief that diamonds were poisonous, Don Carlos swallowed a diamond ring to no avail. When the weather in Madrid turned hot in June and July, he would drink huge quantities of ice water, sleep without clothes, and put ice in his bed. Malarial fever may help to explain some of this, but such extremes would certainly have taxed his already frail physique. Sometime around the middle of July, he gorged himself on a spicy partridge pie, and then slaked his thirst with huge amounts of ice water. This was followed by violent indigestion, vomiting and diarrhoea. He died on July 24, 1568, just two weeks after his twenty-third birthday.

Philip's treatment of his son has raised many eyebrows. It seems likely that he never saw his son again after his arrest. According to a contemporary biographer, Luis Cabrera de Cordoba, Don Carlos on his deathbed asked to see his father. Philip rushed to his son's bed, where he made the sign of the cross over him. Cabrera, however, was a secretary of Philip's and his biography is very favorable to the king. It is surely significant that no other contemporary source mentions such a scene. Indeed, the secrecy which surrounded Don Carlos's imprisonment and death gave rise to nasty gossip, all of which may be safely discounted, most notably that Don Carlos and the queen, Elizabeth de Valois had been carrying on an affair under the king's nose, and that Philip conspired to murder his son and his wife. On the other hand, Don Carlos's death was convenient for Philip in that it saved him the trouble and embarrassment of disinheriting his only son. The fullest explanation in Philip's own words comes from a letter written to the Pope in May 1568:

[I]t was not the passion or the fault of the prince, nor any intention on my part to chastise or correct him, for if this had been my motive I would have taken other measures, without going to this extreme. . . . But since, for my sins, it has been God's will that the prince should have such great and numerous defects, partly mental, partly due to his physical condition, utterly lacking as he is in the qualifications necessary for ruling, I saw the grave risks that would arise were he to be given the succession and the obvious dangers that would accrue; and therefore, after long and careful consideration, and having tried every alternative in vain, it was clear that there was little or no prospect of his condition's improving in time to prevent the evils which could reasonably be foreseen. In short, my decision was necessary.

There can be little doubt that Philip was shaken by the death of his only son. According to one of his principal secretaries, he wept for three days. He ordered nine days of national mourning for his son, and his court to wear mourning clothes for a year. No doubt he was terribly conflicted. Don Carlos was his son, but one who had proved completely unfit for the job to which he had been born. Philip had done the best for him that he knew how, based on his own relationship his own revered father. Nothing had worked. In the end, he felt that he had no choice but to do what he had done. The interests of millions of his subjects in stable government had to come before the interests of one man and one family.

Don Carlos was followed to the grave several months later by the queen, Elizabeth de Valois who died in October 1568 of complications following a premature stillbirth. These deaths ushered in the bleakest period in Philip's life, combined as they were with the problems in the Netherlands and the Muslim revolt in Granada. He would write in despair to one of his chief advisors:

> . . . certainly I am no good for the world of today; I know very well that I should be in some other station in life, one not as exalted as the one God has given me, which for me alone is terrible. And many criticize me for this. Please God that in heaven we shall be treated better. . . . Do not be sad at what I have written, for as I cannot unburden myself with anyone but you, I cannot refrain from doing so.

* * *

In the English-speaking world there is a persistent view of Philip II as a zealously intolerant tyrant. In the nineteenth century, the American historian of the revolt of the Netherlands John Lothrop Motley would write of him: "if there are vices . . . from which he was exempt, it is because it is not permitted to human nature to attain perfection even in evil." Certainly the fate of Don Carlos played a significant role in the construction of what is known as the "Black Legend": that Spain under Philip II and his successors was the epitome of political tyranny, religious fanaticism, barbarous cruelty, and the enemy of liberty and truth in any form. Certainly Philip's enemies seized on the fate of Don Carlos to vilify him. In 1581, William of Orange, then in full revolt against Philip published a famous *Apology*, a particularly effective piece of propaganda justifying his rebellion. In it Philip was accused of murdering Don Carlos and Elizabeth for their supposed affair, of incest in marrying his niece Anne of Austria, and of complicity in the death of his cousin and father-in-law Holy Roman Emperor Maximilian in 1576.

This version of events has lived on in art and literature. Rumors of an affair between Don Carlos and the queen combined with the prince's desire to flee to the Netherlands to produce a picture in which Don Carlos emerges ludicrously as a wronged lover and champion of liberty and tolerance murdered by a tyrannical and jealous father. *Don Carlos, Prince of Spain* (1676) by the English playwright Thomas Otway and a play of the same name by Friedrich Schiller (1787) were both based on a French novel of 1671 by César Vichard de Saint-Real, and all emphasize the love between Carlos and Elizabeth de Valois. Schiller's play provided the story for at least five operas, most notably by Giuseppe Verdi in 1867.

In hindsight, it is very difficult to see what Philip could have done differently in his relations with his son. It is easy to fault him for his coldness, "tough love" perhaps, but harder to find plausible alternatives given that the troubles between them involved not only the happiness of one family but the fate of a worldwide empire and its millions of subjects. To return to the theme of the family business, for a time Philip allowed the ethos of the family to predominate over that of the business. He attempted to educate his son in the same way he had been, to cultivate the same sort of relationship he had had with his own illustrious father. Don Carlos's conduct, however, eventually made it apparent to Philip that his son would never be capable of governing. Accordingly, in the arrest and imprisonment of Don Carlos, Philip allowed the ethos of the business to triumph over that of the family, or as he himself said at the time, to treat his son "not as father, but as a king."

Chapter 4: "Unworthy of the name of son": Peter the Great and Tsarevich Alexei

In the case of Philip II and Don Carlos, we saw a father and ruler who had successfully taken the reins of a thriving concern from his own father, but who had very grave — and justified — doubts about the capability and competence of his heir. The case of Tsar Peter I, or Peter the Great, of Russia (1671–1725) and his eldest son, tsarevich Alexei (1692–1718) bears some similarities.[47] In both cases, the father feared for the future if his eldest son succeeded him on the throne. In both cases, there was a long history of contention between father and son, and in both cases, the father had his son imprisoned where he died under mysterious circumstances. There are, however, a number of important differences, both in the nature of the individuals involved, and in their historical and political contexts.

Historians of Russia have long debated the basic nature of the country. Is it essentially a European or Asian country? Or something else? This is one of those questions that has no real answer, but the debate itself is instructive. Until the seventeenth century, Russia was on the fringes of European civilization. In Western and Central Europe, it was considered a far-off and exotic land, of which few had direct, first-hand knowledge, in much the same category as Persia or Siam. Communication with and transportation to Russia were both difficult. To the south, it was bordered by the Muslim Ottoman Empire which controlled not only modern Turkey, but most of the middle east and the Balkans, as well as the Black Sea. To the west was

---

[47] In Russia the heir to the throne was known as the tsarevich. The tsar's wife was the tsaritsa, and the royal princesses (the tsar's sisters, nieces, and aunts) were tsarevnas.

the sprawling commonwealth of Poland-Lithuania, a traditional rival and enemy. The newly powerful kingdom of Sweden controlled not only Finland, but most of the Baltic coast. Russia's only seaport was Archangel, on the far northern White Sea, which was cut off by ice for much of the year.

Culturally, Russia was also isolated from Europe to the west. It had not been affected by the great cultural, artistic, and intellectual movements which were changing the face of Europe in the sixteenth and seventeenth centuries, such as the Renaissance and Reformation and the development of modern science. Religiously too, Russia was a world apart. Earlier in the middle ages, Russian rulers had been converted to Christianity by missionaries from the Byzantine Empire; Russia therefore was Eastern Orthodox in religion, rather than Roman Catholic. With the fall of Constantinople to the Muslim Ottoman Turks in 1453, Russians came to see themselves as the true heirs of Orthodoxy with a divine mission to preserve its purity from corruption both from Muslim infidels and Catholic (and later Protestant) heretics.

For most of the middle ages, the term "Russia" was a cultural or geographical concept, rather than political, for there was no single Russian state. Rather, there were a number of smaller competing states and rulers. Earlier in the middle ages, the most powerful of these states was that of Kievan Rus, based in the city of Kiev, and ruled by a series of powerful Grand Princes. This flourishing state was, however, devastated by the Mongol invasions of the thirteenth century. These invasions had a catastrophic effect on Russian civilization as a whole, as the Mongol Khans and their successors exerted their dominance through the imposition of tribute and repeated raids and invasions.

In the course of the fifteenth and sixteenth centuries, however, one of these competing states rose to a position of dominance in Russia. This was the state ruled by the Grand Duke of Moscow, or Muscovy as it is often called. The rise of Muscovy was facilitated by several factors. First, it was located north of the grassland or steppe, which was dominated by Mongol cavalry. It also stood at the center of a network of rivers which aided in trade and communication. It was also fortunate in the longevity, stability, and competence of its rulers. In the course of two centuries, from 1389 until 1584, it had only five rulers. The Grand Dukes of Moscow were also extremely shrewd in their relations with the Mongol (or Tatar) khans who ruled the territories which succeeded the Mongol empire of Genghis Khan. They curried favorable relations and acted as collectors of the tribute paid by other Russian rulers. This put them in position of power relative to other rulers. Then, in the fifteenth century, Grand Duke Ivan III asserted his independence from the khans.

There was also a religious element to Muscovy's rise to dominance in Russia, which is extremely important in our understanding of subsequent Russian history. Earlier in the middle ages Russia had been converted by missionaries from the Greek-speaking Byzantine Empire to the eastern orthodox form of Christianity. This imparted to Russians a feeling of religious superiority and exceptionalism when compared to Roman Catholic form of Christianity which dominated the rest of Europe to the west. From a relatively early date the metropolitan or chief official of the Orthodox Church in Russia was based primarily in Moscow, and the Grand Duke of Moscow established a reputation as the leading patron and protector of the Russian Orthodox Church. When the Byzantine capital of Constantinople fell to the Ottoman Turks in 1453 putting an end to the thousand-year-old Byzantine Empire, the Russian Orthodox Church became essentially independent, and in 1589 the metropolitan of Moscow was raised to the rank of patriarch. This sense of a special religious destiny was expressed in the Russian saying: "two Romes have fallen [Rome itself and Constantinople], a third stands [Moscow], and a fourth there shall not be." There was a deeply ingrained sense that Russia, and especially Moscow, possessed a divine destiny to preserve and restore true Christianity.

By the early sixteenth century, the point of no return had been passed in Muscovy's rise to dominance in Russia. This was achieved largely during the reigns of Ivan III, the Great (1462–1505) and his son Vasily (or Basil) III (1505–33). By the time of Vasily's death in 1533, the territories of Muscovy were three times larger than at the time of Ivan III's succession in 1462. Ivan III was first Muscovite ruler to use the title Tsar, derived from the Latin *caesar*, or emperor, indicating that he was not merely one Russian ruler among many, but the rightful and supreme ruler of all the lands inhabited by Russian-speaking Orthodox Christians.[48] Ivan III also ceased the practice of paying tribute to the Mongol khans, establishing Muscovite independence, although Russian rulers would contend with invasions from the east for some time yet.

The accomplishments of the Muscovite rulers came perilously close to catastrophe during the reign of Ivan IV, the Terrible, from 1533 to 1584. He came to throne as an infant, and during his childhood, the government was dominated by cliques of *boyars*, or great nobles. For his whole life, Ivan cultivated a bitter hatred for the *boyars*. Although there were some positive accomplishments early in his adult reign, by the 1560s Ivan's hatred of the *boyars* had clearly gained the upper hand, compounded by his foul temper

---

[48] Although Ivan III used the title, his grandson Ivan IV (the Terrible, r. 1533–84) was the first to be vested with the title at his coronation.

and cruelty, in large part due to chronic pain and the alcohol and drugs with which he self-medicated. During the 1560s Ivan effected a disastrous revolution in the Russian state. Approximately half of the territory was to be assigned to the tsar's personal estate, or *oprichnina*, and in essence became his personal property. The other half, the *zemshchina*, was to be governed by a *boyar* council or *Duma*, with only the greatest matters of state to be referred to the tsar. Ivan's motives are not entirely clear, but it is certain that whatever other reasons there may have been, the *oprichnina* was intended to destroy *boyar* power at its roots. For within the *oprichnina*, *boyar* lands were held under conditional tenure at the pleasure of the tsar. Opposition to the *oprichnina* was widespread and it was brutally suppressed, with Ivan giving free rein to his hatred and paranoia. Metropolitan Filipp of the Orthodox church was deposed and strangled on Ivan's orders. The large and prosperous city of Novgorod was sacked on unfounded suspicions of plotting with the King of Poland.

Ivan's reign was disastrous, bringing political instability and economic chaos. The division between the *oprichnina* and the *zemshchina* made rational government impossible.

In his family life as well, Ivan's reign brought disaster to Russia. In 1581, in a fit of rage he beat to death Dmitri, his eldest son and heir. When Ivan finally died in 1584, he was succeeded by a younger son Fedor, who was a pious imbecile. When Fedor died without heirs in 1598, the direct line of the royal family came to an end, since another younger son of Ivan the Terrible, also named Dmitri, had died in an accident in 1591. For a time, the brother-in-law of Tsar Fedor, Boris Godunov, attempted to rule Russia, but when he died in 1605 there was an extended period of instability in Russia, known as the Time of Troubles. Various pretenders claimed the throne and fought against each other. The King of Poland invaded, attempting to have his son made tsar, and the Polish army occupied Moscow for a period of several years.

In 1613 a young Russian nobleman, Michael Romanov was elected tsar by an assembly of *boyars*. Indeed, the Romanov dynasty would rule Russia down to the Russian Revolution of 1917. The real ruler of Russia, however, was Michael's father Filaret, the patriarch of the Orthodox Church, at least until his death in 1633. When Michael died in 1645, he was succeeded by his son Alexei (r. 1645–76). Given the disasters of the reign of Ivan the Terrible and the Time of Troubles, Russia underwent a remarkable recovery under Michael and Alexei. Politically, Russia continued to develop along the lines laid down under the Grand Dukes   of Moscow. The Tsar ruled as an autocrat, but he was dependent on the nobility to implement his authority throughout Russia's vast territory. In return, the Tsar allowed nobles virtually complete power over their own estates and their peasant inhabitants. Indeed, it was in the mid-seventeenth century that serfdom was legally entrenched as the foundation of the Russian economy and society.[49]

Over the course of the sixteenth and seventeenth centuries, ties between Russia and Europe were expanding and strengthening. Periodic Russian embassies to European capitals in search of alliances against the three major Russian foes of Poland, Sweden, and the Ottoman Empire brought increased European awareness of Russia, and vice versa. Many Russians were quick to observe the superiority of European military tactics and technology, with the result that there were hundreds of foreigners serving as officers in the Tsar's army. Most of the still meagre trade between Russia and Western Europe still passed through Poland and Sweden which dominated the Baltic Sea and its coastlines, but by the middle of the sixteenth century English sailors and merchants had established trade through Archangel on the far northern White Sea.

In religion too, foreign influence was increasing in Russia. The annexation of Ukraine in the mid-seventeenth century brought Catholic and Jesuit influence in the form of the Kiev Academy, which influenced a generation of Russian clergy.[50] At the same time, partly in response to these foreign influences, Patriarch Nikon of the Russian Orthodox Church attempted to implement a reform of church practices and liturgy. Based on religious scholarship which had become known in Russia since the fall of Constantinople, he and his supporters had come to believe that many church practices in Russia had over time been corrupted and misunderstood. He sought to restore them to the original forms of the Orthodox Church as expressed in original documents and scholarship. Many of these issues seem trivial to us, for example the proper spelling of the name of Jesus or whether to cross oneself with three fingers (Nikon's position) or with two (the traditional practice). In the minds of many Russians however, these practices were not "mere ritual," but rather the essence of the Orthodox faith itself. God's favor to His true church rested on the correct performance of liturgical ritual, and any deviation threatened the special relationship between the Russian people and the Almighty.

---

[49] A serf was not a slave, at least not in the sense that his person was owned by a master. A serf was a peasant farmer whose personal freedom was restricted in certain important ways. For example, a serf was bound to the land of his master; he could not leave. He was also obligated to perform labor services for his master.

[50] Ukraine was much more exposed to European influence by virtue of its border with Poland and indeed by long periods of Polish rule. In religious terms, the chief expression of European influence was the Ukrainian Greek Catholic Church, or Uniate Church as it is sometimes called. Founded in the late sixteenth century, it followed Eastern Orthodox rites and liturgy but was under the jurisdiction of the Pope.

Nikon's reforms caused a schism within the Russian Orthodox Church, as many rejected his reforms as "Greek innovations" and a sign of the Antichrist. "Old Believers" fled to the margins of Russia, effectively beyond the government's reach, where they could continue to practice their traditional faith. Nikon also fell afoul of Tsar Alexei, although not for his religious reforms, which the Tsar supported. Rather, Alexei and the *boyars* came to fear and resent Nikon's political ambitions and efforts to subjugate the state to the church. Thus, even as the government promoted his religious reforms, Nikon was deposed as Patriarch in 1666.

By the middle of the seventeenth century, then, Russia was slowly but surely reorienting itself to the west. European influence was growing and European culture was making inroads among the elite, but this was a gradual and incremental process. The increasing presence of foreigners and foreign influence in Russia posed difficult problems for a culture characterized by its sense of religious difference and purity and its fear of external corrupting influences. We can see these tensions at work in the reign of Tsar Alexei, Peter the Great's father. Some later Russian historians saw in Alexei the antithesis of his son Peter, whom they detested for his Westernizing reforms. They saw in Alexei a pious and gentle soul, devoted to Russian tradition and the customary role of the Tsar. This picture is completely misleading, for Alexei was very much a modernizer. He continued the military reforms begun by his own father, Tsar Michael, as well as the practice of recruiting foreign officers and experts. At the same time, however, he established a special district in Moscow to house foreigners, known as the "German Quarter." (To Russians, all foreigners were "Germans," regardless of their actual origins.) Although this has sometimes been seen as an indicator of increasing openness to the west, in fact it was precisely the opposite: a means of protecting Russia from foreign corruption by quarantining the foreigners in their own settlement. By all accounts, the German Quarter was a little piece of Western Europe in the heart of Muscovy. At the same time, it was at Tsar Alexei's urging that foreigners presented Russia's first theatrical performance in 1672, with the director and actors supplied by the foreigners living in the German Quarter.

Tsar Alexei's chief advisor for much of his reign was Artamon Matveev, who was one of the leading advocates of Westernization. It was Matveev who encouraged the performance of plays for the Tsar and the court. Married to a Scottish woman, his household broke from many Muscovite traditions. His son Andrei (later an important diplomat for Peter the Great) was given a thoroughly Western education. There were also close ties between Matveev and the Naryshkin family of Tsar Alexi's second wife Natalia, Peter the Great's mother.

Alexei's first wife had been Maria Miloslavsky, of a noble family but not of the highest rank. Among their surviving children were two sons, Fedor and Ivan, and six daughters. Fedor, the heir to the throne was intelligent but sickly, while Ivan was handicapped both mentally and physically (he was nearly blind). Among the daughters, only Sophia would play an active role in government. Traditionally the royal princesses or *tsarevnas* lived a secluded though privileged existence. They were typically not married, for marriage to a royal princess might strengthen one boyar clan over another. Only Sophia would break the mould, as we shall see.

Maria Miloslavsky died in 1669 in giving birth to her thirteenth child, but with only two surviving sons in doubtful health, the Tsar's remarriage was inevitable.[51] In 1671 he married Natalia Naryshkin, the daughter of a minor noble. Although there were close ties between the Naryshkin family and Artamon Matveev, the Tsar's principal advisor, there are some fairly durable myths surrounding her background. One of these myths has Natalia living in the household of Matveev as his ward, where she was exposed to his Westernizing ways. It was allegedly in Matveev's home where the widower Tsar was struck instantly by the young Natalia. Matveev then supposedly arranged for Natalia's presence in the *smotriny*, a traditional ceremony in which the Tsar viewed prospective brides. The fix was in, however, as the Tsar had made up his mind to marry Natalia and the other women were simply window dressing. In the words of one modern historian, however, these stories are "romantic nonsense."[52]

Another misconception is that prior to Tsar Alexei's death in 1676, the families of two wives formed opposing factions within the royal court, one devoted to preserving the ways of old Muscovy (Miloslavsky) and the other pressing for greater ties with Europe (Naryshkin). In fact, the factional rivalry would emerge only after Alexei's death, and it had no basis in attitudes towards Westernization. It was a power struggle between two noble clans and their supporters.

The marriage of Alexei and Natalia quickly bore fruit. Their first child was a large and healthy boy born on May 30, 1672.[53] Named Peter, his birth was cause for celebration as were all male royal births. In this case, however,

---

[51] Tsar Alexei's first-born son Dmitri died in infancy in 1651, while his second son, Tsarevich Alexei died at the age of fifteen in 1670, which no doubt underlined the importance of the Tsar's remarriage.

[52] Paul Bushkovitch, *Peter the Great: the Struggle for Power, 1671–1725* (Cambridge: Cambridge University Press, 2001), 58. All of the evidence for this version of events is based on recollections of parties who had political motives for propounding it.

[53] Dates given are (except where noted) according to the Old Style (OS) of the Julian calendar which was in use in Russia until the twentieth century. Most of the rest of Europe (England excepted) adopted the more accurate Gregorian calendar (or New

given the poor health of his two elder half-brothers, Peter's birth and his robust health were all the more welcome as dynastic insurance. Before his death at the age of forty-seven in 1676, Alexei would father two more children with Natalia, both girls: Natalia (1673–1716) and Fedora (1674–78).

When Alexei died in 1676, he was succeeded on the throne by his eldest surviving son, who became Tsar Fedor III at the age of fifteen. With a young and physically weak Tsar on the throne, his mother's relatives, the Miloslavsky family, took control of the government. Artamon Matveev was deprived of his powerful positions an exiled to a minor post in the far north. Fedor's brief reign was filled with factional fighting among the courtiers and *boyars*, most especially between the families of Tsar Alexei's two wives. Never healthy, Fedor died in 1682 at the age of twenty-one.

Peter, now ten years old, had been relegated to the margins of the royal family with the death of his father. Fedor was married, but in 1681 both his wife and infant son died. He remarried, and though he would have no more children before his death, no one could have known it at the time. Then there was Ivan; although physically and mentally disabled, he was capable of fathering children. Any of Ivan's sons would be obstacles to Peter's eventual accession. In fact, Ivan did marry, but any potential threat to Peter's succession was averted by the fact all of his five children were daughters. The odds of young Peter eventually assuming the throne were therefore long indeed. On the other hand, his health, vitality, and native intelligence posed a very dramatic contrast to his two elder half-brothers. Moreover, in Russia the practice of the eldest son succeeding his father on the throne was not as ironclad as elsewhere in Europe. It was certainly the norm, but precedents existed in Muscovite history for conferring the throne on someone other than the eldest son. Ironically, later in his life Peter would be confronted with this dilemma when he became persuaded of his son Alexei's incapacity to rule.

For the first decade of his life, Peter lived a life of what might best be called benign neglect. His formal education was quite rudimentary, limited to basic literacy and numeracy, and to religious instruction. Indeed, even as an adult Peter's handwriting and spelling were atrocious. His older half-brothers Fedor and Alexei (d. 1670) on the other hand, received a more advanced "Western" education, with instruction in Latin, Polish, and poetry. As an adult, Peter felt keenly that his education had been sorely lacking. His daughter Elizabeth recalled how he would visit she and her sisters at their

---

Style — NS) in the course of the sixteenth and seventeenth centuries. During Peter's life, there was a discrepancy of eleven days between the two.

lessons and remark how lucky they were: "I was deprived of all that in my youth."

With Fedor's accession to the throne and the ascension of his Miloslavsky relatives to power, Peter and his mother Natalia were relegated to a decidedly subordinate position in the royal family. Indeed, for a time, Natalia feared for her own life and that of her son, but Fedor never showed any animosity towards them. Indeed, as mentioned above, few people could have suspected that Peter would one day ascend to the throne.

When Fedor died with no surviving children, Muscovites were faced with a difficult dilemma. Ordinarily, Ivan would take the throne as the next eldest son of Alexei. But Ivan was neither physically nor mentally capable of ruling the country. Peter, on the other hand, although he was only ten years old, seemed more promising royal timber. He was healthy and vital, obviously intelligent and curious about the world and people around him. And, as mentioned above, there was in Muscovy some precedent for choosing as tsar someone other than the eldest surviving son of the previous Tsar. Also working in Peter's favor was that he had a living mother who could act as regent until he attained the age of majority.

Upon Fedor's death, Orthodox Patriarch Joachim seized the initiative and convened an assembly called a *zemsky sobor*, or assembly of the land, to recognize Peter as tsar rather than Ivan. Artamon Matveev was recalled from exile and the Peter's Naryshkin relatives assumed powerful positions. Peter's supporters, however, reckoned without two crucial factors. One was the ambition of Ivan's Miloslavsky relatives, particularly his older sister Sophia. The other was the dissatisfaction of the *streltsy*.

Sophia was one of Ivan's five surviving sisters, and the only one to play an overt political role. Muscovite princesses typically led a secluded life where contact with male non-relatives was strictly limited, and although in certain instances they could exercise significant political influence, it was usually from behind the scenes. Sophia, on the other hand, whom one contemporary described as "ambitious and power hungry" was certainly exceptional in her boldness and political intelligence. Her chief aim was to secure her brother Ivan on the throne and by extension to preserve her political power and that of her mother's family, the Miloslavskys. By this time, Sophia had formed a close relationship with one of Tsar Fedor's closest advisors, Prince Vasily Golitsyn. Eventually the two were to become lovers, but it is not clear that they were at this point.

By itself, Sophia' ambition would have achieved little, but it combined in a powerful way with the unrest among the *streltsy*. The *streltsy* were a body of musketeers established in the sixteenth century, and had become the backbone of the garrison guarding Moscow. In order to support themselves and their military function, they were granted a number of privileges, such as tax exemption. Over time they had become a hereditary class of merchants and craftsmen, with their military duties seen largely as a sideline. By the later seventeenth century military developments had rendered them largely obsolete on the battlefield, but they still prided themselves on their guardianship of Moscow and especially on their devotion to the ways of old Russia — Old Belief was strong among their ranks.

At this moment in 1682, the *streltsy* were in a particularly foul mood over disputes regarding their pay and rumors of corruption and injustice in high places. There were rumors that Ivan had been murdered and that these conspirators would attack the *streltsy* next. In particular, *streltsy* anger was focused on Ivan Naryshkin, the brother of Tsaritsa Natalia, who was accused of trying on the crown. Sophia's role in fomenting this unrest, if any, is unclear, but she was certainly able to capitalize on it.

On May 15, 1682, the *streltsy* marched on the Kremlin and demonstrated their anger, some shouting that Ivan should be tsar rather than Peter. Natalia displayed Ivan and Peter on a balcony to demonstrate that nothing had happened to either boy. Alongside them was Artamon Matveev, now restored to power. Matveev was hurled off the balcony and torn to pieces by the angry *streltsy* below. Likewise Ivan Naryshkin was murdered along with about forty others, including some of the most prominent *boyars* in Russia. This episode left an indelible mark on ten-year-old Peter, demonstrating to him lengths to which "old Russia" was willing to go to resist change and the necessity of force to counteract it. Decades later, when faced with another *streltsy* revolt, Peter would crush it with brutal violence.

On May 23, Ivan and Peter were declared joint tsars, with Ivan as senior tsar and Peter as junior, although this distinction could not have meant much given their respective conditions and characters. Sophia took the reins of actual power as regent in the names of her two younger brothers. For the next seven years, Sophia governed Russia, closely assisted by Vasily Golitsyn.

Although Sophia was a Miloslavsky princess, other members of the family played little part in the government, much to their dissatisfaction. At the same time, Sophia attempted to balance factions by giving important positions to members of the Naryshkin family and Peter's supporters among the nobility. Natalia, however, believed that her family and most especially her son were being marginalized, and Peter grew up believing that the Miloslavskys were his implacable opponents. Sophia's inescapable problem was, however, that Peter was growing up and that unless she took decisive action her authority had an inevitable if still undetermined expiry date.

Beyond the factional infighting, however, Sophia's government broke no new ground when it came to policy. The cautious and incremental Westernizing reform of Russia which had been underway for at least a century was continued. Indeed, Vasily Golitsyn had been largely responsible for one of the major reforms of Fedor's reign, the elimination of the code of precedence in the government and army.[54] Golitsyn was highly Westernized for a Russian noble of his time, speaking both Latin and Polish. Under Sophia, Catholic priests were allowed into Russia to minister to foreigners in the German Quarter. Her government also offered refuge to French Protestants fleeing the persecutions of Louis XIV, and established Russia's first institution of higher education, the Slavonic-Greek-Latin Academy.

During Sophia's regency, Peter and his mother were largely absent from Moscow and the Kremlin, spending long periods of time in the nearby village of Preobrazhenskoe. This suited both Peter and his half-sister. Peter escaped the formal rituals and ceremonies which tsars customarily participated in, and Sophia was happy to have these performed by Ivan and increasingly herself.

During the years of Sophia's regency, Peter's formal education was discontinued and he was able to indulge his interests and proclivities. Disdaining palaces, he lived in a humble wooden house. He indulged his endless curiosity about how things worked, learning all he could about various trades and crafts becoming, among other things, an accomplished carpenter. Above all, he was fascinated by weapons and warfare. He organized his playmates, nobles and commoners alike, into play regiments, supplying them with uniforms and wooden weapons. Eventually two regiments evolved, named for the villages of Preobrazhenskoe and Semenovskoe.[55] Nor did Peter insist on command, as one might expect. He served as a non-commissioned officer, and labored alongside his friends at building fortifications and digging ditches. By the later 1680s when Peter was in his mid to late teens, the two regiments had developed from a bunch of boys playing soldier into real, if somewhat unofficial, military units, trained according to the most current practices from Western European standards.

During these years Peter also became acquainted with a number of the foreigners living in Russia, although his contact with the German Quarter was still quite restricted. Foreign military officers directed Peter and his playmates in their military endeavors. Peter also made the acquaintance of

---

[54] Previously nobles had refused to serve under the command of nobles of lesser rank. This frequently made it impossible to appoint men of ability to important positions because nobles of higher rank would refuse to serve under them.

[55] The Preobrazhensky and Semenovsky regiments would remain the elite units of the Russian Imperial Guard right down to the Russian Revolution of 1917.

two Dutchmen, Frans Timmermann and Karsten Brandt. Timmermann was a Dutch merchant who taught Peter navigation and by extension arithmetic, geometry, and the science of fortification. Brandt was a carpenter and shipbuilder who had lived in Russia since 1660 and supported himself as a carpenter in the German Quarter. It is arguable that Russian history changed forever in June 1688 when Peter and Timmermann, on one of their habitual forays into the countryside, came up on a disused and decrepit sailboat. Peter was instantly captivated and Timmermann and Brandt helped him refurbish it and taught him to sail. From then on, Peter remained fascinated by sailing and the sea. He went sailing whenever he could on nearby Lake Pleschev (Pleshcheyevo), much to the dismay of his mother and other traditionally minded Russians who feared the sea and sailing. One of Peter's great accomplishments as tsar was the founding of the Russian navy. Much later, Peter's original little sailboat would be given a place of honor in the Maritime Museum in St. Petersburg as the "grandfather of the Russian navy."

Peter passed an important threshold in January 1689, when he married, at the age of seventeen. His bride was twenty-year-old Evdokia Lopukhina, daughter of a noble family of middle rank. Contemporary descriptions of her looks and intelligence vary, so we are probably justified in assuming that she was average on both counts. Certainly she had been conventionally brought up to become a proper Russian wife, that is, submissive and retiring. As one contemporary observed, she was "no match for her husband in character." All the evidence suggests that Peter complied with his mother's wishes to marry and with her choice of bride without demur. Involved as he was with sailing, his "play regiments," and indulging his wide-ranging curiosity, his marriage seems to have been a very minor concern. He and his wife led completely separate lives. She would write him formulaic letters inquiring about his health, but no letters from Peter to Evdokia have survived, if indeed any were ever written. Even so, Peter and his bride did fulfill the main function of a dynastic marriage, for on February 18, 1690, the tsaritsa gave birth to a boy, who was named Alexei after his grandfather. The following year she would bear another son, named Alexander, who would die before his first birthday. Peter was otherwise engaged, and he was so indifferent to his wife by this time that he did not attend the funeral.[56]

Peter's marriage and impending fatherhood were further signs that he was coming into maturity, which served to reinforce the inherent limitations on Sophia's power. Sophia and Golitsyn were also damaged by two failed military campaigns in the Crimean peninsula against the Tatars. Sophia acted

---

[56] Some sources refer to a third son, Paul, who was said to have died in 1693, but the official palace records do not mention him.

as if they were great victories and gave Golitsyn a hero's welcome, but the truth became widely known. Peter and his supporters were increasingly and openly critical of Golitsyn's and Sophia's government, as well as expressing discontent over Sophia's increasing appropriation of the powers and symbols which belonged rightly to her brothers, the tsars Peter and Ivan. Moreover, as Peter matured, more and more important figures came to understand that the future belonged to Peter, and that if they wanted to advance their positions, they had better establish good relations with the young tsar.

On the night of August 7, 1689 Peter was awakened with news that the *streltsy* were marching on Preobrazhenskoe in order to kill him. The *streltsy* were indeed gathering, but to accompany Sophia on a procession to a nearby monastery. It is certainly possible that Peter's supporters created such rumors in order to force a confrontation, but it is impossible to know for sure. In any case, Peter (who was, after all, still only seventeen) fled in panic to the strongly fortified Trinity Monastery along with his "play" regiments (now growing into manhood as was Peter himself). Over the next month, a standoff ensued, with the balance increasingly favorable to Peter. Eventually, Patriarch Joachim declared his support, as did a majority of the *streltsy* and the foreign officers, leaving Sophia without armed support of any kind. The government was purged of Sophia's supporters, Golitsyn was exiled to the far north, and Sophia was imprisoned in a convent, though not at this time forced to take a nun's vows.

As a result of these events, Peter was now the unquestioned ruler of Russia, although not yet eighteen years old. He was always very solicitous of and protective towards his elder half-brother Ivan, until his death in 1696 Peter's co-tsar, and officially at least, the senior tsar. Ivan continued to reside in the Kremlin, taking part in the traditional rituals of the tsar and the court, freeing Peter from these detested tasks. For the next several years, however, Peter was content to leave the actual conduct of the government in the hands of his mother Natalia and her advisors, drawn mostly from her own Naryshkin family and its supporters. Peter occupied his time as he had before, with sailing, military affairs, and practical craftsmanship. Now that he was an adult and had overthrown Sophia, he was able to freely indulge his appetite for both alcohol and for increased contact with foreigners.

The young Peter left an indelible impression on all who met him. At the age of eleven, the secretary of the Swedish ambassador mistook him for sixteen, and praised "his frank and open face ... and his great beauty." In 1683 a German physician described the young tsar:

> He is a remarkably good looking boy, in whom nature has shown her power; and has so many advantages of nature that being the son of a

king is the least of his good qualities. He has a beauty which gains the heart of all who see him and a mind which, even in his early years, did not find its like.

When Peter was fully grown his height reached 200 cm (6'7"), impressive even today, and all the more so when average heights were less than now. Everyone who described him made note of his prodigious energy and enthusiasm and his inability to be still for any length of time. Perhaps the best word to describe his personality is mercurial. He had a fearsome temper, and when agitated suffered from facial tics and on occasion full-blown convulsions, involving loss of consciousness. Although the younger and junior co-tsar, he certainly made a more favorable impression than Ivan. The Swedish ambassador's secretary went out of his way to contrast the two: Ivan "sat motionless with downcast eyes . . . gave his hand to be kissed at the wrong time," and greeted the ambassadors with a kind of "babbling noise."

As mentioned, after Sophia was overthrown, Peter was content to leave government in the hands of his mother and her advisors, freeing him to indulge his appetites and curiosity. Much to the dismay of his mother and the more conservative courtiers, he began to spend a great deal of time in the German Quarter, and made some very close friends among the foreigners there. There was Patrick Gordon, the veteran Scottish soldier who became a kind of mentor to the young tsar. There was also Franz Lefort (1655–99), a Swiss adventurer and playboy, renowned for his capacity to party and his way with women. Among the Russians who accompanied Peter was Alexander Menshikov (1673–1729), who would become Peter's best friend, confidant, and drinking buddy. Life for Peter and the "Jolly Company" in the German Quarter was one long party, with stupendous bouts of drinking, smoking, and chasing women. Peter began a twelve-year-long affair with Anna Mons, the daughter of a German tavern keeper.

Peter's antics caused a great deal of consternation among conservatively-minded Russians such as his mother and the new Patriarch Adrian. (Joachim had died in 1690 and was replaced–against Peter's wishes–by the more conservative and insular Adrian.) As if to deliberately scandalize his critics, Peter created mocking parodies of court and church life. He and his friends constituted an "All-Jesting, All-Drunken Synod" presided over by a mock "Prince-Pope" and a mock "Prince-Caesar." They conducted drunken parodies of church and state rituals according to rules drawn up by Peter himself, although the young tsar occupied a subordinate rank, just as he had when forming his own regiments.

With the death of his mother Natalia in early 1694, Peter began to actually rule, as well as to reign. Over the next two decades, he would dramatically transform his country. Russia had been growing closer to Western Europe for some time, as we have seen, but Peter transformed this incremental and evolutionary change into a revolution. He modernized the army, according to the latest European standards, and single-handedly founded the Russian navy. He fought successful wars against the Ottoman Turks (1695-96), Sweden (the Great Northern War, 1700-21), and Persia. In 1697 he led a group of 250 on a grand embassy to the west. Attempting to travel incognito as "Peter Mikhailov," he spent a period of months learning shipbuilding in the shipyards of the Dutch East India Company in Amsterdam, laboring alongside his best friend Menshikov. In Amsterdam, and later in England, he toured incessantly, visiting museums, churches, observatories, and even attended human dissections for anatomy students.[57] Above all, his time in the west convinced Peter (not that he needed any further convincing) that Russia was hopelessly backwards and primitive. On his return to Russia, he brought with him some 750 foreign experts and craftsmen, whom he had recruited, from mining engineers to shipbuilders, and architects to soldiers.

In the summer of 1698, while still abroad, Peter received word of an abortive revolt among the *streltsy*. They were upset by Peter's unconventional lifestyle and the foreign novelties he had introduced. In addition, Peter had not forgotten their earlier revolt and he seized any chance to humiliate them as the representatives of Old Muscovy. The mutiny was repressed without much trouble, but Peter was still dissatisfied. He saw in the revolt — rightly —widespread opposition to his policies, and — wrongly — scheming by the Miloslavskys and Sophia. He rushed back to Moscow where he ordered and supervised brutal torture, interrogation, and execution of the offending *streltsy*. Their regiments were abolished and they were scattered throughout Russia in exile. Sophia was exiled to a more remote convent and forced to take vows as the nun Suzanna.

Upon his return to Russia and the suppression of the *streltsy*, Peter begin the work of Westernization in earnest. Over the next twenty-five years, administration was reformed, the military modernized, mines and factories founded. For Peter, Westernization was primarily about technology and the military; he had little interest in the arts, philosophy or culture. He did his best to "encourage" Russian nobles to adopt Western ways. He founded a system of secular schools — the first in Russian history, including academies for the study of mathematics, navigation and engineering. He forced a number of nobles to send their sons to the west for their education. Even further, he passed a law which required that nobles to prove they had completed their

---

[57] Dissections were open to the public and a common form of entertainment.

education before they could marry. Opposition to this was so severe that even Peter had to relent.

This Westernization also had a side that seems trivial to us, but was very distressing to more traditionally-minded Russians. Peter returned from Western Europe determined to follow Western fashions in everything. The style for men in Europe at the time was to be clean shaven, whereas Russian men typically took enormous pride in their beards, which had great religious significance. Immediately upon his return, Peter insisted that his courtiers be clean shaven, going so far as to shave the beards of some prominent boyars himself. Eventually, Russian men were allowed to keep their beards, if they so wished, by paying an annual tax. In return they received a medallion to be worn around the neck which stated that they were legally entitled to their beards. Peter also insisted that the boyars dress in "German" style clothing, as he had done for years, rather than the traditional robes with their long flowing sleeves. Peter would carry scissors with him and cut off the sleeves of those who wore traditional dress. Peter had also been exposed to tobacco in the German Quarter, and he now insisted that his courtiers take up its use.

All these changes shocked and disturbed the more traditionally-minded among Peter's subjects. Patriarch Adrian wrote: "Latin Jesuits, Dominicans, Bernadines and others not only shave their beards, but also their mustaches and look like apes or monkeys." From another writer:

> Look often at the icon of the Second Coming of Christ, and observe the righteous standing at the right side of Christ, all with beards. At the left stand the Muselmen [Muslims] and heretics, Lutherans and Poles, and other shavers of their ilk, with just whiskers, such as cats and dogs have. Take heed whom to imitate and which side you will be on.

The most visible and enduring symbol of Peter's vision for a new Russia was the new capital city he had built, St. Petersburg. To Peter, Moscow represented the backwardness of traditional Russia. Begun in 1702 on land wrested from Sweden, St. Petersburg was to be both a grand city in Western style and Peter's "window to the west" — a port city on the Baltic with direct access to Western Europe. The land, however, was marshy and thousands of serfs labored and died in the construction of Peter's grandest monument. Peter insisted that anyone who wanted his ear and favor had to be physically present in St. Petersburg. And so, the aristocracy reluctantly and unhappily followed the tsar to the northern marshes, far removed from their estates and traditional haunts. From then until the Russian Revolution of 1917, and in some ways to the present day, the dichotomy of St. Petersburg (renamed Leningrad after the Revolution and since reverted to its original name) and

Moscow have represented the fundamental ambivalence of Russian history. Moscow was situated in a central position to govern a vast empire which straddled Eurasia. St. Petersburg, on the other hand, was situated at the far western extremity of the empire, but in a position which reflected Peter's overarching ambition to remake Russia into a European power.

Upon his return from his grand tour of Europe, Peter also determined to rid himself of his unwanted, unloved, and thoroughly traditional Russian wife. Evdokia made no secret of her disapproval of her husband's conduct, especially of his contacts with the polluting foreigners. For his part, Peter made no secret of his affair with Anna Mons, keeping her in grand style. Upon his return to Russia, he went to visit her before his wife. Even while on his voyage to the west, Peter instructed important nobles to pressure Evdokia into becoming a nun, which would have the effect of ending their marriage and sparing Peter an embarrassing mess. The whole eighteen months Peter was absent from Russia, he appears not to have written her a single letter. Evdokia steadfastly refused to accommodate Peter, citing her duty to their son Alexei, now a boy of eight. She suspected, rightly, that if she entered a convent, she would never see her son again.

Peter now took decisive action. In September 1698, Evdokia was removed from the palace and confined to the monastery of Suzdal under armed guard. Several months later, her head was shaved, the traditional rite of initiation undergone by nuns. Shortly afterwards, she renounced her vows as coerced and resumed her secular life, although still confined to the convent, even eventually taking an army officer as a lover. This would later come back to haunt Peter: if Evdokia were not a nun, then she and Peter were still married, and Peter's later marriage was bigamous and any children it produced were illegitimate and ineligible to inherit the throne.

When Alexei was born in 1690, Peter greeted the birth of an heir with great fanfare and joyous celebrations. It seems, however, that he was a very remote presence in Alexei's life. The young prince lived with his mother, and visiting Alexei also meant seeing Evdokia, with whom Peter was increasingly disenchanted. Besides, Peter's time was more than occupied with other things: partying with his friends in the German Quarter, his affair with Anna Mons, the "All-Drunken, All-Jesting Synod," learning the military sciences of navigation, artillery and fortification, and ultimately, the grand tour of Western Europe. Could it be that since Peter's own father died when he was very young, that he had no notion of a normal or healthy father-son relationship, even given the different standards prevailing among royal families? In addition, Peter's own temperament and personality no doubt played a large role. He was a dominant and domineering individual, with seemingly boundless reserves of energy and enthusiasm. He knew what he wanted to do, and heaven help anyone who stood in his way — just ask Sophia or the *streltsy*. He was not sentimental or affectionate; he was emotionally close to very few: his mother, his sisters, and his second wife Catherine topped the list. Lefort and Menshikov were his closest male friends, and even they felt his considerable wrath on occasion. With Peter, you were either for him or against him, and those whom he considered obstacles to his ambitions suffered the consequences.

We can safely assume that Alexei's earliest education was heavily influenced by his mother's conservative Muscovite inclinations. We may also assume that at some level the boy came to resent his father's treatment of his mother. According to the Imperial ambassador, Alexei scolded Peter's uncle, Lev Naryshkin, who had been pressuring Evdokia to take monastic vows:

> "It is well known that you are the reason that I and my mother suffer so much and must innocently bear so much. And yet I know that many heads are stuck up before the Tsar's Kremlin who have not sinned so much as you. . . ." During this speech the tsarevich became so angry that he fell into Naryshkin's hair and was immediately ordered out of the room . . .

With his mother shut up in the monastery at Suzdal, Alexei's care was confided to Peter's sister Natalia. As to his education, he was given a series of German tutors, and a thoroughly Western education, according to Peter's wishes. He was to be taught French, German, Latin, mathematics, history and geography. He was to read foreign newspapers and become adept in physical activities such as fencing, dancing, and riding. He made good progress in his studies. In a letter to the great philosopher Leibnitz, Alexei's tutor Heinrich von Huyssen wrote:

> The Prince lacks neither capacity nor quickness of mind. His ambition is moderated by reason, by sound judgement, and by a great desire to distinguish himself and to gain everything which is fitting for a great prince. He is of a studious and pliant nature, and wishes by assiduity to supply what has been neglected in his education. . . . he loves mathematics and foreign languages and shows a great desire to visit foreign countries.

It seems as if Peter was determined to supply his son with the formal education that he had never had. At the same time however, Peter showed no compunction in interrupting his son's studies for what he no doubt considered a practical introduction to the arts of ruling and war. In 1702, when Alexei was twelve, his father took him to Archangel as he prepared to meet a rumored Swedish attack. At thirteen, he was enlisted as bombardier in an artillery regiment. Peter's attitude towards his son was similar to his attitude towards most everything: sudden bursts of enthusiasm followed by long periods of indifference punctuated by outbursts of annoyance.

As Alexei grew older, he was given more responsibility and more important tasks. At sixteen he was sent to Smolensk to requisition supplies for the army and to gather recruits. At seventeen, he was put in charge of Moscow's defenses. It is more than evident that Peter intended his son to follow in his footsteps and was attempting to provide a suitable apprenticeship. It is also evident that he cared not one bit about Alexei's wishes and inclinations. Alexei was clearly neither stupid nor incompetent. He was simply different than his father. To return to the analogy of family business, he was ill-suited to take over the business from his father and would have been much better off making a career of his own choosing. As heir to throne, however, this was impossible. Besides, Peter seemed temperamentally incapable of perceiving the viewpoint of anyone else. Of course Alexei would do what he wanted; he was Peter's son, that was his duty. The ethos of the "business" has triumphed over the ethos of the family. Peter is the archetypal "founder" and displays the personality characteristics noted in Chapter 1. He was certainly charismatic, capable of insincerity and manipulation. He was narcissistic as well, narrowly concerned with his own agenda and goals, lacking empathy with others. His work (and his play) were all-consuming, a classic workaholic with little or no time for cultivating relationships.

In 1709, Russian forces won a crushing victory over Sweden at the Battle of Poltava. Russia and Sweden had been at war since 1700, the central issue being which power was to dominate the Baltic Sea and northern Europe. In 1700, Peter's army had been embarrassed by a humiliating defeat at the Battle of Narva. This caused Peter to accelerate his program of Westernization and modernization of the military. Although the war would drag on until 1721, the outcome was effectively decided at Poltava in 1709, which gave Peter increased freedom of action. At this point, Peter made two decisions regarding his son's future: he was to be sent to Western Europe to continue his education, and he was to take a European wife.

Alexei was therefore sent to the beautiful and cultured city of Dresden, the capital of the Elector of Saxony, Augustus the Strong. Augustus was also the elected King of Poland and an important ally of Peter's in the war against Sweden.[58] A marriage was negotiated to Princess Charlotte-Sophie-

---

[58] Besides his enormous physical strength — he was said to be able break horseshoes by hand — Augustus was a voracious womanizer. He is reputed to have fathered over three

Christine of Brunswick-Wolfenbüttel. She was related to many of the leading royal houses of Europe including the Habsburgs, as her sister was married to Archduke Charles, who would later become Holy Roman Emperor Charles VI. Politically and dynastically, this was a good match, although it goes without saying that neither Alexis nor Charlotte had any choice in the matter. The two young people met and seemed relatively happy with each other, or at least accepting of their fate. On October 14, 1711, twenty-one-year-old Alexei and seventeen-year-old Charlotte were married in the palace of the Queen of Poland at Torgau, with Peter in attendance. According to the terms negotiated, Charlotte was permitted to keep her Lutheran faith, but any children were to be raised in the Orthodox Church.

Four days after the wedding, Peter dragged his son away from his young bride, saying that his presence was required with the army in nearby Pomerania. Charlotte eventually joined Alexei in the town of Thorn, where she stayed for six months while Alexei was frequently absent on his father's business. Charlotte wrote to her mother of their miserable conditions there, and Menshikov was shocked by their poverty when he visited them, persuading Peter to send them money. In October 1712, Peter commanded Charlotte to relocate to St. Petersburg and wait for her husband, who was occupied with his military duties. Alexei, who had been with Peter on a military tour of inspection in Finland joined her there in the summer of 1713. Living together for an extended period for the first time, their relationship quickly began to sour. Alexei began to drink heavily and to treat his wife badly, ignoring her in public, and telling his friends that he had never loved her, that she was too skinny and pockmarked. He began an affair with a woman named Afrosina Fedorova, who had been a serf belonging to his tutor. This in itself was not unusual, but he installed her in the same palace as Charlotte, a deliberate slight. As a further rebellion against his father, it seems, he began to consort with people opposed to Peter's reforms. The Imperial ambassador wrote that

> the tsarevich had brought little German inclination and customs back from Germany and passed most of his time with Muscovite priests and bad common fellows, and at the same time was strongly given to drink.

The Swedish ambassador also conveyed his impressions:

> [I]n everything apart from outer clothing, he keeps to the old Russian customs and it seems the prince only outwardly follows foreign

---

hundred children by his numerous mistresses.

manners and is polite to foreigners more out of fear of his father than by his own inclinations and wishes.

A further source of tension, both within Russia as a whole and between father and son, was Peter's remarriage. His affair with Anna Mons had ended by 1702. She would eventually marry the Prussian ambassador and would live in the German Quarter until her death in 1715. At about the same time, Peter began an affair with a Lithuanian orphan named Martha Skavronska (1684–1727), later known as Catherine (Russian: Ekaterina Alexeevna), who would eventually become his wife and would succeed him after his death as Empress Catherine I. She was living in the town of Marienburg as a sort of servant and foster child in the home of a Lutheran pastor when the town was taken by Russian army in the summer of 1702. She became a servant in the household of General Sheremetev, the Russian commander who had conquered the town. When Peter's closest friend Alexander Menshikov was visiting Sheremetev, he spotted the attractive Martha and recruited her for his own household. By the fall of 1703 she was living in Menshikov's household in Moscow. It is certainly possible that they had an affair, but circumstances seem to weigh against it. Whatever the case, the two formed a close and lifelong friendship and political alliance due in part, no doubt to their rather humble origins.[59] Sometime in late 1703 or early 1704, she became Peter's mistress. They had a son named Peter in 1704, and another named Paul in 1705. Altogether she would bear Peter ten children, of whom only two survived into adulthood.[60] Peter and Catherine were married in a small private ceremony in 1707, and on February 19, 1712, in a large and public — though unusual — ceremony. Peter chose to be married as a rear-admiral rather than as a tsar, and the ceremony and banquet were held in Menshikov's palace. There were many foreigners present, who were typically barred from Muscovite weddings. There were none of the traditional trappings of the wedding of a Russian

---

[59] Menshikov's precise origins are obscure, at least partly due to his later efforts to fabricate an ancient and noble lineage for himself. One story had it that his father was a Lithuanian peasant who apprenticed his son as a pastry cook. It was while hawking his pies on the street as a boy that Lefort noticed him and from there was enlisted into Peter's play regiments. This story is lent some credence by a later episode in which Menshikov appeared with a tray of pies as a joke. More likely, however, his father was Lithuanian soldier who had been captured and later settled in Russia, converting to Orthodoxy. Certainly noble Russians looked down upon him. Said one: "By birth, Menshikov is lower than a Pole." Peter referred him as "child of my heart," "my dearest comrade," "my best friend." Although practically illiterate, Peter gave Menshikov huge responsibility, and Menshikov seized the opportunity to amass great wealth. Peter was often irritated by his excesses, and several times forced him to disgorge some of his booty, on occasion even striking him, but their friendship survived until Peter's death.

[60] These were Anna (1708–28) who became Duchess of Holstein and was the mother of Tsar Peter III (r. 1761–62) and Elizabeth, who was empress from 1741–61.

tsar. Conspicuous by his absence was Tsarevich Alexei, who may have been upset that his father's wedding eclipsed celebrations of his own birthday on February 18.

In Catherine, Peter found his closest companion and friend. She accompanied him on many of his military campaigns, and when they were separated they wrote very affectionately to each other. She shared his sense of humor and his taste for alcohol, but she was also able to serve as a calming and moderating influence when he flew into his occasional rages. Their marriage attracted much negative comment, mostly due to her low birth and because she was a foreigner. There was also a substantial body of opinion which held that the marriage was bigamous, since Peter's first marriage to Evdokia had never been legitimately ended.

It is difficult to pinpoint exactly when relations between Peter and Alexei began to deteriorate. Given the circumstances, it would certainly be surprising if there were no tension between father and son. To Peter, Alexei must have represented a reminder of Evdokia and his unhappy marriage. More than that, he threatened all that Peter had accomplished, either through his perceived incompetence and laziness, or because he advocated a return to the traditional insular Muscovy of the past.[61] From Alexei's perspective, it must have been impossible to live up to the demands and expectations placed on him by his father. Like many sons of hard-driving and overbearing fathers, Alexei seemed to simply follow the path of least resistance, whether it was grudging obedience or a kind of "out of sight, out of mind" negligence. This only served to further enrage Peter, who could never seem to grasp that this son might have different inclinations and abilities.

Already upon his return to Russia in 1713 we see Alexei's fear of his father and Peter's demands upon his son. Peter required that his son undergo a series of examinations to test the knowledge he had acquired abroad. Struck by terror at the prospect of disappointing Peter's expectations, he attempted to escape the exam in drawing by shooting himself in the right hand. As it turned out, his hands were shaking so badly that the ball missed his hand; he did, however, suffer significant powder burns. In the winter of 1714-15, pleading ill health, Alexei once again left Russia for Germany, in order take the waters at Carlsbad. Commanded to return promptly by his

---

[61] Paul Bushkovitch has rebutted the conventional view that Alexei was a cultural and religious conservative, ably demonstrating that in his own education and outlook, Alexei was very Western. However, those who opposed Peter's Westernizing policies looked to the tsarevich for hope for the future, even if he did not entirely share their conservative outlook. See Paul Bushkovitch, "Power and the Historian: the Case of Tsarevich Aleksei 1716-1718 and N.G. Ustrialov 1845-1859," *Proceedings of the American Philosophical Society* 141 (1997), 177-212.

father, Alexei, in the words of the Hanoverian diplomat Weber, "shewed but little inclination upon receipt of the letter." Upon Alexei's return to Russia in January 1715, Peter wrote to his son:

> Have you assisted [me] since you came to maturity of years in [my] labors and pains? No, certainly, the world knows you have not. On the other hand, you blame and abhor whatever good I have been able to do, at the expense of my health, for the love I have borne to my people, and for their advantage; and I have all imaginable reason to believe, that you will destroy it all, in case you should survive me.

As we have seen, Peter and Catherine's 1715 wedding revealed further bad blood. Even the birth of two children to Alexei and Charlotte could not restore the tsarevich to his father's favor. The first was Natalia (1714–28) and the second was Peter (1715–30), who would reign as Tsar Peter II from 1727–30. The unhappy Charlotte died nine days after giving birth to her son on October 12, 1715. The birth of an heir to the throne would normally have occasioned much rejoicing. In this instance however, it was overshadowed not only by Charlotte's death, but the birth of a healthy son to Peter and Catherine on October 29, also named Peter.[62] Peter Alexeievich's birth was barely acknowledged, while Peter Petrovich's was celebrated with fireworks, artillery salutes and free beer and vodka on the streets of St. Petersburg.

It seems that this sudden explosion of male heirs gave Peter an impetus to deal with his recalcitrant son. Even before the birth of the two boys, on October 11, Peter dictated a long letter to Alexei. This letter was however not delivered to Alexei until October 27, the day of Princess Charlotte's funeral and even before the birth of Peter Petrovich. In this letter, he catalogued his long list of disappointments in his son and delivered an ultimatum:

> [A]t the time that I am viewing the prosperity which God has heaped on our native country, if I cast an eye upon the posterity that is to succeed me, my heart is much more penetrated with grief on account of what is to happen, seeing that you, my son, reject all means of making yourself capable of governing well after me. I say your incapacity is voluntary because you cannot excuse yourself with want of natural parts and strength of body, as if God had not given you a sufficient share of either; and though your constitution is none of the strongest, yet it cannot be said that it is altogether weak. . . .

---

[62] To distinguish between the two princes, I shall follow the Russian custom of assigning them a patronym, derived from their father's name. Alexei's son is thus Peter Alexeievich and Peter's son is Peter Petrovich. Peter Alexeievich would reign briefly as Tsar from 1727–30, while Peter Petrovich, never healthy, would predecease his father in 1719.

You say that the weak state of your health will not permit you to undergo the fatigues of war. This is an excuse which is no better than the rest. I desire no fatigues but only inclination, which even sickness itself cannot hinder. Ask those who remember the time of my brother [Ivan]. He was of a constitution weaker by far than yours. He was not able to manage a horse of the least mettle, nor could he hardly mount it. Yet he loved horses, hence it came that there never was, nor is there actually now in the nation, a finer stable than his was. By this you see that good success does not always depend on pains, but on the will. . . .

I am a man and, consequently, I must die. To whom shall I leave after me to finish what I have partly recovered? To a man who like the slothful servant hides his talent in the earth — that is to say, who neglects making the best use of what God has entrusted to him?

Remember your obstinacy and ill-nature, how often I reproached you for it and for how many years I almost have not spoken to you. But all this has availed nothing, has effected nothing. . . . You do not make the least endeavors, and all your pleasure seems to consist in staying idle and lazy at home. Things of which you ought to be ashamed (forasmuch as they make you miserable) seem to make up your dearest delight, nor do you foresee the dangerous consequences of it for yourself and for the whole state. . . .

After having considered all those great inconveniences and reflected upon them, and seeing I cannot bring you to good by any inducement, I have thought fit to give you in writing this act of my last will with this resolution, however: to wait still a little longer before I put into execution to see if you will mend. If not, I will have you know that I will deprive you of the succession, as one may cut off a useless member.

Do not fancy that, because I have no other child but you [Peter Petrovich would not be born for several weeks yet], I only write this to terrify you. I will certainly put it in execution if it please God; for whereas I do not spare my own life for my country and the welfare of my people, why should I spare you who do not render yourself worthy of either? I would rather choose to transmit them to a worthy stranger than to my own unworthy son.

Alexei responded with a total capitulation, offering to renounce the succession:

I have nothing to reply to it [Peter's letter] but that if your Majesty will deprive me of the succession to the crown of Russia by reason of my incapacity, your will be done. I even most urgently beg it of you because I do not think myself fit for government.

This was clearly not the response Peter was looking for. He intended his ultimatum to whip Alexei into shape. Instead, he meekly gave in, reinforcing in Peter's mind his perception of his son as lazy and weak-willed. Alexei was in the classic double-bind, no-win situation. He could seemingly never satisfy his father's exacting standards. On the other hand, giving up was seen as shirking.

The dangers of Alexei succeeding to the throne were underlined when Peter fell seriously ill in late 1716, even having the last rites administered to him. Even if Alexei were to renounce the succession, Peter feared what might happen after his death. In particular, he doubted the sincerity of any renunciation, as Alexei might be persuaded by the "big beards" (the conservative clergy) to take up the throne after Peter's death. Therefore, on January 19, 1716, Peter issued to his son another ultimatum:

. . . I cannot resolve to let you live on according to your own free will, like an amphibious creature, neither fish nor flesh. Change therefore your conduct and either strive to render yourself worthy of the succession, or turn monk. I cannot be easy on your account, especially now that my health begins to decay. On sight therefore of this letter, answer me upon it, either in writing or by word of mouth. If you fail to do it, I will treat you as a criminal.

Alexei was stunned; he did not particularly want to rule, but he had no desire to become a monk either. After consulting with his friends and advisors, Alexei agreed to become a monk. One of his advisors, Alexander Kikin, allegedly told him, "Remember, they do not nail a cowl to a man's head." In other words, Alexei could easily renounce his vows if he wished to do so at some point in the future.

About to depart on another long European journey, which in the course of eighteen months would take him through northern Germany, Denmark, the Netherlands and finally to France, Peter relented and gave Alexei a six-month long reprieve to consider his decision. When the deadline passed, and Alexei still had not given a decision, Peter summoned his son to join him in Copenhagen. After having borrowed substantial sums of money, Alexei set out, ostensibly to join Peter. On Kikin's advice, however, once out of Russia, he headed not for Denmark but for Vienna, where he hoped for the protection of his dead wife's brother-in-law, Holy Roman Emperor Charles

VI. Accompanied by his mistress Afrosinia disguised as a page, and three servants, the tsarevich arrived in Vienna on November 10, 1716.

For a period of several months, no one was quite sure what had happened to the tsarevich. There were rumors that Peter had had him seized and confined to a monastery or had even had him killed. Others said that he had been attacked and taken prisoner (or killed) by bandits in Germany. Peter, still absent from Russia, sent agents throughout northern Europe to try to pick up Alexei's trail.

Alexei's flight was a problem for all concerned. Peter was furious and ashamed that this son had betrayed him in such a public fashion. Moreover, with the tsar's long absence from Russia and his controversial and widely unpopular behavior and policies, the flight of the heir posed a distinct and possibly severe threat. Might Alexei be seeking foreign support for an invasion whose goal would be to overthrow his father and take the throne for himself? Clearly, the possibility could not be discounted, and in Peter's mind it was rendered all the more dangerous by the connection he perceived between Alexei and the "big beards." For Emperor Charles VI, Alexei's uninvited presence was both a danger and a potential opportunity. The danger was that of arousing the ire of a powerful and volatile neighboring ruler, who moreover had large army not far away in Poland and northern Germany. On the other hand, turning away a family member in need of protection would not look good. Then, of course, there was the possibility of using Alexei to head up an invasion to overthrow Peter.[63]

Alexei was at first kept in a castle in the Tyrol under conditions of strict seclusion. By March of 1717, one of Peter's agents had approached the castle near enough to catch sight of him. A letter from Peter was submitted to the Emperor requesting that his son be returned forthwith. Charles prevaricated, saying that he doubted that Alexei was in the Tyrol, but that he would investigate. At the same time, he sent an emissary to Alexei, who showed the tsarevich Peter's letter and asked if he was willing to return to Russia. Alexei was frantic at the thought. Not willing to turn over to Peter a reluctant son by force, Charles arranged for Alexei to be hidden in Naples, then an Austrian possession.

---

[63] This possibility had long been discounted by historians. More recently, however, Paul Bushkovitch has brought to light documents indicating that the Austrians did indeed give serious thought to this course of action before their doubts regarding Alexei's suitability for such a role caused them to reconsider. In addition, the Swedes also contemplated something similar. See Paul Bushkovitch, "Power and the Historian: the Case of Tsarevich Aleksei 1716-1718 and N.G. Ustrialov 1845–1859," *Proceedings of the American Philosophical Society*, 141 (1997), 177-212.

Alexei's presence in Naples was soon sniffed out by Peter's main agent in this business, Alexander Rumantsiev, who informed the tsar who was in Germany on his way back to Russia. Peter then entrusted the return of his wayward son to Peter Tolstoy, a trusted diplomat. Peter gave Tolstoy two letters. The first was to Emperor Charles VI, demanding the immediate surrender of his son, and hinting at the unpleasant consequences that might follow a refusal. The second was to Alexei himself, and promised clemency if Alexei submitted:

> If you are afraid of me, I assure you and I promise to God and His judgment that I will not punish you. If you submit to my will by obeying me and if you return, I will love you better than ever. But if you refuse, then I as a father, by virtue of the power I have received from God, give you my everlasting curse; and as your sovereign, I declare you a traitor . . . .

Once again, Emperor Charles VI was put in a difficult situation. He did not want to be seen as forcing an unwilling Alexei to return to a vengeful father and a potentially unpleasant fate. On the other hand, Peter had made it abundantly clear that he was willing and able to make life very difficult for Charles. Clearly the best outcome for the Emperor would be if Alexei agreed to return Russia of his own free will.

To that end, in September 1717 Rumiantsev and Tolstoy were granted access to an unwitting Alexei. Tolstoy, an experienced and wily diplomat, played the tsarevich like the proverbial fiddle. He gave him Peter's letter and intimated that the Emperor was about to withdraw his protection, and that Peter was willing, if necessary, to invade and seize his son by force. Tolstoy quickly realized that the secret to manipulating Alexei lay with his beloved mistress Afrosinia, now pregnant. Tolstoy persuaded the governor of Naples to have her removed from the castle which had been their home. Alexei pleaded with Tolstoy to come see him and negotiate a solution. Tolstoy then persuaded Afrosinia to urge Alexei to return home.

An emotionally and psychologically-abused Alexei now agreed to return to Russia on condition that he be allowed to marry Afrosinia and to live quietly in the country. Tolstoy quickly agreed and relayed the conditions to Peter, who also agreed. In a letter dated October 4, 1717, Alexei informed Peter of his decision to return, signing the letter, "your most humble and worthless slave, unworthy of the name of son." Escorted by Rumantsiev and Tolstoy, Alexei slowly made his way through Italy and Austria. The pregnant Afrosinia was left in Venice to spare her the difficult journey through the Alps in winter. By January 1718, Alexei was in Moscow, waiting for his father's instructions.

He quickly discovered that Peter had now imposed two conditions to his supposedly unconditional pardon promised in Naples. He had to renounce the throne, and name his accomplices in his flight and his alleged conspiracy against the tsar. The first was no problem, as he had already offered to do so on several previous occasions. On February 3, 1718, a formal ceremony of renunciation took place in the Kremlin before an assembly of the tsar, his leading advisors, great nobles, and leading churchmen. Alexei was brought in without a sword, indicating his status as a prisoner. Peter gave a speech in which he recounted his son's failings. He had resisted all his efforts to make him into a worthy heir. He had consorted with bad company and had dishonored his wife, taking up with "an idle, common serving wench."

> We could not keep an heir who would lose everything that with God's help his father had obtained and who would overturn the glory and honor of the Russian people, for which I spent my health, in some cases not even sparing my life.

Two-year-old Peter Petrovich was declared the new heir, and all who continued to regard Alexei as heir were condemned as traitors. Alexei fell on his knees and confessed his guilt, pleading for Peter's forgiveness. Peter forgave him, provided he name the accomplices in his flight. Alexei agreed, signed the renunciation and swore allegiance to his little half-brother, as did the assembled luminaries.

Fulfilling Peter's second condition proved much more difficult, for he refused to believed that there was not a widespread conspiracy to put Alexei on the throne. Peter created a special court to investigate the alleged conspiracy, the Chancellery for Secret Inquisitorial Affairs. According to Alexei, only Alexander Kikin and his valet Ivan Afanasiev had known of his plans to flee. Kikin, in particular according to Alexei had played a central role, urging him to seek refuge with the Emperor. He categorically denied that Afrosinia had had any prior knowledge, and that he had more or less duped her into accompanying him. Beyond that, Alexei confessed that he had spoken with many others regarding his relations with his father. Among these were many prominent nobles and government ministers. Some of them expressed sympathy for the tsarevich and discontent with some of Peter's policies, particularly the costs of the continuing war with Sweden. Prince Vladimir Dolgoruky, a powerful noble from one of Russia's most distinguished noble families allegedly told Alexei, "if it were not for the tsaritsa's [Catherine's] influence on the sovereign's cruel character, our life would be impossible." Among others implicated in this general sympathy for Alexei and general discontent with Peter were his half-sister, tsarevna Maria

Miloslavsky, Avram Lopukhin (brother of Peter's first wife Evdokia), as well as Alexei's tutor and his confessor.

Subsequent interrogations, many under torture, did not reveal a widespread conspiracy to put Alexei on the throne. What they did reveal, however, was in some ways even more troubling to Peter. They revealed substantial, if disorganized, resentment of and opposition to some of Peter's most cherished plans and policies: the war with Sweden and its attendant taxation and burdens, required residence in St. Petersburg, and Peter's reliance on his "low born" wife Catherine and chief advisor Menshikov. What was not revealed was any desire on the part of those implicated in this opposition to return to the traditional ways of Old Muscovy. There is no doubt that many of those who did wish to turn back the Westernization of Russia did wish for Peter's death and Alexei's succession. There is also no doubt that Peter suspected Alexei of such aims, and that he feared the influence of the "big beards." But it is wholly inaccurate to see this as a conscious aim of Alexei's or of those at court and in the government who expressed sympathy for the heir and opposition to Peter's policies.

Peter's vengeance on those implicated in his son's flight was severe. Kikin was arrested and interrogated under torture. He admitted his role in Alexei's flight, but denied having told him that a monk's cowl "was not nailed to a man's head." Eventually, he was slowly tortured to the point of death before Peter relented and ordered him beheaded. Afanasiev was also executed for his role in Alexei's flight. Others who paid the ultimate price were Avram Lopukhin, and the Bishop of Rostov, who had both allegedly wished for the tsar's death. Many of those who had merely expressed sympathy for Alexei or opposition to Peter were punished more lightly, usually by fines or exile or both. Some who were implicated, however — not in Alexei's flight but in the general discontent — were not punished at all. Clearly, the discontent was so widespread among the political elite that they could not all be punished. And punished for what? For a general discontent with the current state of affairs? For expressing loyalty to and sympathy for the rightful heir to the throne? For daring to imagine that one day, Peter (frequently ill as he was) might die and Alexei sit on the throne?

An interesting tangential development concerned Alexei's mother, the long since spurned Evdokia. On the same day that Alexei had renounced the succession, Peter sent an agent to the convent at Suzdal where she had lived for the past nineteen years. Peter's agent quickly discovered that she had not been living as a nun, but rather as a royal princess. It was further discovered that she had taken a lover, Stephen Glebov, an army officer. Both Evdokia and Glebov were interrogated (he under torture) as to the details of their plotting with Alexei and his supporters. There was in fact no plot. There were some innocuous letters between mother and son, but there was no evidence of any conspiracy. Glebov was tortured for several days and finally executed by the very painful method of impalement. Evdokia was removed to a very remote convent on Lake Ladoga, north of St. Petersburg, with only a female dwarf for company.[64]

In March of 1718, Peter returned to St. Petersburg from Moscow, bringing Alexei with him. Alexei lived in small house on the grounds of the Peterhof palace, and was closely watched by armed guards. Alexei begged Catherine to intercede for him with his father, to allow him to marry Afrosinia. Peter, however, was still clearly not satisfied that he had rooted out, or even identified all those who conspired against him. To that end, Afrosinia was interrogated regarding Alexei's activities in exile. Elicited without torture, her testimony doomed her lover, and it is hard to imagine that she could not have known the implications of her statements.[65] She informed the tsar that his son had been in contact with various senators and bishops while he was in exile, but could not provide names. Further, she testified that Alexei frequently complained about his treatment at his father's hands. He had hated watching ships being launched. When rumors had reached him of an alleged uprising in the Russian army in Germany, she reported that he reacted with glee. He had rejoiced when he heard that Peter Petrovich (his infant half-brother) was ill. He expected revolt in St. Petersburg at any time, and had spoken repeatedly of the succession. When he became tsar, he had allegedly told his mistress, there would be big changes:

> When I am ruler, I shall live in Moscow and leave St. Petersburg as a mere provincial town. I shall keep no ships and an army only for defense, and I want to wage no wars with it. I shall be content with the old dominions: in the winter I shall live in Moscow and in summer at Yaroslavl.

No doubt this partly reflected Alexei's views and actual statements. It also likely reflects, at least in part, what Afrosinia believed the tsar wanted to hear about his son. Whether or not Alexei desired a return to traditional Muscovite ways (and the preponderance of the evidence is that he did not), these statements still represent a repudiation of Peter's life's work. Further,

---

[64] After Peter's death, she would return to court in 1728 during the reign of her grandson Peter II (Alexei's son). She died in 1731.

[65] By this time she had presumably given birth to the child she was carrying. Its fate is unknown.

she continued, she had only left Russia with Alexei because he had threatened to kill her, and she had only ever slept with him because of his threats.[66]

Confronted with Afrosinia's testimony, Alexei denied many of the specifics. The interview between Peter and his son has been immortalized in the nineteenth-century painting by Nikolai Ge. Further interrogations brought further confessions, and Alexei began to name those on whom he had been counting for support. He still denied, however, that he planned to mount a revolt against Peter, and that he had communicated with any of his named supporters while in exile.

By June 1718, Peter had decided that some sort of trial for his son was necessary. The grounds for such a trial were that he was still not satisfied that Alexei had confessed all of his misdeeds. On June 14 1718, Alexei was put on trial for treason before the Chancellery of Secret Inquisitorial Affairs, many of whose members had themselves been implicated as sympathetic to Alexei. The specific charge was high treason: that Alexei had, with the aid of the Holy Roman Emperor, planned a rebellion which was to end in his father's death and Alexei's accession to the throne.

On June 17, Alexei appeared before the court and made several admissions. He had "hopes in those people who loved the old ways." He had counted on the support of ordinary people against his father. Peter announced that his son had broken his promise to tell all he knew. Alexei fell at his father's feet and begged forgiveness and mercy. Finally, he raged at Peter, that he had never treated him as an heir, and had preferred lesser men over him:

> [T]he whole country is with me, no one excepted, and I see that for you it is matter of my life, and if you call me a thief, a rogue, and murderer, I want to be one, and I am one and I will gladly die, but see what happens to you after my death.

The Dutch ambassador reported that nothing like it had happened since Philip II and Don Carlos.

Over the next several days, Alexei was subjected to several more interrogations, this time under torture. Torture was a standard judicial procedure not only in Russia, but in other parts of Europe whose legal systems were based on Roman law. It was intended not, in the first place, as punishment, but rather to ensure that the accused was holding nothing back. In Alexei's case, the torture was intended to confirm information elicited from others. In Russia, the usual method was flogging with the knout, a short, thick whip. Fifteen to twenty-five strokes were usual; more

---

[66] Afrosinia was eventually pardoned and released. She married an army officer and lived in St. Petersburg until her death thirty years later.

than that could be fatal. On June 19, Alexei received twenty-five blows, and admitted that he had told his confessor, Father Iakov Ignatiev, that he had wished for his father's death. On June 24, he was questioned three times. On the first occasion, he received fifteen blows, on the second, twenty-five, and on the third, another nine. Several more admissions were forthcoming, none of which added much to the general picture.

In the evening after the initial session of June 19, Peter sent Tolstoy to ask his son some questions, "not for the investigation, simply for knowledge." Why had he disobeyed his father despite the potentially severe consequences? Alexei blamed his upbringing, which, in a way, deflected responsibility back on Peter himself. As a boy, living with his mother, his education had been neglected, and by the time Peter took charge of him, it was too late. Kikin had only been a catalyst.

Peter had already canvassed the opinion of a number ecclesiastical members of the court as to what punishment his son deserved. They responded very evasively. The Old Testament prescribed punishment, but the New recommended mercy. It was not up to them to decide: "the heart of the tsar is in the hands of God." Now, on June 24, the question was put to the secular members of the court. Alexei was unanimously pronounced guilty of treason and was sentenced to death, with the final decision in Peter's hands. Among those who signed the verdict were virtually all those who had been named as Alexei's supporters. Still, Peter was not satisfied that all had been revealed. On the morning of June 26, Alexei was tortured yet again, this time in Peter's presence. By seven o'clock that evening, he was dead. Officially, his death was ascribed to a stroke.

There is no doubt that his son's death spared Peter an acute dilemma. Would he have had his own son executed? This would have presented enormous problems, domestically and abroad. On the other hand, allowing Alexei to live posed equally severe problems. Conceivably, Alexei could have continued to serve as a focal point for those opposed to Peter's policies. Despite his renunciation, there was no guarantee that Alexei would not at some point claim the throne for himself, especially given Peter's poor health and the youth and poor health of Peter Petrovich. The convenience of Alexei's death certainly did not escape contemporaries, and almost immediately rumors began to circulate that he had in fact been murdered. None of the evidence is compelling, and in the end, the most likely explanation is the most obvious. Never very healthy, Alexei had been weakened by bouts of severe physical, emotional, and psychological abuse and succumbed to his injuries.

True to form, Peter's reaction to his son's death was conflicted, to say the least. The very day after Alexei's death, Peter participated fully in the anniversary celebrations of the victory at Poltava. On June 29, the day before Alexei's funeral, he celebrated his name-day with the usual abandon, and on the day after the funeral, he attended the launch of a new warship. In other words: business as usual. Yet, Alexei's funeral on June 30 was a solemn state affair, but attendees were told not to wear mourning clothes since he had died as a condemned criminal. A sermon was given on King David's words of mourning for his own rebellious son: "O Absolam, my son, my son!" One observer reported that Peter was "bathed in tears." Afterwards, his body was accompanied to the royal mausoleum by Peter, Catherine, Menshikov and important government officials, where it was laid to rest beside his widow Charlotte.

For many (probably most) other people, such a troubled relationship with such a tragic ending might have produced some soul-searching: Where did things go wrong? What might I have done differently? But for Peter, unlike Philip II, there is absolutely no evidence of any such introspection.

If anything, these events had the opposite effect on Peter. He was more determined than ever to change Russia forever, to make his reforms irreversible. The period after Alexei's saw some of Peter's more far-reaching reforms:

> After the death of the tsarevich in 1718 came the major results of the Petrine era, principally in government, but also a continued reform of Russian culture. The case of [Alexei] was the greatest spur to Peter's reform in the history of the reign, greater even than the Northern War.[67]

The extent of sympathy and support for Alexei among aristocrats and courtiers underlined the importance in Peter's mind of restricting their access to the levers of power. To that end, Peter created a system of nine colleges or administrative boards to carry out the business of government. This system was modelled on the Swedish government, and plans for it were underway before Alexei's trial and death, but when it was instituted, the presidents of the college were generally not drawn from among the high nobility. Within each college, moreover, decisions were reached by majority vote, further diluting aristocratic influence.

In 1722, after several years of work, Peter decreed a new Table of Ranks which organized and rewarded service to the state, and was intended primarily to bind nobles to government service. Nobles were required to

---

[67] Paul Bushkovitch, *Peter the Great: The Struggle for Power, 1671–1725* (Cambridge: Cambridge University Press, 2001), 425.

service in the civil service, the court, or the military, each of which was organized in fourteen precisely defined ranks. Promotion from one rank to another was dependent on merit and service, rather than birth or influence. The system established by Peter would endure unchanged until the mid-nineteenth century, and in modified form until the Russian Revolution of 1917.

Mindful of Alexei's supporters among the "big beards" and "those who loved the old ways," Peter carried out a series of reforms in the Russian Orthodox Church which effectively made it into a department of the government. When the conservative Patriarch Adrian died in 1700, Peter had simply not filled the position, and appointed Stephen Iavorsky, Metropolitan of Ryazan, as administrator of the patriarchate. Much church revenue was redirected into the royal treasury. Iavorsky over time grew bolder in his authority, and in 1712 gave a sermon which was highly critical of government policy. He even referred to tsarevich Alexei as "our only hope." He was, however, among those who signed Alexei's guilty verdict in 1718. Shortly after Alexei's death, Peter directed another important clergyman, Feofan Prokopovich, Archbishop of Pskov, to draw up plans to reorganize the church. In 1721, church administration was reorganized along the lines of the colleges. The position of patriarch was abolished and replaced by a Holy Synod, a board of clergy and laymen appointed by the tsar.

At the time of Alexei's trial and death, as we have seen, Peter decreed that his heir was his infant son Peter Petrovich, his son with Catherine. There is a good deal to suggest that like many driven men who have alienated and/or ignored a first family, Peter was determined not to make the same mistake twice. Peter Petrovich's care and education were closely monitored, and the toddler appeared periodically at court ceremonies riding a pony. Catherine would write to Peter:

> And please take care, Dad, because he [Peter Petrovich] has a bone to pick with you; when I remind him that his papa has gone away he doesn't like it; he likes it much better and is pleased when you tell him that papa is here.

Shortly after, she informed the proud father that little Peter liked to drill his soldiers and fire his toy cannon, just as his father had. Sadly, however, Peter Petrovich was small and frequently ill, and noticeably lagged in development his nephew, Peter Alexeievich, four weeks his elder.

In April 1719, the young tsarevich died at the age of three and a half. His father's reaction to his death was very different than his reaction to Alexei's death not even a year earlier. Peter suffered convulsions, and shut himself up in his room for three days. It is, of course, very possible that had he lived, Peter Petrovich might have had the same sorts of conflicts with his father that Alexei had had. Peter and Catherine now had three surviving children, all daughters: Anna (1708-28), Elizabeth (1709-61), and Natalia (1718-25). In all, Catherine gave birth to twelve children, six girls and six boys. Of these, only Anna and Elizabeth lived beyond their seventh birthday.

With the young tsarevich's death, the succession seemed to settle on Peter's sole male heir, his grandson and Alexei's son, Grand Duke Peter Alexeievich. Yet he was never formally granted the title of tsarevich, or recognized as heir to the throne. It is likely that the tsar feared that his grandson might serve as rallying point for opposition, just as his father Alexei had done. He was not mistreated, but rather ignored.

In 1722 Peter the Great attempted to seal the future of his reign and reforms in a Law of Succession, which allowed the tsar to name his own heir. Explicitly citing the "Absolam-like wickedness" of Alexei, it stated:

> We deem it good to issue this edict in order that it will always be subject to the will of the ruling monarch to appoint whom he wishes to the succession or to remove the one he has appointed in the case of unseemly behavior, so that his children and descendants should not fall into such wicked ways as those described above, having this constraint upon them.

Peter, however, never designated a successor before his death in 1725. According to one story, on his deathbed, he is supposed to have scribbled "Leave all to . . ." and summoned his elder daughter Anna. This account, however, appears only in the memoirs of Bassewitz, secretary to Anna's fiancé, Duke Karl-Friedrich of Holstein-Gottorp. Indeed, this law was a direct result of Peter's experience with Alexei, and was to cause a great deal of political turmoil in Russia before its repeal in 1797. Upon Peter's death, his widow Catherine took the throne as Empress Catherine I with the support of Menshikov and a group of "new men" who feared the resurgence of the old nobility[68]. Menshikov persuaded Catherine to name Grand Duke Peter Alexeievich as her heir, hoping thereby to preserve his own power, as he planned to have him marry his daughter. When Catherine died at the age of forty-four in 1727, the ten-year old Grand Duke became Emperor Peter II. He died of smallpox in 1730 before having named a successor. The Supreme

---

[68] In 1721 in the celebrations of the Treaty of Nystad which ended the long-running war with Sweden, Peter accepted the titles of "Father of the Fatherland, Peter the Great, Emperor of All Russia." From then on Peter preferred the title of Emperor to that of Tsar, with its connotations of "backward" Old Muscovy. From this point until the Revolution of 1917, all Russian rulers were technically emperors (*imperator*) although the title tsar would continue to be used popularly and almost interchangeably.

Privy Council invited the widowed Duchess Anna of Courland to become Empress. She was the daughter of Ivan V, Peter the Great's half-brother and co-tsar until his death. This invitation came hedged with conditions: she was not to remarry or name a successor, powers of war and peace would remain with the council, as would powers of taxation and spending. Upon assuming the throne, she quickly ignored the conditions and ruled as an autocrat until her death in 1740. She named as her successor an infant, the grandson of her older sister, who became Tsar Ivan VI at the age of two months. At the age of fifteen months, he was overthrown in a military coup and replaced by Peter the Great's surviving daughter Elizabeth. Elizabeth reigned until her death in 1762, naming as her successor the son of her older sister Anna, who became Emperor Peter III. He in turn was overthrown by his wife, who would reign as Catherine II, or Catherine the Great until her death in 1797. It was her son Paul, who detested his mother, who in 1797 overturned Peter the Great's Law of Succession.

Peter the Great died in January 1725, at the age of fifty-two, likely of an infection of the urinary tract. Long years of hard work, military campaigning, incessant travel, and repeated bouts of heavy drinking had taken their toll. If we ever needed proof that one individual can change the course of history, Peter is it, for he single-handedly altered the development of Russia. In his reforms, his unhappy history with Alexei played an important role, spurring him to take measures that would ensure the permanence of his legacy.

CHAPTER 5: "A MONSTER AND THE GREATEST VILLAIN THAT EVER WAS BORN": *GEORGE I AND GEORGE II*

On August 1, 1714 Queen Anne of Great Britain and Ireland died without surviving children.[69] During her lifetime, she had been pregnant eighteen times and given birth to five live children. Only one of these survived infancy, and he died in 1700 at the age of eleven. With her death, the Stuart dynasty of British monarchs was at an end. Quite improbably, at least so it seems to us, the new king was the fifty-four-year-old ruler of a mid-sized German state. This was Georg Ludwig, Duke of Brunswick-Lüneburg, Prince-Elector of the Holy Roman Empire, more commonly known as the Elector of Hanover, after his capital city. As King George I he was the only English king in modern times not to speak English. The complex series of circumstances which brought about this improbable event take us back into the recent, and not-so-recent, histories of England and Germany. Over the course of his reign, he would feud bitterly with the Prince of Wales, his eldest son and heir (later King George II) expelling him from the royal court, cutting off access to his son's children, and severely restricting his financial allowance. For his part, the prince set up a rival court where he openly encouraged opposition to his father's policies.

These episodes illustrate several important themes. First, the unlikely series of events which made Georg Ludwig of Hanover King George I of England demonstrate the crucial importance of the dynastic linkages that

---

[69] Prior to 1707 she and her predecessors had been rulers of England and Scotland, which were separate kingdoms with their own governments, Parliaments, laws, and institutions. The Act of Union of that year united the two kingdoms into a single Kingdom of Great Britain.

drove politics and diplomacy and that lay behind the marriage and family practices of royal dynasties. Second, their hostile relationship demonstrates how divisions within the ruling family both reflected and exacerbated political rivalries in the kingdom. Finally, if we needed any further proof, their poisonous relations underline the intergenerational nature of family dysfunction, for the relations between George II and his eldest son and heir were if anything more poisonous than between George and his own father

The events which would lead to George becoming King of England had their roots in the recent English past. In the 1640s England had undergone a vicious civil war in which the forces of King Charles I (r. 1625–49) fought those of Parliament. A number of issues lay behind this conflict. Charles tried to tax his subject without seeking parliamentary consent. He reformed the Church of England in ways that made it seem more Catholic, outraging zealous Protestants, or Puritans. He ruled England for eleven years without Parliament, violating what many saw as their traditional rights and liberties as free-born Englishmen. The royalist forces eventually lost the civil war, and the king himself was captured, tried for treason, and executed in 1649. England was declared a republic and for a decade struggled to find political stability under its military strongman Oliver Cromwell. After Cromwell's death in 1658, all control was lost as the country slid into anarchy. Finally, in 1660, one of the generals contending for power arranged for the restoration of the monarchy in the form of the son of the executed king who had been in exile in the Netherlands. Thus, in 1660, Charles II became king, bringing to an end the interregnum and England's experiment with republican government.

Charles II, rather being vindictive or vengeful was magnanimous in victory, pardoning all but a very few rebels. He was, as he put it, determined "not to go again on his travels." For most of his reign therefore, he ruled in cooperation with Parliament, remembering what had happened to his father. Although a secret Catholic (he would formally convert on his deathbed), he knew better than to meddle with the Protestant Church of England. There was, however, a huge cloud on the political horizon: he and his queen, the Portuguese princess Catherine of Braganza, had no children — there was no legitimate heir to throne. Charles II was a renowned ladies' man and had many mistresses and illegitimate children. He freely acknowledged at least a dozen bastards by seven different women. However, in the absence of a legitimate child, the heir apparent was Charles's younger brother, James Duke of York.

James was an adult convert to Catholicism, and unlike Charles, made no secret of his innermost beliefs. Thus, when Charles II died in 1685, James assumed the throne as King James II. Most Protestant Englishmen were willing to put up with a Catholic king because they believed it would be a temporary interlude, for James's only two surviving children by a previous marriage, his daughters Mary and Anne, had both been raised as Protestants. Indeed, Mary, the elder daughter, was married to William III, the Prince of Orange, the effective ruler of the Protestant Dutch Republic and one of the leading Protestant rulers in Europe.[70]

Over the next several years, however, James actively alienated Protestants among the political elite of England. He openly — and illegally — placed Catholics in positions of power, and refused to enforce laws which discriminated against non-Anglicans, whether Protestant or Catholic. James was faced with a rebellion by the Duke of Monmouth, an illegitimate son of Charles II. The revolt was repressed without much trouble, but James refused to disband the army which Parliament had agreed to pay for. Many Protestants feared that James would use military force to undo the limitations on royal power established earlier in the century.

All political calculations were undone in June 1688, when James once again became a father, this time of a healthy baby boy. (His first wife, Anne Hyde — the mother of Mary and Anne — had died in 1671. He subsequently married a Catholic, the Italian princess Mary of Modena.) As a male, baby James Francis Edward took precedence in royal succession ahead of his two older half-sisters. Now, Protestant Englishmen were faced with a Catholic royal dynasty into the indefinite future, rather than just a temporary Catholic interlude. Leading politicians began to correspond with James's son-in-law Prince William III of Orange, and invited him to invade England to preserve their religious and political liberties against an unjust and tyrannical king (James II). In November 1688, William landed in England with a large force. Many leading English commanders defected to William, or at least refused to fight for James. The panic-stricken king fled to France, after tossing into the River Thames the Great Seal of England. Since the winners generally get to write the history books, this series of events has become known as the "Glorious Revolution."

William convened an extraordinary assembly called the Convention to decide what to do.[71] The Convention declared that by his flight, James had abdicated his throne, which was now vacant, and then declared that William

---

[70] Although technically not a monarch, the Princes of Orange exerted great power as governor or *stadholder* in the seven provinces which comprised the Dutch Republic. They were also commanders in chief of the army and navy.

[71] An extraordinary assembly was required, since Parliament had to be called by the king, and obviously James did not call this assembly.

and Mary were to rule jointly as king and queen.[72] William and Mary reigned jointly until her death in 1694, remaining childless, and William reigned solely until his death in 1702. Upon William's death, the crown passed to Mary's younger sister Anne. But the genealogical and dynastic tribulations of the English crown were not yet finished. For Anne herself was, as we have seen, tragically childless. Her only child to survive infancy, the Duke of Gloucester, had died just after his eleventh birthday in 1700. William showed no interest in remarrying, and thus would father no children to succeed him on the throne. Clearly, some further arrangement was necessary in order to prevent the Catholic James II or his heirs from reassuming the throne.[73] A further complication presented itself in that besides the "Old Pretender," all of the leading claimants to the English throne were Catholic. By some calculations, the first fifty-four claimants by hereditary right were all Catholic. Clearly, this would not do; English had not invited a foreign invasion and overthrown a Catholic king simply to have a Catholic assume the throne a generation later.

Accordingly, in 1701, Parliament passed the Act of Settlement, declaring that in the absence of surviving children of William or Anne, the throne should pass to a German princess, Electress Sophia of Hanover, or "heirs of her body, being Protestant."[74] Sophia was a granddaughter of James I of England (James VI of Scotland), the father of the executed Charles I. Since Sophia predeceased Anne by two months in 1714, it was her son Georg Ludwig who became King George I upon Anne's death. But George's own family background and dynastic history were if anything even more complex and convoluted than those of the English monarchs.

---

[72] William maintained that the Convention had not granted him the throne but merely recognized his accession, which came through hereditary right and right of conquest in a just war. Besides his marriage to Mary, William himself was a grandson of Charles I. Scotland likewise recognized them as monarchs, while Ireland remained loyal to James II. To enforce his authority there, William led a bloody war of conquest, which lay at the root of much of Ireland's troubles down to the twentieth century.

[73] James denied that he had abdicated the throne, and maintained to his dying day that he was the rightful King of England. Upon his death 1701, his son James Francis Edward (whose birth in 1688 had precipitated the Glorious Revolution) claimed to be King James III of England, and James VIII of Scotland. His supporters in England were known as Jacobites (from the Latin Jacobus = James). His opponents called him the "Old Pretender." His son, Charles, the "Young Pretender," or "Bonnie Prince Charlie" launched an ultimately unsuccessful rebellion from Scotland in 1745.

[74] These arrangements would also precipitate the Act of Union of 1707, uniting England and Scotland into a single kingdom. Many in the Scottish Parliament were reluctant to accept Sophia or George as their future ruler, and some mused about restoring the Stuart dynasty in the person of the "Old Pretender." Eventually, enough English pressure was applied that Scotland accepted union with England in order to prevent the re-emergence of an independent and possibly hostile kingdom of Scotland.

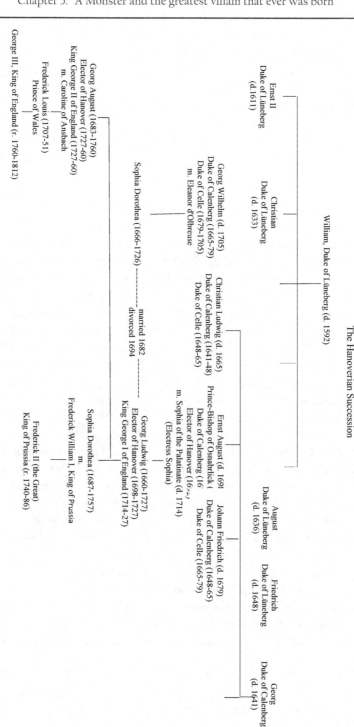

The Hanoverian Succession

The political history of Germany in the early modern period is extraordinarily complex. As we saw in Chapter 3, Germany was theoretically the Holy Roman Empire, descended from medieval attempts to revive the Roman Empire. By the end of the middle ages, Holy Roman Emperors had lost effective control over all but their own hereditary lands. Emperor Charles V (r. 1519–56) strove mightily to re-establish imperial authority in Germany, but his efforts were foiled by the religious divisions brought by the Protestant Reformation, and by the political self-interest of individual German princes, whether Protestant or Catholic. In the early seventeenth century, Emperor Ferdinand II (r. 1619–37) once again tried to impose his authority, but he succeeded only in prompting the disastrous Thirty Years War (1618–48), the most vicious and destructive war in European history prior to the twentieth century. After 1648, each individual German prince was recognized as sovereign in his own territory, and the imperial title signified a certain prestige and status, but virtually no effective power in Germany as a whole. Real political power in Germany lay with individual princes and a series of independent cities. There were approximately 300 individual territorial rulers and 150 imperial cities, as well as a handful of territories ruled by powerful prince/bishops. Among the larger territories were Saxony, Bavaria, Brandenburg, Brunswick, Hesse, and the Palatinate.

To complicate the picture even further, the principle of primogeniture among ruling dynasties was less prominent in Germany than elsewhere in Europe.[75] As a result, rather than leaving their territories to a single heir (usually the eldest son), German rulers frequently arranged for their territories to be divided on their death among all their sons. For German dynasties, therefore, calculations of marriage and inheritance were vitally important, as they sought to reunite territories divided up in earlier generations. German states split and recombined at a dizzying rate, resulting in a tongue-twisting roster of hyphenated states: Holstein-Gottorp, Braunschweig-Wolfenbüttel, Calenburg-Göttingen, Hesse-Darmstadt, and Mecklenberg-Schwerin, to name only a few.

The future George I of Great Britain was descended from the Welf dynasty of Saxony, one of the most ancient and august princely families in Germany. He could claim among his ancestors Henry the Lion (1129–1195), Duke of Saxony and Bavaria, and Holy Roman Emperor Otto IV (d. 1218). In the following centuries, the family's holdings came to be known as the Duchy of Brunswick

---

[75] In the case of ruling dynasties, primogeniture dictated that the title and power were inherited only by the eldest male heir. The contrary practice was that of partible inheritance, where the territory was divided among heirs, usually only the sons. Primogeniture was on the increase in Germany, but it was still contending with partible inheritance.

(German: Braunschweig), and underwent a number of divisions in order to accommodate all the sons of the respective Dukes. In the thirteenth century, a younger son of the duke was given part of the family's lands to rule as the Duke of Brunswick-Lüneburg, while the senior branch of the family continued as Dukes of Brunswick-Wolfenbüttel. Parts of the Duchy of Brunswick-Lüneburg were themselves given to younger sons over the generations as the duchies of Brunswick-Bevern, Brunswick-Grubenhagen, Brunswick-Celle, Brunswick-Calenberg, and Brunswick-Göttingen.

George's father was Ernst August, the fourth son of Georg, Duke of Calenberg, himself the younger son of Duke William of Brunswick-Lüneburg.[76] His three older brothers all ruled as Dukes of Brunswick-Lüneburg, while Ernst August was successively Prince-Bishop of Osnabrück and Duke of Calenberg after the death of his older brother Johann Friederich in 1679.

George's mother was Sophia of the Palatinate. The Palatinate was a populous and prosperous territory along the Rhine river in western Germany. It was ruled by the Elector Palatine, traditionally one of the seven electors of the Holy Roman Emperor. They were thus in a position to extract concessions from current emperors who wanted their sons to succeed them, or from hopeful would-be emperors. The electors occupied a special rank within the Empire, as the emperor had long before given up any claim to power within their territories. The electors also monopolized the major ceremonial and administrative posts of the Empire, which conferred prestige and not infrequently substantial revenue. Sophia's father, Elector Frederick V had, however, lost a serious gamble which had severe consequences for his family and in European diplomacy. In 1619 at the outbreak of the Thirty Years War, he had agreed to be elected King of Bohemia by the rebellious Bohemian nobility in place of the detested Ferdinand of Habsburg (soon to be Emperor Ferdinand II as well as King of Bohemia). The luckless Frederick not only lost his new Kingdom of Bohemia, but was also driven from the Palatinate. He and his family took refuge in the Netherlands, while the electoral dignity was transferred to his Catholic kinsman the Duke of Bavaria.[77] Sophia, also a granddaughter of James I of England, therefore, grew up in circumstances that ill suited her exalted rank, all the more so since she was the twelfth of thirteen children. Her marriage to Ernst August was therefore seen by many as beneath the dignity of her family. Certainly, she was driven by the desire

---

[76] George's German name was Georg Ludwig, but for the sake of simplicity, we shall refer to him as George.

[77] In the Peace of Westphalia (1648) which ended the Thirty Years War, the family lands were restored to Sophia's elder brother, as was the electoral title, while the Duke of Bavaria kept his, thus adding an eighth electorate to the Holy Roman Empire.

to regain the status of which war and circumstances had deprived her and her family.

Their marriage can legitimately be seen as a reasonably happy one, given the circumstances and the times. Although Ernst August did have his mistresses and bastards, he always treated Sophia well, and she was confident of her place in his affections. They were likewise united by their political ambitions: she to restore the tarnished luster of her family, he to reunite the separate territories of the Brunswick-Lüneburg inheritance and to achieve the family's crowning glory — an electorate of the Holy Roman Empire. The eldest of Ernst August's brothers, Christian Ludwig, died without heirs in 1665. His younger brother and successor as Duke of Brunswick-Lüneburg, Georg Wilhelm, had only a daughter — Sophia Dorothea, of whom we shall have much to say later, and the third brother, Johann Friedrich (d. 1679), had only daughters. The dynastic stars were thus aligning nicely for Ernst August or his heir to reunite the various territories under their rule.

All the available evidence points to relatively happy and "normal" childhood for young George, born in 1660. No doubt Sophia remembered less than fondly her own childhood in a relatively poor exile with a distant single mother. (Her father, Elector Palatine Frederick V had died when she was two years old.) She took an active interest in the education and rearing of young George and his younger brother Friedrich August, born in 1661. In 1664 Sophia left her young sons to join her husband on an extended tour of Italy. Although she enjoyed herself immensely, she discovered just how attached she was to "Görgen" and "Gutschen," and on her return she determined to never be separated from them as long again. Other children followed: Maximilian Wilhelm in 1666, Sophia-Charlotte in 1668, Karl Philipp in 1669, Christian Heinrich in 1671, and Ernst August in 1674.[78] But George, as the eldest, was clearly the most important, carrying with him as he did, the family's hopes of advancement and power. As he grew older, his father played an increasingly large role in his upbringing, preparing him for his future role as ruler of the reunited lands of Brunswick-Lüneburg. Young George and Friedrich August joined their father hunting as soon as they were able. At fifteen, his formal education came to an end, and George joined his father on military campaign, prompting effusive praise from his father

---

[78] Friedrich August died in battle in 1690, as did Karl Philipp. Maximilian Wilhelm likewise made a military career for himself in the service of the Holy Roman Emperor, converting to Catholicism and was almost completely estranged from his family. Sophia Charlotte ("Figuelotte') was married to Prince Frederick, heir to the Elector of Brandenburg, later King Frederick I. Christian Heinrich was killed in battle in 1703. Besides the estranged Maximilian Wilhelm, only Ernst August lived to see George become King of Great Britain, becoming Duke of Albany and York and Earl of Ulster.

in a letter to his mother. By the age of eighteen, he was experienced enough to assume independent command. At about the same time, he discovered that other traditional noble pursuit (besides hunting and war): chasing women. At sixteen he was discovered to have impregnated one of his sister's governesses. In order to avoid future embarrassment, it is possible that Ernst August arranged for the younger sister of his own mistress to become the mistress of his son.[79]

In short, whatever problems emerged later in George's life with his own wife and his own eldest son, we cannot impute those problems to his upbringing. His relationship with his mother was loving and supportive, and his relationship with his own father was dutiful, and gives no hint of the bitter conflict between George and his own son.

Not all was sweetness and light in the Brunswick-Lüneburg family, however. Upon the death of Christian Ludwig in 1665, the third brother, Johann Friedrich quickly occupied his duchy of Celle. This violated their father's will which had stated that in the event of Christian Ludwig's death without heirs, the second brother Georg Wilhelm was to have his choice between Celle and Calenberg. For a time, war between the brothers looked imminent, with Ernst August siding with Georg Wilhelm. In the end, Johann Friedrich knuckled under and Georg Wilhelm became Duke of Celle. In all likelihood, this spat among brothers reinforced in Ernst August's mind the dangers of partible inheritance. In 1682 he planned to institute primogeniture in his lands in order to preserve their reunification under George for which he was planning. In 1683 he obtained the approval of Holy Roman Emperor Leopold I, and in 1684 he revealed his plans to his family at large, causing great consternation among George's younger brothers, and certainly undermining family harmony. Friedrich August rejected all offers of compensation and plotted with the senior Brunwick-Wolfenbüttel branch of the family to spoil his father's plans. Maximilian Wilhelm at first agreed to the primogeniture clause, but after Friedrich August's death in battle attempted to revoke his earlier agreement. He too plotted with foreign rulers and was imprisoned for a time for his actions. No doubt these events played a large role in his conversion to Catholicism and his eventual near-total estrangement from his

---

[79] One of George's biographers states that "It was customary for royal and princely parents to arrange (more or less discreetly) for their sons at the age of sixteen to find a trustworthy and healthy sexual partner.... [I]t would be in character for Ernst August to create a situation whereby the sister of his own mistress became the mistress of his son. Through Klara [the elder sister] he could control Mlle von Meysenberg [the younger sister]. She was good-looking and lively but of an age to be sensible (some five years older than George) and could be relied upon not to create trouble when the time came for George's marriage." Ragnhild Hatton, *George I: Elector and King* (Cambridge MA: Harvard University Press, 1978), 36.

family. In fact, we could say that this is an excellent example of the ethos of the business (the interests of the ruling dynasty) prevailing over the ethos of the family.

Besides the reunification of family lands under George, there was an even more ambitious prize which tempted Ernst August and Sophia: an electorate of the Holy Roman Empire. The emperor had created an eighth electorate in 1648, so why not a ninth? This distinction would mark the family's ascent to the highest level of European nobility, and would be a fitting restoration of lost status, for was not Sophia the daughter of an elector and the granddaughter of a king? Was not Ernst August descended from a Holy Roman Emperor? But in order to achieve this goal, the family's lands would have to be substantial enough to justify the electoral dignity, and to maintain the greater political, diplomatic and military roles demanded of an elector.

Dynastically speaking, there was one threatening cloud on the horizon: Sophia Dorothea, the daughter of Ernst August's elder brother Georg Wilhelm, Duke of Celle. Indeed, her very existence was both a threat and a problem of long standing. The original plan had been for Sophia to marry Georg Wilhelm instead of Ernst August, but the elder brother decided that he enjoyed life as a bachelor too much to marry. In order to sweeten the pot for his younger brother, in 1658 Georg Wilhelm signed an agreement that he would never marry, meaning that Ernst August or his heir stood a good chance of inheriting his lands when he died. By 1665, however, Georg Wilhelm had fallen deeply in love. The object of his affection was Eléonore d'Olbreuse, a Protestant French noblewoman of a minor provincial noble family. Georg Wilhelm now wanted to settle down with the beautiful, gracious, and talented Eléonore. Prevented from entering into a formal marriage by the agreement of 1658, she agreed to a "marriage of conscience," and the 1658 agreement was reconfirmed and now explicitly stated that no son of theirs could inherit Celle. Nevertheless she continued to press for a legal marriage, and Georg Wilhelm remained caught between his agreement with his brother and his desire to please Eléonore. Their daughter Sophia Dorothea was born in 1666, and in 1675, Eléonore and Georg Wilhelm were formally married, with the blessing of the Holy Roman Emperor. From the perspective of Ernst August and Sophia, not only did this violate the 1658 agreement, but any future sons could conceivably inherit their father's lands. As it turned out, they had no more surviving children, but the existence of the now legitimate Sophia Dorothea still posed a threat. Should she marry, her husband might feel compelled to press her claim to part of the Brunswick-Lüneburg legacy, and thus set to naught all of Ernst August's and Sophia's carefully-laid plans. The solution to this dilemma was blindingly obvious: let Sophia Dorothea marry George!

But it was not as simple as all that, for in the status-conscious world of seventeenth-century nobles, Sophia Dorothea's rank was far below George's, a discrepancy sensed especially acutely by George's mother. His father was more inclined to view the political and territorial advantages of the match, a point of view to which his wife eventually came around. Indeed, contrary to much contemporary gossip (especially in light of later events), there is a good deal of evidence that Duchess Sophia made an effort to make her daughter-in-law feel welcome at the Lüneburg court. Accordingly, on November 22, 1682, sixteen-year old Sophia Dorothea married twenty-two-year-old George. As was normally the case with dynastic marriages, the wishes and feelings of the bride and groom were not a consideration. George's mother, Duchess Sophia would write that her son "would marry a cripple if it were to benefit *la maison*." Certainly George thought his new wife attractive enough, and they wasted no time in producing the required offspring: Georg August (the future George II of England) was born less than a year after his parents' wedding, and a daughter, named Sophia Dorothea after her mother, was born in 1687.

In light of subsequent events, however, it is very easy to see this marriage as doomed from the start, and certainly much salacious gossip emerged after the fact. There is no reason to suppose that George and Sophia Dorothea should have been any unhappier than any other young couple who married for purely dynastic reasons. As it turned out, however, the two were badly mismatched in terms of temperament and personality. George may not have been boorish ogre later lampooned by his English critics, but no one found him especially warm or charming. Even his most sympathetic biographer admits that in public he appeared sullen and wooden, and "was not a glamorous figure."[80] He had been raised as the privileged eldest son of powerful and ambitious parents, and he was conscious of his exalted position. Sophia Dorothea, on the other hand, was lively and vivacious, the spoiled, vain, and frivolous daughter of doting parents.

She soon became bored with the elaborate court protocol imposed by her in-laws, and her subordinate place in court life. She could stomach her inferiority to her mother-in-law, but repeatedly ran afoul of Countess von Platen, Ernst August's long-time mistress, who played an important role at court and wielded significant power. With George gone for long stretches with the army, Sophia Dorothea occupied herself with clothes, jewellery, and behaving impulsively. (It is all too easy to forget that she was still in

---

[80] Hatton, 173.

reality an adolescent girl.) George soon acquired a mistress, Melusine von der Schulenberg, whose compliant personality he contrasted to his wife's fits of jealousy.

It is hardly surprising then that Sophia Dorothea was unhappy and open to temptation: a high-spirited young woman married to a dull husband who, when he did not ignore her, compared her unfavorably to his mistress; a mother-in-law who harbored a grudge against her mother and tolerated her for the good of the family's political interests; and a day-to-day life both tedious and tense, restrained by court protocol, and surrounded by courtiers only too ready to spread gossip. Temptation soon came in the dashing person of the Swedish nobleman Count Philipp von Königsmarck.

Königsmarck was one of a familiar species in seventeenth-century Europe: minor noblemen who sought employment in the court or army of a foreign prince as means of advancing their own wealth and interests. Germany, with its plentiful courts and rulers, provided ample opportunities for this early modern Eurotrash. Already an experienced soldier, in 1689 he received a commission as a colonel in the Hanoverian army. With his wealth, dashing good looks and romantic aura, he soon assumed a prominent place in court life, becoming friendly with George's younger brother Karl Philipp. Karl Philipp was enamored of his beautiful sister-in-law, and it was he who introduce her to Königsmarck in 1689.

What began as playful flirtation soon evolved into a full-fledged affair, and it is certain that by 1692 they had become lovers. Passing letters through go-betweens, they tried to maintain a veil of discretion, but inevitably tongues at court began to wag. Both lovers were recipients of not-so-veiled warnings: Sophia Dorothea from both her mother and mother-in-law, and Königsmarck from his fellow officers, from George's brothers, and from the commander-in-chief of the army. Clearly, however, their passion blinded them to the dangers of their behavior, and they began to plan to run away together.

On the night of July 1, 1694, Königsmarck entered the palace at Leineschloss and made his way towards Sophia Dorothea's chambers. It is unknown whether or not he reached them; what is certain is that he was never seen again. He was certainly murdered, whether by design or in resisting arrest is unknown. There is, however, some very compelling evidence that this was a contracted murder. A contemporary diplomatic report stated that the killing blow had been struck by one "Montalban." A short time later, the treasury recorded a payment of 150,000 taler to one Niccolò Montalbano. This was a huge sum, considering that the highest-paid government minister earned 1,500 taler annually.[81] Much of the salacious gossip which soon erupted sought to lay the blame on George, the cuckolded husband. According to some versions, he caught his wife and Königsmarck *in flagrante* and murdered the count in a jealous rage; this despite the fact that he was demonstrably in Berlin on the night of July 1, 1694. Other versions laid the blame on Ernst August's mistress, Countess von Platen, who had become enraged when the glamorous Königsmarck spurned her amorous advances. The payment to "Montalban" and the apparent synchronization of events would seem to indicate some level of official complicity, but we are unlikely ever to know the exact sequence of events. Whatever the case, Königsmarck had been "disappeared" and Hanoverian envoys throughout Europe were instructed not to comment on the matter.

On the same night that Königsmarck was murdered, Sophia Dorothea was confined to her rooms, the search of which resulted in the discovery and confiscation of Königsmarck's letters. Within a few days, Königsmarck's apartments were searched and Sophia Dorothea's letters seized. There could thus be no doubt about the true state of affairs, and it was agreed upon by all involved — George himself, Sophia Dorothea, Ernst August and his wife, Georg Wilhelm and Eléonore — that a quick divorce was the only solution. Nevertheless, to avoid scandal, it was determined that Königsmarck's role, and even his name, were to be completely suppressed. Rather, Sophia Dorothea's refusal to cohabit with her husband were the formal grounds for divorce. At first, Sophia Dorothea readily agreed, for still ignorant of her lover's fate, she imagined freedom and an eventual reunion. Even after she must have known that he had to be dead, she likely imagined a quiet and dignified retirement in the country.[82]

In September, she willingly left the court in Hanover to take up residence in a small château near the village of Ahlden. When the divorce was finalized later in 1694, she discovered all her expectations betrayed: her father refused to see her and agreed to a relatively strict confinement in Ahlden, her ex-husband kept her dowry, ostensibly for the support of her two children, and she was to be denied access to her children. Sophia lived in isolation as the "Duchess of Ahlden" until her death in 1726.[83]

---

[81] Hatton, *George I*, 59.

[82] As the party in the wrong in the divorce, she was forbidden to remarry, while George, as the wronged party, was free to do so. Officially, he never did, although he later lived as husband and wife with his mistress Melusine von der Schulenberg with whom he had three daughters. They may have been parties to a morganatic marriage, but the evidence is inconclusive.

[83] The isolation of Sophia Dorothea of course gave rise to all kinds of gossip and suspicion in the courts of Europe. It is likely, however, that it was motivated by political considerations rather than fear of scandal. A free Sophia Dorothea posed a threat to the

While the Königsmarck affair was playing out, the longstanding political ambitions of the House of Brunswick-Lüneburg were finally realized, and in 1694 Ernst August was officially installed as the ninth Elector of the Holy Roman Empire. George, his eldest son and heir would henceforth be known as the Electoral Prince of Hanover. In January 1698, Ernst August died and George inherited his titles as Duke of Brunswick-Lüneburg and Prince-Elector of the Holy Roman Empire, although the electoral title would not be confirmed by the Imperial Diet or Reichstag until 1708. As the icing on the cake, in 1705, George's uncle and former father-in-law, Georg Wilhelm died, and the Lüneburg and Celle territories were united under one ruler. In fact, however, the territories and their governments had increasingly been operating as a single entity in recognition of their coming union.

It was during the 1690s as well that succession to the English throne became a real possibility rather than a distant dream. The death of Queen Mary in 1694 made the possibility of a direct heir much less likely, as did King William's subsequent disinclination to remarry. Princess Anne was the heir apparent, but given her sad reproductive history, no relief was likely to come from that quarter. Indeed, in 1700, her only surviving child, the Duke of Gloucester died at the age of eleven. Thus it was in 1701 that Parliament passed the Act of Settlement which fixed the succession on Sophia or her heir, when the throne should become vacant without a direct heir, as would eventually transpire in 1714.

At the time of their parents' divorce, young Georg August was ten years old and his sister Sophia Dorothea was seven. It is difficult to say what impact these events might have had on the children. Like most children of the elite, they were raised mostly by a succession of wet-nurses, nannies, governors, and tutors, rather than their parents. So their mother's confinement and absence might not have had the same impact that they would have on children of divorced parents in our own day and age. There are, nevertheless, indications that the young prince was profoundly affected by his parents' divorce and the treatment of his mother. We do know that Georg August never saw his mother again. We also know that although he was raised primarily by his paternal grandmother, the Electress Sophia (as she was now known), he did spend time at Celle with his maternal grandmother Eléonore who, we may assume spoke sympathetically to the young prince of the plight of her daughter, and his mother. There are unverifiable stories that he attempted to see his mother, and that when he succeeded his father

eventual union of the Brunswick-Lüneburg territories. As the prospect of the English succession grew more probable, she could also serve as focal point for the opposition to the Hanoverian succession, most especially the Jacobites, the supporters of the exiled James II and his descendants.

as King of England in 1727, he displayed her portrait, which previously been forbidden. There are equally unverifiable reports that he altered in his views towards his mother when he later examined for himself the evidence of her adultery.

Although there is no direct evidence for it, we may reasonably suppose that a boy of ten was going to miss his mother when all contact was forbidden. We may equally suppose that he would resent his father for it. By the same token, we may also surmise that to the father, the son pining for his absent mother would be a constant reminder of her betrayal.[84] Certainly, relations between father and son were difficult from early on, and it is virtually certain that the adultery and divorce were at the root of the problems.

The education of the electoral prince was entirely traditional for the day, consisting of languages, primarily French, Italian and English, history, military affairs, and etiquette. (His grandmother Sophia was especially insistent on his learning English in preparation for a possible future as a King of England. In contrast to his father, Georg August read and spoke English very well, although he spoke with a thick German accent.) He was especially fond of military history and administration, and genealogy, which perhaps speaks of a mind for detail without great depth or subtlety. His father, it seems, was largely absent from the prince's youth, both before and especially after the divorce, occupied as he was with governing the electorate and participating in the convoluted diplomacy and wars of the late seventeenth and early eighteenth centuries.

As the heir to the Electorate of Hanover, and after 1701 to the British throne, the question of Georg August's marriage was of some import. Fortunately for all concerned, in this case the marriage of the heir was concluded in a way that left everyone reasonably happy. His choice fell on a young German princess, Caroline of Brandenburg-Ansbach. Orphaned at the age of thirteen, she had become a ward of her relative, King Frederick I of Prussia, whose queen, Sophia Charlotte was the sister of George of Hanover, and thus the aunt of the prospective bridegroom. A beautiful and intelligent young woman — she was a correspondent of the famous philosopher Leibnitz — she had already turned down a very prestigious offer of marriage to Charles of Habsburg, soon to become Holy Roman Emperor Charles VI, rather than convert to the Roman Catholic Church. Georg August paid her an unofficial visit and was immediately smitten. The proposal of marriage was soon on its way; it was accepted and the couple was married on September 2, 1705.

---

[84] Some of George's English opponents liked to taunt him by calling his son (Georg August) "young Königsmarck," even though he was born years before the affair. There was never any real question of the prince's paternity.

By the standards of royal marriages, theirs was unusually happy and stable. Georg August would later have his mistresses, but Caroline took this in stride and until her death in 1737 was her husband's closest confidante and advisor. The required children and heirs soon followed: Friedrich Ludwig in 1707 (about whom more later), Anne in 1709, Amelia in 1711, Caroline in 1713, George William in 1717 (died in infancy), William in 1721, Mary in 1723, and Louis in 1724. The Elector was very fond of his daughter-in-law, and remained so despite the tensions that would emerge between him and his son. Indeed, it seems likely that George would come to envy his son for his happy marriage and easy relationship with his wife, an unhappy reminder, perhaps, of his own disastrous marriage.

There is precious little evidence of any collaboration between father and son during Georg August's formative years. Indeed, the Elector seems to have gone out of his way to maintain and even increase the distance between them. Not only, it seems, was the young prince's very existence and appearance a constant reminder of his wife's adultery (for Georg August was said to resemble his mother), but he was also temperamentally very different from his wooden and sullen father. Observers remarked on his affability and ease in society, which no doubt only intensified his father's resentment.

As had his father, Georg August began his military career at a young age, as was common among princely families, and the nearly continual wars of the period provided ample opportunity. From June to October to 1708, the twenty-four-year old prince was on campaign with the English, Dutch, and German forces in the Netherlands which opposed the aggressive and ambitious policies of King Louis XIV of France. In July he took part in the important battle of Oudenarde under the command of John Churchill, Duke of Marlborough, one the leading generals of the day. The prince distinguished himself on the battlefield, prompting Marlborough to praise him to the Elector. English writers praised him as "Young Hanover Brave," anticipating the day, they said, when such a valiant warrior would be their king. It was a defining experience in Georg August's life, one that he loved to recount, and that he longed to repeat. (Indeed, years later as King George II he would be the last King of England to personally lead his army in battle.)

It was, however, not to be, for as his father's only son, and as heir to the thrones of both Hanover and Great Britain, he was too valuable to be risked on the battlefield. He did by this time have an infant son, but given the demographic realities of the time, this was meagre insurance: Georg August was the heir, and there really was no "spare." Indeed, had not three of his paternal uncles been killed in battle? So, from the Elector's perspective, this seemed an entirely sensible precaution, and so it was. Yet if his father was proud of his son's exploits, he did a very good job of concealing it. He might have given Georg August his own regiment to command, or a decoration of some sort, neither of which were forthcoming. The young Electoral Prince was to have no further opportunity to display his prowess in battle. Although there is no positive evidence for it, it is reasonable to surmise that he would resent this treatment, and that it contributed to the tense relations between father and son.

Indeed, this is a classic case of the "double bind" in which many heirs find themselves, as discussed in Chapter 1. Georg August's success in battle provoked his father's jealousy and resentment. On the other hand, had he not distinguished himself, it would have been taken as obvious proof of his incapacity to lead and eventually to rule. Either way, the heir loses. By way of comparison, if the tsarevich Alexei had proved to be an effective military commander and dynamic leader, Peter the Great would likely have been just as unhappy with him.

Another cause of conflict between father and son had to do with the impending change of ruling dynasty in Great Britain, specifically with the question of how involved they were to be with Great Britain before the death of Queen Anne. In fact, the prospect of the English succession had earlier caused considerable tension between Elector George and his mother the Electress Sophia. Having succeeded in restoring her family's luster, with the prospect of even further glory in the near future, Sophia was keen to become acquainted with her prospective new kingdom and subjects. She offered several times to come to England, and carried on a correspondence with a number of English politicians. Queen Anne, however, was less than thrilled with this for any number of reasons. There was the possibility that the presence of the heir presumptive in England would create a rival center of power, as Anne's opponents would seek to curry favor with the next ruler. On the more personal side, the prospect of the Hanoverian succession must have been for the Queen a continual reminder of her own inability to provide an heir, not to mention her incredibly sad reproductive history. She also considered Sophia's eagerness unseemly, to say the least, as if the heir presumptive were impatiently awaiting the Queen's death. As Anne put it, having a Hanoverian at court in England would be forcing her "to look at her coffin every day that remained of her life." George was more circumspect and tried to restrain his mother's British ambitions, which did cause some conflict between them.

The prospect of England likewise caused further tension between George and his own son. Queen Anne had been persuaded with difficulty to confer a number of English titles and honors on Georg August, in recognition of his status as third in line for the throne, after his grandmother Sophia and his father George. In 1705, he became a naturalized British subject, and in 1706 he was granted the titles Baron of Tewkesbury, Viscount Tallerton, Earl of Milford Haven, and Duke of Cambridge. In addition, he was invested with the Order of the Garter, the highest honor bestowed by the English Crown. Elector George proved less than gracious in his conduct, refusing to allow any grand presentation of these honors to his son, as he was not formally able to hold audiences during his father's lifetime. George suggested that the requisite notifications could be delivered by a footman, which enraged Lord Howe, the English representative in Hanover, who insisted that a formal ceremony was necessary to receive "the highest gift the Queen had to bestow." In the end, the honors were conferred at a private ceremony. Queen Anne was furious at being snubbed, and Georg August did his best to atone for his father's conduct. Lord Howe reported that the Electoral Prince was blameless, and Georg August himself wrote suitably grateful and humble letters to the Queen.[85]

From the beginning, Georg August and Princess Caroline showed an inexplicable antipathy towards their eldest son, Friedrich Ludwig (Frederick Louis), born in 1707. It may be that the very circumstances of his birth reminded them of their bitter relations with the baby's grandfather. Ordinarily the birth of a princely son was greeted with celebration as a bolstering of political stability. The circumstances that surrounded the birth of "poor Fred," as he would become known, were very different. Upon being notified that his daughter-in-law was in labor, the Elector prohibited any of the family from entering her apartments, including the prospective father and his own mother, Electress Sophia, who was very fond of the young princess and had promised to be present during labor. The Elector even posted guards to ensure that his orders were carried out. He denied requests from the English government to have a representative present at the birth. Official announcements of the birth would not be forthcoming for a week, and the baby's christening was hastily improvised and held on very short notice, almost in secret.

Although George was very fond of his daughter-in-law Caroline, he did seem to envy her happy marriage, and probably could not help contrasting it with his own. It also seems likely that he was resentful of his son's increasing

---

[85] Queen Anne further displayed her pique, when Caroline gave birth to her daughter Anne in 1709. Georg August wrote to the queen, asking her to be godmother, and for permission to name the child after her. The queen consented, but named as her proxy the baby's maternal great-grandmother, the duchess of Celle, Eleonore, mother of the disgraced Sophia Dorothea. It is hard to imagine a candidate less acceptable in the Hanoverian court.

public profile, and was very reluctant to share public attention with him. Moreover, Georg August had been raised largely by his grandmother Sophia, and George may also have resented his mother's attention to his son. Whatever the reasons, the Elector scrupulously excluded his son from decision making and the levers of power, a pattern that would continue and intensify in England.

Queen Anne finally died in 1714 at the age of 48, worn out by repeated pregnancies and chronic illness. Since Sophia had died two months earlier, her son the Elector of Hanover now became King George I of Great Britain. In hindsight, it is easy to assume that all was preordained and took place without a hitch. In fact, however, the change of dynasty was in some jeopardy. The "Old Pretender" still claimed the throne as James III, and there were a large number in England and Scotland — known as "Jacobites" — who looked sympathetically on his cause and might be prepared to support it if the opportunity arose. A number of these had been influential in the later years of Anne's reign, and it was by no means certain that they would support the Hanoverian claim. In the end, however, their leaders lost their nerve, and the succession passed smoothly to the House of Hanover.

With great pomp and celebration George I travelled to his new kingdom with his son Georg August, now styled Prince of Wales. Nothing, however, changed in their relationship, which remained frosty at best. Although the Prince of Wales was given a place in the Cabinet, this was a largely ceremonial body which gave formal approval to decisions already taken in the inner council or Closet, from which he was pointedly excluded. This exclusion was demonstrated for the world to see in 1715 when there was a Jacobite rebellion in Scotland. As a grown man with military experience, the Prince of Wales might have been expected to play a role in the suppression of rebels. Even if, as heir to the throne, his life was too valuable to be risked on the battlefield, he might have been given some position to fulfill where he would not be too exposed to danger. From a public relations point of view, what could be better than the heir to the throne bravely defending it against a would-be usurper? Instead, he spent the rebellion in forced idleness at his home in St. James Palace in London.[86]

Excluded from any meaningful role in political life, George Augustus (we shall now begin referring to him with the English form of his name) and Princess Caroline embarked on an active social life, designed in part,

---

[86] In contrast, after he became King George II, when he was confronted with another Jacobite rebellion in 1745, that of "Bonnie Prince Charlie," he gave command of the army to his own son, William, Duke of Cumberland. Granted, William was his second son ("the spare, not the heir"), but he was also considerably younger that George Augustus had been in 1715.

no doubt, to enhance the prince's popularity among his future subjects, at the expense of his father's, if necessary. Indeed, the contrast between the two men was notable. George I, then in his mid-fifties spoke no English, and was considered dull and cheap. His son, on the other hand, spoke English well (having learned it in childhood), although with a thick German accent. King George made no secret of his preference for Hanover, travelling there whenever possible, and surrounded himself with his German friends and mistresses.[87] The latter were Melusine von der Schulenberg, with whom George had three daughters, as mentioned earlier, and Sophia Charlotte Kielmansegge, daughter of his father's mistress, Countess von Platen. As the former was tall and scrawny and the latter quite corpulent, they became known in England as the Maypole and the Elephant. George Augustus and Caroline, on the other hand entertained their new subjects lavishly, and their household at first at St. James and then at Kensington, quickly became a center of social life. Princess Caroline played an important role here as well. Well educated and interested in the latest developments, she patronized and hosted a number of the literary and intellectual luminaries of the day, including Sir Isaac Newton. The prince and princess went regularly to the theatre, and were often seen in public, whereas the king shut himself up with a handful of Hanoverian intimates. George Augustus and Caroline went to great lengths to endear themselves to their future subjects, with the prince supposedly exclaiming, "I haff not vun drop of blood in my veins dat is not English." George I, on the other hand, seemed to want nothing more than to return to Hanover as soon and as often as possible.

The tension between father and son, between present and future kings, inevitably became mixed up in English factional politics. As Parliament's role in the government expanded, it increasingly became the forum for factional and policy differences among the political elite. In the later seventeenth century, two major parties had come to dominate, the Whigs and the Tories.[88] Generally speaking the Tories supported the power of the king over Parliament, or to be more precise, they believed that the proper constitutional balance had already been struck, and opposed further

---

[87] Their recent experience with a foreigner as king, the Dutch William III, led British politicians to impose on George I the stipulation that no foreigner could be appointed to a British position. George did, however, bring with him a collection of German friends and advisors, who had no official position in the British government. In a way, this was worse, as their influence was exercised behind the scenes, and they were increasingly seen as unaccountable to anyone.

[88] Although historians call them "parties," they were not political parties in our modern understanding, complete with constitutions, formal structures, official platforms, and so on. Rather, they were relatively fluid and shifting groups of men who shared similar backgrounds, thought alike on most issues, and tended to frequent the same clubs and taverns.

attempts to strengthen Parliament at the expense of the king. The Whigs, on the other hand, generally stood for expanding Parliament's power, and were ever on the lookout for evidence of the arbitrary use (or abuse) of royal power. On religion, the Tories again favored the status quo: an official Church of England which was broadly Protestant in doctrine, but firmly subjected to royal power, and legal discrimination against all non-Anglicans, whether Roman Catholic or non-Anglican Protestants, known as Dissenters or Nonconformists. While the Whigs generally agreed on the need for an official Church of England, they favored more latitude and flexibility, including some tolerance for Dissenters, but most certainly not for Catholics. While there were many exceptions, Tories tended to be of a higher social status, whose wealth derived from the traditional sources of land and agriculture. Whigs, on the other hand, tended to come from more modest backgrounds (although still part of the wealthy and powerful elite represented in Parliament) whose wealth derived more from commerce and industry. Among the Tories as well were the Jacobites, those (a minority) who supported the claim to the throne of the deposed and exiled James II and his descendants, while the Whigs were 100 per cent behind the Protestant Hanoverian succession. All Jacobites were Tories, but not all Tories were Jacobites. On top of these real and meaningful distinctions, there were also more personal and factional divisions, as ambitious men and groups schemed and plotted for power. As in our own day, policies and principles were often compromised or betrayed in the pursuit of power for its own sake.

When George I first assumed the British throne, he strove to maintain a balance between the factions. Although Whigs were certainly favored over Tories, Tories were not excluded, although those known to have Jacobite sympathies certainly were. In the aftermath of the Jacobite rebellion of 1715, however, Tories were rigorously excluded from power, and from then on, through the remainder of the reign, and throughout the reign of George II, power was monopolized by various factions of Whigs. Increasingly the pursuit of power and personal rivalries came to the fore, rather than principles and policy, as the "outs" sought to displace the "ins." The hostility between the ruler and the heir inevitably became part and parcel of this factional conflict. Those politicians excluded from power and influence sought to increase their standing with the next ruler, while George Augustus was more than happy to spite his father by publicly favoring those who opposed his ministers and policies.

Further complicating the situation was the fact that no one then alive in England had any experience of an adult Prince of Wales during the reign of his father. This had not happened since the reign of James I a century earlier, when his son Charles was Prince of Wales. He became king at age 25 upon his father's death in 1625. His own son, later Charles II (born in 1630), grew to manhood during the civil war of the 1640s, and was in exile after his father's execution until the monarchy was restored in 1660. As we have seen, Charles had no legitimate children, and his brother James II fled into exile while his son was still an infant. William and Mary had no children, while Queen Anne tragically had no heirs who lived past the age of eleven. This was, of course, what made the Act of Settlement necessary in the first place. Several generations had thus lived and died with no experience in managing the usual tensions between king and heir, which were in this case compounded by their hostility towards each other, the factional divisions in Parliament, and the fact that theirs was a new and foreign ruling dynasty. By 1714, George Augustus was a grown man of 31, with a family of his own, and (in his own eyes anyways) extensive military experience, who felt himself shut out of any meaningful role by a spiteful and jealous father.

In 1716, George I finally realized his goal of returning to Hanover, from which he had been absent for two long years. If he were to be absent for more than six months, as he planned to be, a formal regency was necessary to ensure continuity, and the Prince of Wales was the obvious choice for regent. The king, however, was extremely reluctant to entrust power to his son: he never had before, why should he start now? His original idea was to appoint a "Council of Regency." Lord Townshend, one of his chief advisors, pointed out that there was no precedent for such a body in English history. Accordingly, George Augustus was named "Guardian and Lieutenant of the Realm," but had his powers as such limited. Historians disagree on whether this was a calculated slight or a sensible precaution, but what matters most for our purposes is that the Prince of Wales felt himself aggrieved.[89]

Father and son also clashed on the makeup of the son's household. Household posts were an important marker of favor and influence, and their appointment gave the holders great access and influence. Not surprisingly, therefore, these posts became mixed up both with the conflict between King and Prince, and with party politics. The Duke Argyll was the Prince of Wales' Groom of the Stole, a very important position which put him in very close contact with the prince. Argyll was a distinguished soldier, and wanted to be named Commander-in-Chief of the Army. The king, however, distrusted

---

[89] George II's most recent biographer emphasizes the limitations of the regent's powers (Jeremy Black, *George II: Puppet of the Politicians?* [Exeter: University of Exeter Press, 2007], 45) while Ragnhild Hatton states that these restrictions were perfectly normal and sensible. She also refers to the conciliatory language in George I's instructions to his son, although it may be that she misreads the usual formulaic language used in such cases. (Hatton, *George I*, 197.)

anyone who was close to his son, and promoted his own candidate instead. Encouraged by his advisors who feared Argyll's opposition, and to spite his son, the king further insisted that George Augustus dismiss Argyll from his household. When the prince protested vigorously, George I threatened to name as regent his younger brother Ernst August, rather than his son. Faced with this prospect, the prince knuckled under and dismissed Argyll.

While the king was in Hanover, the prince and princess took every opportunity to burnish their public image. They dined in public and welcomed all who wished to see them. Although dismissed from his household, the prince continued to show Argyll a great deal of public favor. He reviewed the troops and visited the fleet at Portsmouth to great public acclaim. Within the limits of his regency, he threw himself into government business, so much so that his father, kept informed of developments in England, grew even more suspicious of his son's aims. Rival politicians also saw opportunities to exploit the dissensions in the royal family for their own ends.

The tensions between father and son, king and heir, finally boiled over in 1717 and further display the synergy of family tensions and political quarrels. In 1716, Princess Caroline had given birth to a stillborn son, but she had quickly become pregnant once again, and gave birth to an apparently healthy baby boy on October 20, 1717. The prince and princess asked the king and his younger brother, Ernst August to be the baby's godfathers. The newborn's parents wanted to name the baby William (perceived as a more English name than the Germanic George), while king's advisors insisted on George, since the king was one of the godfathers. Eventually, he was given the compromise name of George William.

Much more serious tension arose, however, surrounding the choice of the baby's other godfather. The king, however, insisted on the traditional choice for royal sons, which was the Lord Chamberlain, the Duke of Newcastle. Newcastle was an ambitious politician, whom the Prince of Wales detested. Princess Caroline suggested a compromise whereby at the christening Newcastle would serve as a proxy for the absent Ernst August. This was rejected as disrespectful to the king. Moreover, the king's ministers insisted that time was of the essence as the king had not been well, and was anxious to leave for Germany to "take the waters." When the christening took place on November 28, therefore, tensions were already high, with the prince and princess feeling that their wishes were being ignored on one issue after another. After the prince escorted his father out of the room, as protocol required, he returned and berated Newcastle, according to some reports standing on his toes, while he shouted: "You rascal! I shall find you out! [ie.

get even with you]." Apparently, with the prince's thick accent, Newcastle had understood him to say, "I shall fight you!" that is, challenge him to a duel. Newcastle reported this "threat" to the king, who was outraged, and chose to treat it as a challenge to his authority. He asked James Stanhope, one of his chief advisors for his advice. Stanhope responded that while the prince was the king's son, "the Son of God Himself was sacrificed for the good of mankind." The king ignored two reasonable letters of apology from his son, and decided on further punishment. On December 2, the king ordered his son to leave St. James Palace, orders which the prince refused to obey until he received them in writing. George Augustus and Caroline vacated the palace, leaving their three young daughters and the infant George William in the care of their grandfather. The king probably expected Caroline to stay behind with her children, and at first allowed her free access to them. When the prince visited the children without informing his father, however, he was explicitly forbidden to do so without royal permission. When George Augustus solicited legal advice, he was informed that in English law, royal grandchildren belonged to the Crown, and that he had no recourse. Caroline was offered the opportunity of staying with her children, but only if she cut off all communication with her husband, which she refused to do. The king attempted to further punish his son by declaring that no one could hold a position in both his own and his son's household, or even be received in both. The Prince of Wales was forbidden to attend the royal church at St. James, as well as the theatre at Drury Lane, which held a royal privilege. The king withdrew his son's guard, and forbade any observance of his birthday. The king further attempted to dictate whom his son could appoint to positions in his own household, until it was pointed out to him that the prince's right to make such appointments was granted in the form of irrevocable letters patent. Then, he tried to withhold the prince's income of £100, 000 a year. This however, was granted by Parliament and could not be revoked solely on the king's command. He then "suggested" that the prince hand over the sum of £40,000 a year for the maintenance and education of young Prince Frederick, who had been left in Hanover. The Prince of Wales responded that nothing would make him happier than to welcome his elder son to England, where his education could be continued at the prince's expense. He knew full well that George would never agree to this, not wanting two heirs in the kingdom. To add insult to injury, the Duke of Newcastle was invested with the Order of the Garter, the most prestigious chivalric order in England.

George Augustus and Caroline rented Leicester House where they established their own rival court, entertaining lavishly and publicly. They also leaked the conciliatory letters which had been brusquely rebuffed by the king:

> I have received with due submission Your Majesty's orders to remain in my apartment until Your Majesty informs me of his further wishes. The strong mark of Your Majesty's indignation has infinitely astonished me, never having had any sentiments towards Your Majesty other than those of a dutiful son. . . The action of the Duke of Newcastle shocked me, and I was so indignant that I could not prevent myself showing it . . . If I have had the misfortune to give unintentional offence to Your Majesty, I ask pardon.

Professions of humility were one thing, the king responded, actions another. His son's professions were empty words, he said, that made him want to vomit. Nevertheless, the king did feel it necessary to assuage public opinion by appearing more in public, which he disliked.

This strife within the royal family attracted a great of public attention, and it is not surprising that there were a number of rumors. One had it that the king would punish his son by sending him into exile, perhaps giving him some position in the American colonies. This may have had its origins in a comment made by the Earl of Sunderland, another of George I's advisors that "He [the Prince of Wales] must be carried off and my lord [Admiral] Berkeley will take him on board and carry him to any part of the world Your Majesty will order, him, whence he would never be heard of more." Another had it that the prince would shipped back to Hanover, and that the two dominions would be separated. George I did, in fact, muse about splitting Britain and Hanover in future generations, but for the present it was too risky, as he had no other son.

The quarrel within the royal family also had political implications, as politicians currently out of favor curried favor with the next king. Chief among these were Lord Townshend and his brother-in-law Robert Walpole. They had earlier been key members of the royal council (or Cabinet as it was beginning to became known), but had lost king's favor when they opposed his policy in northern Europe. George was scheming to gain territory from the crumbling Swedish empire around the Baltic Sea, and Townshend and Walpole rightly saw that this was primarily to Hanover's benefit rather than Britain's. They were replaced by Sunderland and Stanhope as the key voices in the council. Walpole was an extremely shrewd politician (indeed, he would dominate Parliament and the government for most of the first half of the eighteenth century), and he and Princess Caroline saw eye to eye on many issues. So much so, in fact, that there were rumors that they were lovers, which is extremely unlikely. In any case, Walpole saw a political opportunity in the crisis in the royal family. If he curried favor with the next king, he was at the very least well-positioned to dominate politics in the new reign (as indeed he did). On the other hand, if he could effect a reconciliation between father and son, he could garner the gratitude of both the present and future kings. George Augustus's and Caroline's residence first at Leicester House and then at Richmond Lodge became the focal point of opposition to government ministers and their policies, and the court of the king and his mistresses openly mocked.

There were no great issues of principle at stake in this political maneuvering. Rather, the Whigs had split along factional lines, and the factions were quite willing to use whatever issues were at hand to press their advantage or to discredit their rivals, and as we have seen, they were certainly not above using the dissent within the royal family.

As in most situations of family conflict, it was the children who suffered most. Deprived of their parents, the three young princesses and the infant prince George William were cared for by the widowed Countess of Portland. Over time, the restrictions on visits from their parents were relaxed somewhat, and the children's mother was allowed to visit them once a week, but always under supervision. The eldest of the three girls, Princess Anne, born in 1709 is supposed to have said "We have a good mother and father, but we are like orphans." When a visitor remarked that surely the king must visit them, she replied, "Oh no, he does not love us enough for that." Thereafter, the king paid more attention to them, but the rumor was that whenever they heard their grandfather was coming to see them, the children would run and hide. In February 1718, young Prince George William fell ill, and was moved to Kensington Palace where his mother and father were given unrestricted access. The day after he was moved, he died, his parents having arrived just in time to sit with him while he breathed his last. Public opinion of course laid the blame for his death on his grandfather, who had so callously deprived him of the love and presence of his parents. In fact, an autopsy revealed that he had a polyp on his heart, and would likely have died young with or without his parents.

For several years, the king and the prince continued thus, with each attempting to discredit the other, and politicians caught between the two. In the words of one:

> Those who were for the Prince do not speak their minds because the father was king. Those who were for the King were equally backward because the son would be King; these because the King might resent; these because the Prince might remember.

Prince George and the opposition politicians who surrounded him publicly opposed the government on several important issues. Beginning in 1717, George I along with Stanhope and Sunderland had proposed the repeal of two Acts of Parliament which discriminated against the Nonconformists or Dissenters, that is, Protestants who were not members of the official Church of England.[90] Opposition to these bills was led by Walpole and Townshend, with the open support of the Prince of Wales, and they were not afraid to play on fears for the future of the Church of England. In revenge, perhaps, the king and his ministers introduced to Parliament the Peerage Bill. If this passed, the king's powers to create new peers (members of the House of Lords) would have been severely restricted. This would have had the effect of limiting a future king's ability to appoint his own ministers and to pass legislation in Parliament. Whether or not it was his intent, the king's support of this bill was certainly perceived by his son as an attempt to humiliate him and to continue his control from beyond the grave. In the end, the bill was defeated through the political scheming of Walpole and his opposition allies who recognized that it would have excluded them from power.

It was Robert Walpole who was the driving force behind the very reluctant reconciliation of the king and his son. In this, he had a valuable ally in Princess Caroline, who astutely understood the harm that these quarrels threatened for the ruling dynasty. Allowed freer access to her children, she went out of her way to be conciliatory to her father-in-law, hoping above all to have custody of her children restored. There were, however, still a number of obstacles to be overcome. The king wanted guarantees as to his son's future conduct, while the Prince refused to commit himself to support his father's policies sight unseen. Both felt themselves to be the aggrieved party, and both looked to the other to take the first step. Besides Walpole and the Princess Caroline, the king's own ministers were keen to end the rift, recognizing the harm that it was doing the government, not to mention their concern for their own political futures. There was also a more tangible, even mercenary, motive for the reconciliation. The king had amassed £600,000 in debts, and it was widely thought that only Walpole had the ability to get Parliament to grant the money to clear the debts.

A formal reconciliation was held on April 23, 1720. The Prince of Wales gave a speech in which he expressed his regret at having been in father's

---

[90] These were the Occasional Conformity Act and the Schism Act. The former prevented Dissenters from conforming to the Church of England by taking communion in it once a year, and the latter outlawed in practice, if not in theory, Nonconformist schools. They also proposed an act to limit the independence of the universities of Oxford and Cambridge, where most the Church of England's clergy were trained.

displeasure for so long, and his wish that his father would never again have reason to complain of his conduct. According the Princess Caroline, whose account of the meeting is the only source we have, the king appeared pale and nervous and received his son's submission sullenly. The only audible words he spoke were in the French that he habitually used in England: "*Votre conduite, votre conduite*" ("Your conduct, your conduct"). The next day, meeting after church, the two men stood side by side without exchanging a single word.

Although their relationship was officially patched up, it is readily apparent that this reconciliation was a political gesture rather than a real restoration of familial relations, which had never really existed in the first place. Both sides felt that they had been short-changed. The king felt that his son's submission was insincere and motivated only by party politics. He would write to his daughter, Sophia Dorothea, Queen of Prussia "my son's submission . . . would have been better for coming sooner and without the persuasion of the party." Further, when the king finally met with Princess Caroline, privately and for over an hour, he scolded her for her part in the rift. She would later confide to Walpole that the king told her "that she might say what she pleased to excuse herself; that she could have made the Prince better if she would, and that he expected from henceforward she would use all her power to make him behave well." For his part, the Prince of Wales felt betrayed by Walpole and his allies, who, he felt, had not extracted from the king all of the concessions they might have.

From 1720 until the death of George I and the accession of George II in 1727, relations between father and son were officially restored, but were hardly warm or affectionate, not that they had ever been. George Augustus had seemingly learned that there was nothing to gained from opposition to his father. All it had gained him was public humiliation, loss of custody of his children, and isolation of his supporters from power and influence. He was very much holding the weaker hand when it came to confrontation with his father. For the rest of his father's reign, George Augustus played little political role, seemingly content to wait for his father's death, hardly the best foundation for family harmony.[91]

In an interesting epilogue, relations between George II and his eldest son Frederick Louis were even more poisonous than those with his own father. Born in 1707, he had been left in Hanover in 1714 when his grandfather assumed the British throne as George I. It was felt essential that a prominent member of the family be present in Hanover. His father and mother repeatedly implored George I to allow the little prince to join them in England, and

---

[91] See Black, *George II*, 53.

they were continually rebuffed. This was very likely one more instance of George I asserting his authority over his son. Raised by a series of tutors and governors, his only family contacts were with his uncle Ernst August, and with his grandfather during his stays in Hanover. George I lavished as much affection on Frederick as he was capable of lavishing on anyone, once again in all likelihood to spite his son. As a result, Prince Frederick did not again lay eyes upon his parents until after his father's accession as King George II in 1727. Parents and child were essentially strangers. To make matters worse, his younger brother William, born in 1721, became the favorite son, doted on by devoted parents.[92]

After his arrival in England, father and son clashed on a number of fronts. Frederick felt that his allowance was insufficient for his position, and on at least one occasion he got opposition politicians to agitate on his behalf in Parliament for more money. George also insisted that his son live in the royal palace at Hampton Court rather than establish his own household, the better to keep an eye on him. They were also very different temperamentally. George II was a philistine, with little use for the arts and culture. On one occasion he famously said that he hated "all boets and bainters." Frederick on the other hand was an ardent and knowledgeable patron of the arts, and was an accomplished violist and cellist. The dissent between father and son spilled over into the artistic realm. George II was devoted to the music of Handel, whom he patronized generously while Frederick and his supporters ostentatiously preferred Italian music, particularly that of the now largely forgotten Giovanni Buononcini. On the several occasions when the king left Britain to visit Hanover, Frederick was pointedly ignored and Queen Caroline named regent, just as George's own father had sidelined him.

In 1736, Frederick married a German princess, Augusta of Saxe-Gotha, and in 1737 she gave birth to their first child, a daughter named Augusta after her mother. In an eerie echo of the events of 1717, this birth worsened relations between father and son. When Augusta went into labor earlier than expected, her husband hustled her out of the royal palace to ensure that his parents would not be present at the birth. Queen Caroline, who had always made excuses for Frederick and tried to smooth things over between her husband and her son, now turned completely against him: "My first-born is the greatest ass, and the greatest liar, and the greatest canaille, and the

---

[92] The two sons were also very different in appearance. Frederick was small and swarthy, giving rise to unfounded rumors regarding his paternity, while William was large and fair, resembling the rest of the family to a much greater extent. Much has been of George Augustus's and Caroline's dislike of their eldest son from his birth, referring to him as a "griff," a West Indian term for a mixed-race child. It is difficult to impossible to separate this supposed aversion from what would happen later. In other words, subsequent events inevitably coloured interpretations of what happened earlier.

greatest beast, in the whole world, and I most heartily wish he was out of it." George II told his wife:

> I must say you have been an excellent mother to all your children, and if any of them behave ill to you they deserve to be hanged. I never loved the puppy well enough to have him ungrateful to me, but to you he is a monster and the greatest villain that was ever born.

As his father had been, Frederick was expelled from court and the royal palace, and set up a rival court at his residence in Leicester House. Unlike his father, at least after 1720, Frederick openly encouraged opposition politicians and publicly opposed the policies of his father's government. In 1736, he publicly opposed the Gin Act, attempting to restrict consumption of cheap gin. This was a serious problem as consumption increased exponentially in the early eighteenth century with significant social and moral effects. On the very day that the Act came into effect, Frederick made a public show of ordering a shot of gin in a tavern.

As his father done before him in his conflict with his own father, Frederick deliberately cultivated his reputation as English, rather than German. Indeed, it appeared increasingly that for George II this was only done as a way of distinguishing himself from his father. Once he became king, this was largely forgotten and he spent a great deal of time in Hanover.[93] Frederick positioned himself as a future "Patriot King" who would overcome factional division in the interests of the nation.

In 1737, Queen Caroline was taken ill due to complications arising from an umbilical hernia suffered during the birth of her last child in 1724. As she lay on her deathbed, Frederick asked his father for permission to come see his dying mother. The king denied his request, believing his concern to be insincere: "he shall not come and act any of his silly plays here." When the queen asked if her son had asked to see her, she was told that her husband had denied him permission. She accepted her husband's decision, saying that she did not want to see her son again. She sent a message of forgiveness to Frederick before dying on November 20, 1737.

Once more, in an echo of the relations between George I and George II, in 1741, there was a public reconciliation between George II and Frederick. As on the earlier occasion, it was primarily political in motivation, and

---

[93] When, in 1736, the king decided to extend an already lengthy stay in Hanover, a notice was posted at St. James Palace: "Lost or strayed out of this house, a man who has left a wife and children on the parish; whoever will give any tidings of him to the churchwardens of St. James's Parish, so as he may be got again, shall receive four shillings and sixpence reward. N.B. This reward will not be increased, nobody judging him to be worth a crown." This last statement is a pun playing on the meaning of "crown" as both the kingship and a coin.

before long, Frederick was back opposing his father. Politicians favored by Frederick were instrumental in having Robert Walpole dismissed from government in 1742, and in the parliamentary elections of 1747, Frederick openly and actively campaigned for politicians who opposed his father's ministers and policies.

Frederick died in 1751 of a burst abscess in his lung, predeceasing his father by nine years. It is impossible to say what his relations with his own son, later George III, born in 1738, might have been like had he lived. We do know, however, that contrary to all expectations, after his marriage to Augusta, he abandoned his wild oats and became a relatively devoted family man. There is reason to suppose therefore, that had Prince Frederick lived, he might have broken the two generations long Hanoverian tradition of hostility between father and son.

As rulers and as men, George I and George II were both thoroughly ordinary. Neither was as exceptional as Louis XI, Peter the Great, or Philip II. As fathers and as sons they were creations of their times and positions in society. While neither was likely father of the year material, we should not imagine that in other circumstances, their paternal relationships would have been so poisonous and that they would have been so emotionally stunted. Theirs is case where ethos of the business (hereditary monarchy) destroyed family harmony. The dynastic scheming that led to George I's disastrous marriage predisposed him against his son, while the conventions of monarchical rule induced him to isolate his son from power, further poisoning their relations. Upon assuming the British throne, their family conflicts combined with party politics in a particularly destructive fashion. George II's relations with his own son were even more difficult, highlighting the intergenerational aspect of family dysfunctions as well as the threats that dynastic practices posed to family harmony.

These episodes also illustrate quite well one of the justifications for focusing this study on the early modern period. Although royal power in Britain had been limited by the events of the seventeenth century, the monarch still possessed significant power. It still mattered a great deal who the king was, what he thought, and what his policies were. At the same time, in common with other European states, the central government was becoming more powerfully entrenched in the lives of ordinary people. The policies of the king, therefore, had the potential to fundamentally alter the lives of his subjects, as we have seen in the case of the Occasional Conformity Act, the Schism Act, and the Gin Act.

Chapter 6: "Such a Wretch no Longer Deserves to Live": Frederick William I and Frederick the Great

Of all the cases examined in this book, probably none is as notorious or as illustrative of the tensions inherent in relations between kings and their sons as that of King Frederick William I of Brandenburg-Prussia and his son, Crown Prince Frederick, later King Frederick II, better known as Frederick the Great. Indeed, it serves as compendium of almost everything that could go wrong in relations between a king and his son, a "perfect storm" of toxic family and political dynamics. As in the case of Peter the Great and Alexei, Frederick William feared for the future of his kingdom in the hands of his son, and sought to remake his son in his own image. Like Charles VII and Louis XI, Frederick and his father were very different temperamentally, and these differences led to each putting the worst possible interpretation onto the other's words and actions. Unlike George I and George II, with whom he shared extensive and close family ties, Frederick William was very conscious of the need to provide a practical political education for his son. On the other hand, the brutal and inflexible methods he used aroused enormous resentment in his son, which festered all the more precisely because the father was so actively engaged. Eventually, his father's abuse and persecution would drive Frederick, like the tsarevich Alexei, to attempt to flee his father's power. He and his best friend, a fellow army officer, were apprehended before they could escape. They were imprisoned and put on trial for desertion and treason. The young prince was forced to witness his friend's beheading, and for a time he believed his own life hung in the balance, a belief that his father did nothing to discourage.

The state which Frederick and his father ruled was a relative newcomer to European power politics. The founder of the "firm," so to speak, was Frederick the Great's great-grandfather, Frederick William, the Great Elector. Born in 1620, he began to rule in 1640 and before his death in 1688 had taken an ill-assorted collection of territories scattered across northern Germany and laid the foundation for a rising power both in Germany and Europe. Indeed, it was his creation that would eventually unify Germany into a single empire in the nineteenth century under the "Iron Chancellor" Otto von Bismarck.

The core of the state was the Electorate of Brandenburg in north central Germany. Since 1415, members of the Hohenzollern dynasty had served as Electors of Brandenburg, which, as we have seen in the previous chapter not only gave them a role in electing the Holy Roman Emperor, but also an exalted status among German rulers. In 1525, a member of another branch of the family became Duke of Prussia. Technically, as Duke of Prussia he was subordinate to and a vassal of the King of Poland, but in actual fact he was independent of any outside control. As a result of the kind of dynastic recombinations we saw in the previous chapter, in the early seventeenth century, Brandenburg and Prussia were united under the rule of Frederick William's grandfather. At about the same time, the dynasty took over the small territories of Cleves, Mark, and Ravenburg along the lower Rhine River in northwestern Germany.

Although Electors of the Holy Roman Empire, Frederick William's predecessors were exceedingly cautious, and did not play an influential role in German politics, remaining among the second tier of German princes. Their territories were relatively small and poor, scattered across the north German plain, without natural defences. Brandenburg was known as "the sandbox of Europe" because of its poor soil. In total, these territories had a population of about 1.5 million in 1648, and the Elector's capital of Berlin was a smallish town of about 12,000. Prussia was a somewhat more promising territory, as it had several large and prosperous towns, whose wealth was generated by the lucrative trade in Polish wheat shipped down rivers to the Baltic coast where it was loaded onto ships bound for Western Europe. Adding to the Elector's problems was the fact that his territories suffered terribly from the ravages of the Thirty Years War. About half of the population had died mostly from disease and/or malnutrition. Brandenburg's two major towns of Berlin and Frankfurt an der Oder suffered population declines of one-third and two-thirds respectively. The union of these various territories was purely dynastic and personal. There were no common laws or institutions, no common currency or army. The only thing that united them, however tenuously, was that they were ruled by the same man. In short, viewed from the vantage point of the middle of the seventeenth century, there was absolutely nothing to indicate that Brandenburg-Prussia would rise from the second rank of German states, let alone play an important role in European diplomacy in the eighteenth century.

It was Frederick William, the Great Elector who began Brandenburg-Prussia's rise to prominence. In the negotiations that resulted in the Peace of Westphalia that ended the Thirty Years War in 1648, he managed some small territorial gains in northern Germany. It was, however, the creation and expansion of the army that more than anything else was responsible for the growth of his power. He realized that in order to protect his scattered territories, he needed an army large enough and effective enough to deter invasion. In 1656, his army consisted of 2000 men; at its peak in 1678, it had 45,000.

Such an army, however, was very expensive, especially for such a small state, and his subjects balked at paying the required taxes. It was in overcoming his subjects' resistance that Frederick William revealed himself as a ruthless and completely unscrupulous political operator. He prevailed upon assemblies of subjects in his territories to concede exceptional, one-time only grants of taxation. When he continued to collect them after their expiry and his subjects resisted, he used his army to brutally suppress dissent. He twice used his army to crush resistance in the important Prussian city of Königsberg (modern Kaliningrad). He relied for political support on the nobility of Brandenburg and Prussia, known as the *Junkers*.[94] In his struggle for tax revenue, Frederick William deliberately sided with the *Junkers* at the expense of peasants and townsfolk. Townsfolk were forbidden to own land in the countryside, while peasants were legally presumed to be unfree serfs, unless they had written proof that they were free. *Junkers* were exempted from taxation, which then of course fell disproportionately on commoners. The Elector confirmed the *Junkers'* power over their estates and serfs; essentially, the ruler's power ended at the gates to the *Junkers'* estates. In return, they not only supported his domestic policies, but they also served in his army and civil service, which increasingly became the same thing. The army also became at least in part a self-financing venture. Frederick William took advantage of the complex diplomatic and military maneuvering of the later seventeenth century to "rent" his army to the highest bidder, open to

---

[94] The name is derived from the German *jung herr*, or "young lord," and came to be applied generically to the nobility of Eastern Germany. *Junkers* were stereotypically violent and crude, delighting in warfare and hunting. Like many stereotypes, it has just enough truth to it to become a stereotype in the first place.

changing sides or quitting a campaign with a large enough incentive. During the Dutch War of 1672–1678, he changed sides three times.

On his death in 1688, he was succeeded by his eldest surviving son, who became Elector Frederick III. The Hohenzollern dynasty was particularly plagued by intergenerational conflict. On top of the usual tensions inherent in a system of hereditary monarchy, successive generations of Hohenzollerns seem to have swung wildly between extremes of temperament and personality. The Great Elector had been a no-nonsense, tough as nails political operator, with the constitution of an ox. His son and successor Frederick was cut from very different cloth. For one thing, he was never intended to be his father's successor. The Great Elector and his first wife, Louise Henriette of Nassau, had had a son named Wilhelm Heinrich who died at the age of five months in 1650. The next, born in 1655, was Karl Emil, who was very much like his father: high-spirited, physically robust, and as he got older inclined to love hunting and war — a chip off the old block. Frederick, born in 1657 was very different. Physically small, he suffered from asthma, and feet that pointed outward that made it difficult for him to walk. As baby he had been dropped by a careless nurse and suffered an injury to his back which resulted in a twisted spine. Eventually, medical care managed to correct his feet and his back, at least to some degree. He was eventually able to stand erect, and the only visible evidence of his injury was a small node on the back of his neck, which he covered with a wig. He did suffer, however, from chronic back pain his whole life, and possibly due to these childhood traumas, was always very concerned about his appearance to the point of vanity. Unlike his older brother, he disliked physical activity such as riding and hunting. Instead, he preferred the pomp and ceremony of court life, and learned to play the clavichord and flute. Karl Emil was very clearly his father's favorite, while delicate and sensitive Frederick was doted upon by his mother. As a young man in his early twenties, Karl Emil was serving in his father's army when he contracted dysentery and died in 1674, making his younger brother Frederick the heir to the throne, the *Kurprinz*, or Electoral Prince.

Relations between father and son worsened further with Frederick William's remarriage following Louise Henriette's death in 1667. Never very healthy, continued pregnancies were very hard on her, and she survived the birth of her sixth child by less than a year. Although their relationship had its stresses, the Great Elector and his wife had grown to genuinely love each other, and he was devastated by her death. Little more than a year later, however, his loneliness induced him to marry Dorothea of Schleswig-Holstein-Sonderburg-Glücksberg.[95]

In an age of frequent death in childbirth, remarriages and step-parents and step-siblings, what we call "blended families," were very common. The wicked stepmother of fairy tales was firmly rooted in reality, and Dorothea may well be seen as a prototype. She and her new husband would eventually have seven children, six of whom would survive childhood. She did all she could to favor her own children over those of the Elector's first marriage. It was strongly rumored that she tried to persuade her husband to disinherit Frederick in favor of her eldest son, Philip William. Only ten years old when his beloved mother died, Frederick grew to fear his stepmother, and in later years twice suspected that she attempted to poison him.

The question of Frederick's marriage served as a focal point for the hostility between stepmother and stepson. Frederick had grown up believing that he would marry his cousin Elizabeth Henriette of Hesse-Kassel, the daughter of his father's sister Hedwig Sophia. The two were about the same age, were childhood playmates, and as they matured, they fell deeply in love. Dorothea, however, had other plans for her stepson, and convinced her husband to oppose the marriage. The Elector instead wanted his son to marry Eleanor, sister of Holy Roman Emperor Leopold I. In an anticipation of his grandson's escapades, Frederick stood his ground and eventually fled to Hesse-Kassel to seek refuge with his aunt and (he hoped) future mother-in-law. Hedwig Sophia refused to turn Frederick over to his father, and in the end was instrumental in reconciling the two. Frederick was permitted to marry Elizabeth Henriette, although the wedding itself was a very frugal and simple affair, a mark of the Great Elector's displeasure with his son.

Their marriage, although happy, was unfortunately short, as Elizabeth Henriette died in 1683, a mere four years after the wedding. They did, however, have one child, a daughter named Louise Dorothea who was born in 1680. In his second marriage, Frederick would not be so fortunate. His second wife was Sophia Charlotte of Hanover, daughter of Ernst August and Sophia, and therefore sister of the future George I of England. This was a purely political arrangement on both sides. Frederick William wanted a northern German ally against Sweden, then the dominant power in the Baltic, while Ernst August and Sophia sought the Elector's support in their own campaign for an electorate. The two houses of Brandenburg and Hanover over the years became locked in a kind of deadly embrace. They were rivals for influence

---

[95] This an excellent example of the proliferation of hyphenated mini-states that resulted from the practice of partible inheritance, as discussed in the previous chapter. Not only that, she was the widow of Christian Ludwig of Hanover-Celle, and therefore the aunt of both George I of England and of his wife Sophia Dorothea.

in northern Germany, but as fellow Protestant dynasties with similar needs and priorities they also came to rely on each other. Despite this reliance — or more likely because of it — they came to despise each other at the same time that they needed each other.

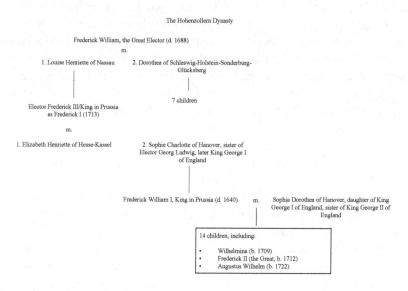

The Hohenzollern Dynasty

Frederick William, the Great Elector (d. 1688)
m.

1. Louise Henriette of Nassau   2. Dorothea of Schleswig-Holstein-Sonderburg-Glücksberg

7 children

Elector Frederick III/King in Prussia as Frederick I (1713)

m.

1. Elizabeth Henriette of Hesse-Kassel   2. Sophie Charlotte of Hanover, sister of Elector Georg Ludwig, later King George I of England

Frederick William I, King in Prussia (d. 1640)   m.   Sophia Dorothea of Hanover, daughter of King George I of England, sister of King George II of England

14 children, including:

- Wilhelmina (b. 1709)
- Frederick II (the Great, b. 1712)
- Augustus Wilhelm (b. 1722)

Strong-willed, intelligent and lively, "Figuelotte," as her family called her, never really fit in well in the Brandenburg court. She remained a Hanoverian through and through, and did not care who knew it. Neither Frederick William nor his second wife cared for her, and continually made snide comments, even questioning her virtue. Relations between in-laws worsened further when Frederick's younger and only remaining brother Ludwig died unexpectedly at the age of twenty-one in 1687. Frederick suspected his stepmother of having poisoned him, attempting to clear the way for her own eldest son to inherit. Electress Sophia (Frederick's mother-in-law) made tactless jokes about "succession powder" (i.e., poison). Once again, Frederick left his father's lands to display his unhappiness, as he and his wife took refuge first with her parents in Hanover and then with his aunt in Hesse-Kassel.

Although Frederick eventually returned to Berlin and resumed his role as heir apparent and electoral prince, family relations remained strained, as one might well imagine. Dorothea continued to scheme on behalf of her children, and Frederick William was extremely secretive about the contents of his will, causing Frederick great anxiety.[96] From 1680 on, the Great Elector was in increasingly poor health, and came to rely on both his wife and his son. Relations between Frederick and his father did improve, and Frederick began to play a larger role in the government.

When the Great Elector, died in 1688 his son became Elector Frederick III. His historical reputation has suffered in comparison with those of his father, son, and grandson. He was obsessed with the details of court ceremony, and spent an enormous amount of time and money emulating the model court of the period, that of Louis XIV in Versailles. The major accomplishment of his reign came in 1700 when, after years of diplomacy and negotiation, he achieved his heart's desire and gained a royal title as King Frederick I. Many, at the time and since, have criticized the time, effort and money that went into this pursuit, when in fact it added not one speck of land or iota of power. Nevertheless, this was an age that valued symbolic display and the trappings of power much more than our own, and there is a compelling argument to be made that in order to be taken seriously as a European ruler of the first rank, he required a more prestigious title than that of Elector or Duke. This was no doubt driven home by recent events. In 1689, as we have seen, Prince William of Orange had become King William III of England. In 1697, Frederick's neighbor and fellow Elector Augustus of Saxony was elected King of Poland. And most significantly of all, in 1692 Frederick's father-in-law Ernst of Hanover gained the rank of Elector, with the further likelihood that the Electress Sophie, or her son George (Frederick's brother-in-law) would one day become monarch of England. This sense of inferiority was supposedly driven home to Frederick when he met with William III of England in Cleves. Frederick had to sit in a mere chair, while William, as a king, was entitled to sit in an *arm*chair.[97] So it was in the depths of winter, on January 18, 1701

---

[96] Despite his frequent statements about the importance of preserving the unity of the family's lands, and despite several historical documents which bound the Electors of Brandenburg not to parcel lands out among their heirs, this is precisely what the will of Frederick William proposed. Upon becoming Elector, Frederick succeeded in overturning his father's territorial provisions for the sons of his second marriage, by buying them off with generous pensions. In this, he was aided by the death of his stepmother in 1689.

[97] The history of the Prussian royal title is a convoluted one. Only the Holy Roman Emperor could grant the title of king. Emperor Leopold I, however, was reluctant to strengthen a potential rival German ruler, and a Protestant one at that. (There was one other king within the Empire, and that was the King of Bohemia, a title held by Emperor Leopold himself.) During the 1690s, however, Leopold required the diplomatic support of Frederick and was persuaded, against much advice, to recognize (rather than grant) the title. Even so, Frederick was not a king in his lands within the Empire. Rather, he was recognized as King in Prussia (*König in* or *zu Preussen*) rather than King of Prussia (*König von Preussen*), although the distinction was lost in French (*roi de Prusse*) and Latin (*rex Borussiae*). This was done largely to placate the King of Poland, who ruled part

the coronation of King Frederick and Queen Sophia Charlotte took place in the Prussian city of Königsberg (modern Kaliningrad). Every last detail was planned by Frederick himself, down to his scarlet coat embroidered with gold and with diamonds for buttons. The coronation and its associated festivities cost 6 million *thalers*, raised through donations and a special tax. By way of comparison, at Frederick's death in 1713, the annual government revenue from all the King's lands totalled about 4 million *thalers*. The newly-crowned Queen Sophia Charlotte viewed the whole experience with a jaundiced eye, calling it "the comedy of the coronation." She was likely minimizing her husband's new royal status in order to downplay the "prestige gap" between Brandenburg-Prussia and her native Hanover.

The relationship between Frederick and Sophie Charlotte was not especially close or affectionate. It was really more of a mutually advantageous dynastic alliance. Nor, on the other hand, was it especially acrimonious, and they were capable of expressing some tenderness towards each other. They were rather more like business partners who at first tolerated each other, and eventually came to like each other. There can be no doubt, however, that they were temperamentally mismatched. Frederick was vain and fussy and, as we have seen, obsessed with the trappings of court life and ceremonial. Sophie Charlotte, on the other hand was bored by the rituals and pomp of court life. Intelligent, lively, and quick-witted, she loved the whirl of social life, the balls, masquerades and concerts. It was observed that she often went to bed as the king was getting up and ate dinner at nine, when the king was retiring for the night. She was well-read and enjoyed keeping up with the latest intellectual trends: she was a frequent correspondent of the great mathematician and philosopher Gottfried Wilhelm Leibniz (1646–1716), who was a resident of Hanover under her father and mother. Increasingly the king and queen led separate lives, and she eventually established her own household and court in the palace of Lützenburg, rechristened Charlottenburg in her honor after her death.

Frederick and Sophia Charlotte nevertheless fulfilled their dynastic duty of procreation, although certainly not as prolifically as they would have wished. The queen gave birth to two sons who died in infancy, and had only one child who lived to adulthood, a son named Frederick William, born in

---

of Prussia. Not until 1772 would the ruler claim the title King of Prussia, when Poland was partitioned by its more powerful neighbors and he could finally claim to rule all of the Prussian lands. The dynastic history of Prussia is further complicated by the fact that from the seventeenth century through the end of the German Empire in 1918, every ruler of Prussia was named Frederick, William, or Frederick William, and even further in that they started renumbering themselves when Elector Frederick III became King Frederick I.

1688, later to become King Frederick William I and the father of Frederick the Great. Once again, we see a son very different from his father. As a child, Frederick William was robust and angelic in appearance, healthy, with bright blue eyes and a round face. His tantrums, however, were legendary, a throwback to his grandfather, the Great Elector. He was a bully, beating up younger boys, even pushing one out of a window. On occasion he would strike and attempt to choke his tutors. On a visit to his Hanover relatives as young boy, he beat up his cousin, the future George II of England, despite the fact that George was four years older.[98] It may be that he suffered from porphyria, the same ailment which might afflicted George III of England, the grandson of George II, as dramatized in the film *The Madness of King George*. (Porphyria certainly has a genetic component, and as we have seen the houses of Hanover and Hohenzollern were closely related.) Although the diagnosis is far from certain, the symptoms certainly fit: seizures, abdominal pain, depression, anxiety, and paranoia.

It was almost as if Frederick William as crown prince observed everything his father did as king, and then determined to do the exact opposite when he would take the throne. Frederick was, as we have seen, devoted to the pomp and ceremony of court life, and willing to spend vast sums on it. Frederick William not only had no use for such things, he so begrudged the sum spent on them that he acquired a deserved reputation as a skinflint and a miser. Whereas Frederick, and especially Sophie Charlotte, were interested in literature, the arts and high culture, Frederick William maintained that all learned men were fools, and threatened to abolish the Berlin Academy of Sciences founded by his father. Above all, Frederick William was devoted to his army and his soldiers. According to his own son, Frederick the Great, under his grandfather Frederick I, Berlin was the Athens of the north, while under his father Frederick William, it became its Sparta. Nevertheless, and this point is absolutely crucial, while his father was alive, Frederick William, however much he disagreed with his father's policies, was scrupulous in his obedience and submission, having a profound belief in the necessity of subordination to divinely-sanctioned authority. When his own son would not only hold different beliefs and attitudes than his father, but upheld them in the face of his father's disapproval and refused to submit himself, the offense was all the greater precisely because Frederick William had subordinated his personal beliefs to the duty of obedience to his father.

[98] The two men held a life-long hostility towards each other, despite (or perhaps because of) the fact that Frederick William married George's sister Sophia Dorothea in yet another example of the deadly embrace of the two families. On his deathbed, Frederick William told his wife to tell her brother that he was forgiven, but only after his death was certain.

The prince who would grow up to become Frederick the Great was born in Berlin on January 24, 1712. His grandfather, King Frederick I lived just long enough to celebrate his grandson's first birthday, dying on February 25, 1713. In a last act of submission to his father, the new King Frederick William I gave the late king a magnificent funeral. He lay in state for eight days on a bed of pearl-embroidered velvet before the state funeral in a splendidly decorated cathedral.

Once his father was buried, however, Frederick William embarked on remaking his lands, his family, and his subjects in his own image. The royal court was drastically restructured and expenses severely curtailed. Upon his father's death, he addressed his courtiers: "Gentlemen, our good master is dead. The new king bids you all to go to hell." Military structure took over the royal court, as the new king established a strict pecking order, in which the field marshal took overall precedence. Court expenses were cut dramatically, and the funds redirected into the army, the exception to Frederick William's miserly nature. The royal stables were reduced from 600 horses to 120, and courtiers told to travel by foot where possible. Royal silverware was sold off, and the royal family ate on wood and pewter rather than china and silver from now on. Palace gardens were transformed into parade grounds. Interiors of royal palaces were whitewashed. At the same time, the army grew substantially in size. Anything that did not have an immediate practical application to increasing the state's power was discarded.

Above all, Frederick William devoted himself to his army and its soldiers. Unlike his approach to everything else, no amount of money was too great for his military. Over the course of his reign, the army doubled in size, from 40,000 in 1713 to 80,000 in 1740. The army consumed more than two-thirds of the government's revenue. By way of comparison, the royal court, to which the old king had been so devoted, now consumed only one per cent. From 1725 on, he habitually wore his uniform as his everyday dress. Frederick William was especially enamored of tall soldiers for his guards regiment and went to great lengths and expense to recruit the tallest soldiers he could find. Some were gifts from foreign rulers, while others were kidnapped and impressed into royal service. No detail of military life and organization was too small to escape the king's notice, from the design of uniforms to the drill-routines to the length of his soldiers' pigtails. If a soldier could not grow a satisfactory moustache, he had to paint one on. The system of conscription was reorganized and streamlined, while the noble officer corps was governed by a strict meritocracy. Discipline was kept through punishments draconian even by the standards of the eighteenth century. Despite this devotion to his army (or more likely because of it), and the lavish resources he expended on it, he was extremely reluctant to actually use it in battle. Moreover, priding himself on his plainspoken and homespun nature, he was suspicious to the point of paranoia of joining in the diplomatic complexities of eighteenth-century international relations. He was afraid, with good reason, of being outsmarted and betrayed by slippery and unscrupulous diplomats and their masters.

Frederick William saw the world through military lenses, and this permeated his views and understanding of his subjects and his family. His subjects were to obey his commands in the same manner that soldiers obeyed their commanders. He took a very detailed interest in all aspects of his subjects' lives, with the goals of economizing and strengthening his government. From the army to the economy, from religion to the law, there was no detail too small to escape the king's attention. In his own words: "I must be served with life and limb, with house and wealth, with honor and conscience, everything must be committed except eternal salvation — that belongs to God, but all else is mine." He was fond of patrolling the streets of Berlin, questioning his subjects on various topics. Given his irascibility and violent temper, any who could fled his approach. On one occasion, the king buttonholed a man who had not managed to escape. When the king asked him why he had tried to flee, the man stammered that he had been afraid. "Afraid?" railed Frederick William while beating the poor soul with his walking stick, "Afraid? You are supposed to love me! Love me, scum!"

His family was not exempt from these demands. Indeed, they were to set an example for his subjects in their frugality, discipline, and obedience. He kept a close eye on household expenses, especially on the grocery bill. His family was expected to subsist on a very frugal diet, consisting largely of bacon, lentils, tripe, and cabbage. His queen, Sophia Dorothea of Hanover, (the daughter of George I of England and the unfortunate "Duchess of Ahlden") felt very strongly that such a humble lifestyle was beneath her dignity. Although the couple managed to produce fourteen children (of whom Frederick was the second eldest), they were very different in temperament. Like her mother-in-law (who was also her aunt), Sophia Charlotte, she was very fond of the social whirl of court life and polite society. She was also intelligent and quick-witted, and her husband often felt inferior in her presence. In the end, she established her own household in her palace of Monbijou where she could indulge her tastes for the finer things. She did all she could to bring the children over to her side and to alienate them from their father. Her fondest wish was that her children would be the means of unifying her own family, that of Hanover, with her marital family. To that end, she schemed endlessly to promote marriage alliances between the two, a further source of discord between she and her children on the one hand, and her husband on the other.

By way of contrast, the king was never happier than at his country lodge at Wüsterhausen, a place his wife and children came to despise for it primitive and Spartan amenities. Here he could hunt and drill his soldiers to his heart's content, away from what he saw as the effete courtiers in Potsdam and Berlin. Apart from his army, and particularly his giant bodyguards or *lange Kerls* (tall fellows), the king's only other indulgence was his *Tabakscollegium* or *Tabagie*, his evening smoking and drinking parties, where the soldiers with whom he surrounded himself could drink themselves into a stupor, recount past glories, and indulge in juvenile pranks not out of place in a fraternity house.

The king's insistence on practicality and his hatred of luxury was also expressed in the education of his son and heir. As an infant, the care of young Frederick was assigned to a Protestant Huguenot refugee from France, Madame de Rocoulles, who had also largely brought up Frederick William. Frederick thus learned French as his mother tongue, and his command of German was always imperfect. Until her death, Madame Rocoulles was for the young prince "his dear, kind, Mama." At the age of seven, Frederick's education and upbringing was assigned to three men. His main tutor was another French Protestant refugee, Jacques Egide Duhan de Jandun. Frederick William had met Duhan on the battlefield and was sufficiently impressed to offer him this important position. Young Frederick's military education and preparation was the responsibility of two prominent army officers, General von Finckenstein and Colonel von Kalckstein. Although the king appointed them because of their military credentials, they were also educated and cultured men as well. Quite unintentionally, therefore, Frederick William's choice of tutor and governors, particularly Duhan, would lead his son in directions quite different from those he intended, with fateful consequences.

In 1718 the king issued a formal Educational Instruction to govern the education of his son and heir. In it, Frederick William directly repudiated the portions of his own education and upbringing which he considered useless: the regal pomp of his father as well as the intellectual pretensions of his mother. The young prince was not to study Latin. Foreseeing that this might be controversial, he declared that "I forbid any one whomsoever to make remarks upon this subject." He was not to study ancient history, but rather the history of his own times, focusing particularly on the history of his dynasty and their lands. Mathematics were emphasized for their military application, particularly "fortifications, the formation of a camp and other sciences of war." Young Frederick "must be instructed in the calling of an officer and a general." His teachers

> must inculcate in my son the veritable love for a soldier's life, impress him with the idea that nothing in the world is more capable of giving a prince more glory than the sword; that he would be a despicable creature, on this earth, if he did not love this sword, if he did not seek in it, and through it the only glory.

The prince's preceptors were to pay special attention to Frederick's moral and religious formation. In contrast to his own upbringing which had emphasized eloquence and the "decorum . . . suitable for a reigning monarch," Frederick William stated simply "See that my son has good morals and befitting deportment, and agreeable manners, but no pedantry." Frederick must be diverted from extravagances such as operas, comedies and other such frivolous and worldly vanities.

The king's instructions on the religious instruction of his son are especially interesting, as it was in this realm that young Frederick would first rebel against his father's authority. The lands of Brandenburg-Prussia had been officially Lutheran since the Protestant Reformation of the sixteenth century. However, in the early seventeenth century the reigning Elector had converted to Calvinism, with the result that both creeds were tolerated. Frederick William enthusiastically supported efforts to reconcile and unite the two faiths, but there were a number of obstacles. Mostly importantly, Lutherans were "universalists" in that they taught that salvation was available for all, that Christ had died for the sins of all. Calvinists, on the other hand, were "particularists" in that they taught the doctrine of predestination: that before Creation God had actively chosen some for salvation and condemned the rest to eternal damnation, irrespective of any merit of their own. In his own youth, Frederick William had had predestination drummed into him, with the result he experienced great anxiety about his own eternal fate. As with most other elements of his upbringing he came to reject predestination. In this, he was influenced by the movement of Pietism, which sought to combine the universalism of the Lutherans with the discipline, asceticism, and activism of the Calvinists. More practically, Frederick William believed that predestination would lead to apathy and fatalism, that mankind in general, and his subjects in particular, required the carrot of heaven and the stick of hell to compel them to fulfill their duties. When it came to the religious instruction of his son, therefore, beyond the usual platitudes about the necessity of fearing God, the king insisted that "You [his teachers] must not make him a Particularist . . . he must believe in universal salvation."

The prince's life was to be conducted according to a rigid schedule. Weekdays and Saturdays, he was to rise at 6 o'clock. Without turning over in bed, he must kneel and say a short prayer. He would then quickly dress, wash his face and hands, and drink his tea or coffee while his hair was being combed. At 6:30, came the reciting of the Lord's Prayer, and a chapter from the Bible and the singing of a hymn, which was to take precisely twenty-three minutes. For breakfast he was allotted seven minutes. From 7:00 until 10:45 came his lessons, after which he was to wash again, put on his coat, and have his hair powdered and then be presented to the king, in whose presence he was to remain until 2:00, when his lessons would resume until 5:00. From then until bedtime the prince was free to pass his time as he wished, "providing he does nothing contrary to the will of God." On Sundays, he was to rise at 7:00, and after the customary prayers and hymn, the preceptor was to read the Gospel selection for that week, and have the prince recite the catechism. After attending church and dining with his father, the rest of the day was his.

It is quite apparent that Frederick William was not only determined to avoid the "mistakes" in his own upbringing, but that he believed that such a rigid and regimented education for his son would turn his son into a miniature version of himself: a hard-working, sober, frugal ruler who governed his family and subjects just as he governed his soldiers. It seems that Frederick William made the exact opposite mistake that his uncle and father-in-law George I of England had made with the Prince of Wales, later George II, or that Charles VII of France made with the future Louis XI. George I and Charles VII saw their heirs as threats, and attempted to isolate them from the levers of power. Frederick William, on the other hand, introduced his son to the duties and responsibilities of power too early, and with absolutely no flexibility. What he wanted was a replica of himself. With a characteristic lack of insight, it does not seem to have occurred to him not only that his son might be a temperamentally different person (just as Peter the Great refused to consider the same for his son Alexei), but that his program of child-rearing might have the exact opposite of the desired effects, something that his own childhood might have suggested to him. Indeed, the ambassador of the Holy Roman Empire perceived this in 1725, when Frederick was twelve years old:

> Even though the king loves the crown prince [Frederick] with all his heart, he wears him out so much with early rising and the strains which carry on all day, that despite his young years he looks elderly and stiff, as if he is already a veteran of many campaigns. The king's view is thus: that by experiencing constant contact with the soldier's world, he will assume with time the remaining virtues of modesty

and thrift . . . What hits you between the eyes, however, is that this way of living runs counter to the crown prince's inclinations and as a result will, in time, produce precisely the contrary effect. . . . [99]

Like Peter the Great, Frederick William exhibited symptoms which might be considered psychopathic, which as we saw in Chapter 1 are common to many successful entrepreneurs. These may aid success in business, but are hardly conducive to a harmonious family. Above all, he was the classic workaholic, single-minded, stubborn, and rigid. He was also narcissistic, concerned exclusively with himself, unable to appreciate, or even understand that others might have different points of view. To a very great degree, the ethos of the business had replaced the ethos of the family. As he himself once said, "You know, my dear son, that *if my children are obedient*, I love them very much" (emphasis added).

Indeed, it was not long before we see the first hints of discord. Unlike his father, who had been a robust and mischievous child, if not downright bratty, Frederick had a frail constitution and in his looks favored his Hanoverian relations. Already, when his son was twelve years old in 1724, one evening at a reception, Frederick William was moved to wonder what "went on in that little head: I know he doesn't think like me, and that there are people who plant other ideas in his mind, and make him criticize everything." Characteristically, he condemned these "people" as "scoundrels," and continued to lecture his son: "Always maintain a good army and have enough money, therein lies the peace of mind and security of the prince." As he hectored his son, he began to give him some light love taps on the cheek, but these soon escalated into real slaps and blows as the king worked himself into a rage.

Throughout his childhood and youth, Frederick was extremely close to his sister Wilhelmina, three years his elder. Indeed, one might suppose that faced with a father who expressed his love through discipline and control, and a mother who saw her children primarily as pawns to be played against her husband, that brother and sister created a kind of substitute family. It was Wilhelmina who first encouraged Frederick to read beyond the dreary fare prescribed by his tutors. He became so enamored of literature that he would sneak past his sleeping governor in order to read late into the night.[100]

---

[99] Quoted in Giles MacDonough, *Frederick the Great: A Life in Deed and Letters* (New York: St. Martin's, 2000), 36-37.

[100] Many of the details of Frederick and Wilhelmina's youth are drawn either from Frederick's own later recollections in letters to friends, or from Wilhelmina's memoirs. It must be said that on many things Wilhelmina's memoirs cannot be taken at face value. Relations between she and her brother later soured, and she became very bitter towards

Like many clever children, and Wilhelmina was at least as clever as Frederick, the pair seemed to delight in mocking and provoking their seemingly obtuse father. They gossiped about prominent figures at court, particularly Grumbkow, the chief minister, and Prince Leopold of Anhalt-Dessau, the "Old Dessauer," the king's oldest friend and closest confidant. They quickly became conscious of the rift between their father and mother. When the king was absent, there were dances and ballets, parties and operas. When he was present, they were subjected to endless military reviews, not to mention his scoldings and ugly temper. Their mother consciously and deliberately turned them against their father. Once, after Wilhelmina had recovered from a serious illness, her father had granted her permission to ask a favor. She asked to be permitted to dress as an adult rather than as a child, to which he assented. She was dressed in a formal gown with a train, and was greatly pleased with the result:

> In short, I was superlatively satisfied with my little figure. I went down with a triumphant mien to the Queen, from whom I expected to have met with a highly gracious reception. ... As soon as the Queen perceived me at a distance she exclaimed: "Oh! Heavens! How she looks! A pretty figure indeed! As like to a dwarf as one drop of water to another!" I stood petrified with astonishment. My little vanity was highly disappointed; and vexation brought tears to my eyes ... she [the Queen] scolded me severely for having applied to the King for any favor. She told me she would not allow any such thing; reminded me that she had ordered me to attach myself to her exclusively, and that if ever I applied to the King on any occasion, she would be excessively angry.[101]

As Frederick matured, conflict with his father persisted and intensified. It seemed that Frederick William actively sought opportunities to berate and humiliate his son. Their relationship seemed doomed: Frederick deliberately provoked his father and in the words of a Saxon diplomat, "[the king] has only to know what will please his son to refuse it to him." Frederick was belittled for wearing gloves while riding on a cold day, and beaten for eating with a fork with three tines rather than two. (For Frederick William, this was an unbearable affectation, a symptom of his son's effeminacy and love of luxury, a theme that would loom large in their relations.) Frederick pointedly held to a belief in predestination in direct defiance of his father. At the age of fifteen, his tutors confessed their religious lessons seemed to be

---

him. Nevertheless, they are a valuable source, especially where she had no reason to deceive and where there is corroborating evidence.

[101] Norman Rosenthal (ed.), *The Misfortunate Margravine: the Early Memoirs of Wilhelmina, Margravine of Bayreuth, Sister of Frederick the Great* (London: Macmillan, 1970), 75.

having no effect. With his characteristic blunderbuss approach, Frederick William ordered his son's religious instruction doubled, with predictable results. By his late teens, he was signing his name "Frédéric le philosophe" indicating his rejection of traditional Christianity and his adoption of the skeptical Deism of the Enlightenment. With the assistance of his tutor Duhan, he surreptitiously acquired a library of almost 4,000 volumes, which included the most advanced and sometimes controversial writers of the time: Descartes, Voltaire, Locke, and Bayle. In order to do this, and to acquire the fine clothes and accessories he loved, he borrowed large sums of money, as bankers were always ready to lend to the next king.

The beatings and humiliations continued. When Frederick William came across his son admiring a new suit of clothes in a mirror, he ripped it off him and threw it into the fire. Frederick was beaten when at Wüsterhausen he was discovered reading a book rather than participating in the hunt. He was beaten when his father burst into his bedchamber, threw him to the ground and forced him to kiss his feet. And yet, like so many victims of domestic abuse (for that is what Frederick was), he still longed for his father's love and approval, even as he provoked and defied him. On one occasion, when in forced attendance at his father's *Tabagie*, Frederick had been made to drink too much and began to complain to Suhm, the Saxon ambassador, about his treatment at his father's hands. "Nevertheless, I love him," Frederick confided. When Frederick William asked what was going on, Suhm tried to explain that the prince was drunk and did not know what he was saying. When the king pressed further, Suhm told him that Frederick had been saying that the king makes him drink too much, and that he loves him. Frederick then threw himself at his father's feet and kissed his hands. Frederick William seemed delighted: "Now, that is well done, just be an honest fellow, just be honest." Frederick had to be helped to bed, but the king was very happy the rest of evening and the abuse abated for a short while. Frederick was clearly in a no-win situation: if he resisted his father, he was rebellious and disobedient; if he obeyed, he was insincere and merely feigning. Frederick William both abused his son, and simultaneously despised his son for tolerating the abuse. After one of the beatings, he shouted at Frederick, "If I had been treated like that by my father, I'd have killed myself; but to you it's all the same, you'll stand for anything." One shudders to think what might have happened if Frederick had resisted.

In 1728, when Frederick was sixteen years old, he was exposed to an entirely different way of life when he accompanied his father on a visit to Dresden, the capital of Augustus the Strong, Elector of Saxony and King of Poland. Augustus was a truly gargantuan, Falstaffian figure. He was said to be able straighten horseshoes with his bare hands. He had almost unlimited appetite for sensual gratification: food, wine, art, and above all, women. He is believed to have fathered over 300 illegitimate children. Dresden, the "Florence of the North" was renowned as a cultural center, as Augustus spent vast sums on architecture and other forms of artistic and cultural patronage. While in Dresden, Frederick was exposed to opera, ballet, grand balls, polite conversation, in short, everything that his father detested. "Fritz," his father told him, "I fear you like it here all too well," to which Frederick responded: "If you did not want me to enjoy myself, why did you let me come?" If Wilhelmina is to be believed, Frederick was also exposed to more carnal attractions as well.[102] On one famous occasion, Augustus treated his Prussian visitors to a kind of peep show. A tapestry was rolled up, revealed a reclining nude woman

> whose beauty excelled that of the finest pictures of Venus and the Graces; her body seemed of ivory, whiter than snow, and better shaped than that of the Venus de Medicis at Florence. The closet which contained this treasure, was illuminated with so many wax tapers that their dazzling light added a new splendor to the beauty of the nymph.

Wilhelmina's version of the story has Frederick William hustling his son away in anger while covering his eyes with his hat. Other versions have Frederick William remarking, "I have to admit, she is rather pretty." Whatever, the case, it seems to have aroused a sexual impulse thus far absent in Frederick. He became enamored of Countess Orczelska, an illegitimate daughter of Augustus, and, according to Wilhelmina, one of his mistresses as well. The countess became Frederick's first, and according to some, his only mistress. Once again, Frederick William had put his son in a no-win situation. On the one hand he was an effeminate dandy; on the other, if he showed an interest in women, he was a debauched libertine, abandoned to "Sardanapalian luxury."

The interlude in Dresden eventually ended, of course, and Frederick returned to his dreary reality, enlivened only by a return visit to Berlin from Augustus and Countess Orczselska. Thereafter, it was back to Wüsterhausen; in Wilhelmina's words: "We had had too much fun in Berlin for it to last too long, and from the Paradise where we were, we plunged into Purgatory." Frederick described the routine in "that terrible place:" "Tomorrow, hunting to hounds, on Sunday, the after tomorrow, hunting to hounds, and Monday, hunting to hounds again." At about the same time,

---

[102] Wilhelmina was not in Dresden. In other respects, however, her account corresponds with other descriptions, so she may be trustworthy on this as well.

Frederick became very ill, which gave rise to gossip and rumors that he had contracted a sexually-transmitted disease in Dresden. The rumor was that treatment was botched, and irreparably damaged his genitals, which would explain his subsequent near total lack of interest in female companionship.[103] Once again, Frederick William's attitude towards his eldest son seemed to soften as he lay ill: "When one's children are well, one does not know that one loves them." The respite was, however, temporary and the physical and emotional abuse resumed.

As in so many cases, the question of the marriage of the heir to the throne both manifested and exacerbated divisions within the royal family, the court, the government, and the kingdom. It had long been assumed that Frederick and Wilhelmina would continue the tradition of marrying their cousins from Hanover, who by now, as we have seen, had become the ruling dynasty in England. The usual scenario had Wilhelmina marrying Frederick Prince of Wales (who had his own difficulties with his own father, King George II) and Frederick marrying Princess Anne, the eldest daughter of George II or Princess Amalia, a younger daughter. In fact, these marriages had been agreed to as part of a British-Prussian alliance in the Treaty of Herrenhausen in 1725. Queen Sophia Dorothea was very much in favor of these English marriages as a way of further cementing ties between the two dynasties, all the more since her children would be marrying into not only her own family, but the royal family of one of the most powerful countries in the world. She did all she could to talk these marriages up to her children, to the point that Wilhelmina and Frederick believed that they were certainties, and Wilhelmina could contemplate a glorious future as Queen of England. While Frederick William was not opposed in principle to English marriages, and at various times agreed to let them occur, a number of forces would eventually sour him on the idea.

First and foremost, Frederick William and his Hanoverian relatives detested each other, none more so than Frederick William and George II. Childhood rivals, they had both pursued the same princess, Caroline of Ansbach, who had in the end married George II and become Queen of England. Now brothers-in-law, they seemed to hate each other all the more. An English observer would note: "our king's contempt for his brother-in-

---

[103] Frederick's sexuality has been the subject of enormous debate. Voltaire, to whom he had earlier been very close, but with whom he later had a bitter fallingout, hinted that Frederick was homosexual. There is no historical evidence for this. He was, on the other hand, almost certainly sterile, possibly as the result of a sexually-transmitted disease and/or its treatment. After these youthful escapades, he certainly had little interest in sex, and he and his wife remained childless. On the other hand, there is significant evidence that they did their conjugal duties, and there is also some evidence that he did have mistresses later in life.

law is as great as one man can have for another, and I dread the probable consequences of a rancor so violent and so reciprocal." The more the queen pressed for the marriages, the more the king resisted: "If you and your English family were at your last gasp, I would not even lend you my doctor." Frederick and Wilhelmina both came to see English marriages as their escape from the tyranny and abuse of their father. Wilhelmina anticipated becoming Queen of England, while for Frederick, England seemed a kind of promised land. According to the English ambassador (hardly an unbiased observer, it is true), Frederick told his father,

> "I respect the English because I know the people there love me"; upon which the King seized him by the collar and struck him fiercely with his cane. . . . There is a general apprehension of something tragicall taking place before long.

The fact that his wife and his children all favored the marriages was enough to sour the king on them all by itself. At one point he proposed a toast in the presence of the queen: "A scoundrel, anyone that is for Hanover." Wilhelmina he condemned as "Hanoverian scum." There were, moreover, political and diplomatic permutations which also predisposed the king against tying his kingdom too strongly to England.

Frederick William was in many ways a throwback to an earlier time in his views on politics and diplomacy. By the eighteenth century, as we have seen in earlier chapters, the Holy Roman Empire was in reality an empty shell. The future of Germany clearly lay with the territorial states and their rulers, such as Frederick William himself and Brandenburg-Prussia. Nevertheless, the king maintained a kind sentimental and anachronistic attitude towards the Empire and the Emperor. All other things being equal, he was predisposed to favor the Habsburg Emperors and Vienna over "foreigners" such as the French and especially English: "no English people or Frenchmen should [have control] over German territories, and I will put pistols and daggers into the cradles of my children so that they can help keep foreign nations out of Germany." He was further concerned that the English marriages would tie Brandenburg-Prussia too closely to England and English concerns, that Prussian concerns and priorities would be subordinated to English ones.

Moreover, the Prussian court was notoriously corrupt and fractious, and the Imperial ambassador, Count von Seckendorff was a master manipulator of these divisions. In this, he was aided immeasurably by the fact that Frederick William's chief advisor, Count von Grumbkow, was in his pay. Seckendorff thus had inside information about royal policies and was able to use it to his own advantage. Not only that, but the king liked and trusted both men. They were both military men, and were frequent participants in the *Tabagie* and never missed an opportunity to advance their agenda and disparage their opponents, in particular the queen. Thus, the royal court was bitterly divided and the question of marriages of Frederick and Wilhelmina assumed political and diplomatic dimensions. Seckendorff and Grumbkow would do all in their power to prevent the English marriages, pressing on the king instead a marriage for Frederick with a minor German princess who happened to be the Emperor's niece. Both Wilhelmina and Frederick despised von Seckendorff and von Grumbkow. Frederick would write of the former:

> He was sordidly scheming, his manners were crude and rustic, lying had become so much second nature to him that he had lost the use of the truth. He was a usurer who sometimes appeared in the guise of a soldier, and sometimes in that of a diplomat.

It is unnecessary to recount all the convoluted maneuvering, but by early 1730, any prospect of the marriages had diminished to the point of invisibility. If Frederick were to marry — his father stated that he was still too immature — the likely choice would be Seckendorff's and Grumbkow's choice, Elisabeth Christine of Brunwick-Bevern, which was what transpired in the end. Whomever Frederick married, he would one day be king. Wilhelmina's future, however, was a different matter, and depended entirely on to whom she was eventually married. Clever and ambitious, she had believed for many years that one day she would be Queen of England. Instead, she was married to the Margrave of Bayreuth, the philandering and undistinguished ruler of a small and insignificant backwater. There is a good deal evidence to suggest that, however illogically, she blamed her brother for her fate, and that this bitterness is what lies behind the sometimes-poisonous pen which emerges in her memoirs.

While all this was transpiring Frederick and his father continued to feud, and Frederick surrounded himself with friends who shared his interests and inclinations, much to the displeasure of his father. Two in particular stand out, both fellow army officers of Frederick. One was Peter Karl Christoph Keith, the elder son of a Scottish military family that had settled in northern Germany. Frederick William responded to this friendship by posting Keith to Wesel in far-off western Germany. The other, whose friendship with Frederick would eventually cost him his life, was Hans Hermann von Katte. With his friends, Frederick experienced a contentment he had never known before: "I am finally learning to be carefree; I am at this moment, despite what might befall me. I play my flute, I read and I love my friends more than I do myself."

It goes without saying that Frederick William disapproved, but so did Wilhelmina. She called Keith her brother's "minister of debaucheries, [who] knew only too well how to worm his way into his [Frederick's] company." Von Katte was an officer in an elite regiment, eight years older than Frederick, and it does not require any great psychological insight to suppose that Frederick saw in him a father figure very different from his biological father. Katte and Frederick had a great deal in common. Katte was a great reader, interested in mathematics and literature, and acquainted with the most advanced thought of the burgeoning Enlightenment. Like Frederick he played the flute, and he could draw and paint as well. Certainly there have been those, both at the time and since, who thought their relationship more than that of friends, that they were lovers. Although it is not impossible, it seems unlikely. Wilhelmina thought he was a worse influence on her brother than Keith and thought him "more repulsive than likable; a pair of black eyebrows hung almost over his eyes. . . . A dark, pockmarked skin added to his ugliness . . . he posed as a wit, and a consummate libertine." It is very likely that Wilhelmina resented anyone who came between she and her brother. Wilhelmina's memoirs were also written much later, and it is certain that her recollections and opinions were greatly influenced by the tragic events yet to unfold.

Given his misery and abuse at the hands of his father, it was only natural for Frederick to contemplate an alternative existence far from his father's reach. It is all too easy to forget that the future Frederick the Great was at this time still an adolescent boy of seventeen. In other words, what we are seeing is evidence of identity exploration, as discussed in Chapter 1. At this stage of life, not only was he able to envision a different life for himself, but his father's brutal abuse drove him to oppose his father in the only realm in which resistance was feasible, that of the mind. He was also at the stage of egotistical self-absorption and the resulting high-risk behavior. Not only was he hounded and abused by his father, he very likely considered that no son had ever been as cruelly mistreated by his father as he had been. Indeed, the next episodes in the prince's life bear out these observations.

In these circumstances, it is hardly surprising that Frederick would contemplate running away, especially since this was practically a family tradition among the Hohenzollerns. Rumors first arose in the autumn of 1729, as the prospects of the English marriages dimmed. He would write to his mother:

> I am in the utmost despair. What I had always dreaded has at length happened. The King has entirely forgotten that I am his son and treated me like the meanest of men.... I am driven to extremes; I have too much honor to submit to such treatment; and I am determined to end it one way or another.

Wilhelmina, who recounts the letter, was in no doubt that this meant he planned to escape. There are vague allusions to an actual attempt in late 1729, but if Frederick really did try to run away, the details have been lost.

Once planted, however, the idea would not go away, and Frederick enlisted a reluctant and fearful Katte in his plans. Frederick saw an ideal opportunity in a month-long reception held by Augustus the Strong near Mühlberg in the spring of 1730. Before he left, he surprised Wilhelmina by appearing in disguise in her rooms. When he informed her of his plans, she argued vehemently against them, no doubt fearing for Frederick, but also for herself, if she were left behind alone to face their father's rage. She thought she had dissuaded him, but once in Mühlberg, Frederick and Katte began to plan once again. The prince asked a Saxon politician for two horses so that he and Katte could visit nearby Leipzig incognito. Fearing that Frederick planned to escape, he refused. Indeed, Katte himself implored him not to grant the prince's request. Frederick held a secret meeting with Guy Dickens, an English diplomat and informed him of his plans to escape first to France, and then to England. Dickens reported this conversation to London, and in early July, Frederick was informed that he would not be welcome in England under the current circumstances. Apart from everything else, the English government feared the reaction of Frederick William and the exposed position of Hanover, right next door to an enraged king with a large and powerful army.

Whatever their differences, Wilhelmina and Katte were undoubtedly correct in fearing the worst if Frederick tried to escape. For one thing, his plans were hardly secret. In Wilhelmina's words:

> The situation of my brother was so deplorable, that I could [not] disapprove of his resolution, and yet I foresaw its terrible consequences. His plan was so badly contrived, and the individuals acquainted with it so giddy, and so little calculated to conduct an affair of such importance, that it could not possibly succeed.

In the end, Frederick lost his chance and the king and his son returned to Berlin. Within, weeks, however, Frederick would be granted another opportunity to escape.

The occasion was a tour through southern Germany as the royal court travelled to Ansbach, to pay visit to Frederick's younger sister Frederica, who had recently married Margrave of Ansbach. Katte had applied for leave on the pretext of a recruiting mission, but whose real purpose was to join Frederick in flight. He and Katte arranged to meet near Stuttgart, and Frederick gave him his valuables for safekeeping. Katte had also received assurances from a French diplomat that the refugee prince would be granted asylum in France.

The whole affair was fraught with obstacles. Plans had to be flexible in order to seize the most advantageous opportunity, but this necessarily meant that details had to left to the last minute. Moreover, Frederick did not realize just how closely he was being watched, especially by a Colonel von Rochow. The previous year, von Rochow had been appointed by the king to his son's household with explicit instructions not to let him out of his sight. It seems that von Rochow became genuinely fond of the young prince, and he sought to protect him by trying to prevent any flight attempt. Besides being continually under surveillance, Frederick's plans were complicated by the absence of his two closest friends, Katte in Berlin and Keith in Wesel. This meant that Frederick had to rely for assistance on men whom he did not know as well and who, in the end, could not be trusted with his secrets. In fact, Katte's leave had been denied, and in letters exchanged through Katte's cousin, they and Peter Keith agreed to travel separately and meet up in The Hague, from where they would travel to Versailles. Unbeknownst to Frederick, Katte's cousin informed von Rochow that something suspicious was going on. The other rather frail reed on whom Frederick had to rely was Peter Keith's younger brother Robert, who was accompanying the royal party as a page. As if these arrangements were not haphazard and fragile enough, Frederick had had a new travelling coat made for himself in bright red, which not only aroused further suspicions but stood out in a crowd when he should have been concerned with being as inconspicuous as possible.

On the night of August 4–5, 1730, Frederick believed that his chance had come. The royal party was lodged for the night in two barns in the village of Steinsfurth, a few miles from the Rhine, across which France beckoned. Having requested Keith to procure horses, Frederick arose at 2:30, thinking to be well away before the rest of the royal party arose. Von Rochow was alerted, and in awkward scene confronted the prince. Von Rochow knew that Frederick had planned to flee, and Frederick knew that he knew, but both pretended that nothing was amiss. When Keith showed up with the horses, he pretended that they were for the pages.

The royal party continued on to Mannheim, the crisis seemingly averted. The next day was a Sunday, and as Frederick William was leaving church, Robert Keith's conscience got the best of him. He fell at the king's feet and confessed that the Crown Prince had attempted to flee. The king summoned von Rochow and asked why he had not been informed of these events. Von Rochow was made responsible for getting Frederick back to Prussian territory "dead or alive," and it was made very clear that should he fail, he would answer with his life. In what was for him a monumental act of self-restraint, Frederick William carried on with the royal tour as if nothing were amiss, no doubt waiting to take action until he was back in his own lands. He could not, however, resist baiting his son when he next saw him. He said he was surprised to see him, that he thought he was already in Paris. Frederick responded that if he had wanted to go to Paris, that is where he would be. In the meantime, it had been discovered that Peter Keith had deserted his post in Wesel and fled to the Netherlands.[104]

On August 12, Frederick was confined in the fortress at Wesel, the nearest Prussian-ruled town, where he his father interrogated him for the first time. According to Wilhelmina and one other account, the king threatened his son with a sword, and the Crown Prince was saved only by a general who interposed himself: "Kill me Sire, but spare your son." This seems rather melodramatic, and is unsupported by any corroborating evidence. "Why have you attempted to desert?" asked Frederick William. Frederick replied: "Because you have not treated me as you son but as a worthless slave." "Then you are nothing but a worthless slave," retorted the king. "I have as much honor as you; I have only attempted what you told me a hundred times you would do if you were in my place." Frederick maintained that France, rather than England was his ultimate destination. He was concerned, among other things, to protect his mother and sister, and his own correspondence with the English government. He also maintained that he would have returned once his father had assured him of better treatment. This was contradicted by Robert Keith's statement that the prince had told him "Once I am gone, I do not ever intend to return." Several subsequent interrogations only poked more holes in Frederick's story. Frederick William clearly feared the worst: that Frederick's flight and connivance with the English was a prelude to his own overthrow. This was never in the cards. Frederick's attempt to flee was strictly personal, a means of escaping the abuse of a brutal father. The

---

[104] He was convicted of desertion in absentia and condemned to death, and hanged in effigy. He would serve in the Portuguese army and return to Prussia after Frederick came to the throne. He was made a royal equerry, lieutenant-colonel and member of the Academy of Science, but still felt he had not been adequately compensated for his loyalty and sacrifice. He died in 1756.

English, far from conspiring against Frederick William, did everything in their power to dissuade Frederick from his desperate plans, precisely out fear of arousing the king's paranoia and suspicion.

In the meantime, Frederick William wrote to his wife about their son. The letter itself has been lost, but Wilhelmina recounts its contents: "I have had that rascal Fritz arrested; I shall treat him as his crime and cowardice dictate; I no longer recognize him as my son, he has dishonored me and my entire house, such a wretch no longer deserves to live." [105] Dissatisfied with Frederick's answers and attitude, the king ordered him confined in the fortress of Küstrin, east of Berlin. To get there from Wesel, however, required crossing territory not under Frederick William's control. Fearing further attempts to escape or to liberate the Crown Prince, he gave very precise orders: the coaches which carried Frederick and his guards were not to stop until they reached Prussian territory; when the prince needed to relieve himself, he was to do so in the open, well away from any trees or bushes that might provide cover for escape; cold food was provided to avoid stopping for meals at inns.

In the meantime, Frederick's accomplices were taken into custody. Peter Keith had already fled to the Netherlands. Robert Keith had saved himself from repercussions by informing the king of Frederick's attempted flight. Two of Frederick's fellow officers, lieutenants von Ingersleben and von Spaen were arrested for little more than having been the prince's friends. A young woman named Doris Ritter, on whom Frederick had had a brief crush and to whom he had given a number of gifts was ordered flogged through the streets of Potsdam and confined to the spin-house of Spandau for the rest of her life.[106]

Lieutenant von Katte was of course the big fish, and his behavior is very puzzling. Orders for his arrest were not issued until August 27, giving him plenty of time to flee. Indeed, as early August 15, a fellow officer, spying him in the street, asked him "What, are you still here?" to which Katte replied that he was leaving that night. Still, he remained in Berlin. Perhaps he naively believed that he would be exonerated. He had written earlier to Wilhelmina that he had done nothing to encourage Frederick's flight, and that he had refused to follow him. Prophetically, he would add, "If he [Frederick]

---

[105] Some historians have disputed the existence and/or contents of this letter, as we have only Wilhelmina's account of it. At the same time that the King is supposed to have written this letter, he also wrote a letter to the Queen's chief lady-in-waiting , in which adopted a much more tender tone: "I beg you to inform my wife [of Frederick's arrest] in a manner calculated not to alarm her." It would, however, be quite in keeping with Frederick William's character to have written both letters, as different as they may seem.

[106] She was released in 1733 after a petition from her father.

undertakes such a move, I shall answer with my head." He did, however, take the precaution of destroying his correspondence with the prince. The officer sent to arrest Katte gave him three hours warning, plenty of time to escape, and "was very annoyed" to find that he was still there.

Very precise instructions were given for Frederick's imprisonment at Küstrin: his books, flute, and sheet music were confiscated. None of his guards were to speak to him, the door was to be permanently locked and opened only three times a day. Food was brought at noon and 6:00 PM. At 8:00 PM he was to be brought a basin and water and had precisely seven and a half minutes to wash.

Frederick William could not and did not believe that there was no widespread conspiracy. Indeed, the queen and Wilhelmina were especially suspect. And even if they had not colluded in Frederick's attempted flight (in fact, Wilhelmina had tried strenuously to talk her brother out of it), there was still plenty of evidence of their collusion with England, which the king would surely take as evidence of complicity in a plot against him, not to mention many passages extremely critical of Frederick William. According to Wilhelmina, she and her mother destroyed all compromising evidence and then fabricated 600 or 700 letters in case the king wondered why there were no letters at all.

Frederick William insisted on charging his son with desertion. Indeed, whenever other words found their way to the record, such as *retraite* (retreat) or *retirade* (withdrawal), he angrily scratched them out and wrote "desertion" in their place. Auditor-General Christian Otto Mylius, was put charge of the investigation that would precede the inevitable court-martial. Together, he and the king came up with a list of 185 questions for the Crown Prince. A number of the questions focused on the issue of filial love and loyalty: Had the king's love for his son not been sufficient? Had he not done everything to make his son love him? To both questions Frederick responded that his father's love had been sufficient. He continued that although he had sometimes disobeyed the king, he had never held animosity towards him. Other questions focused on the issue of English complicity, and the roles played by the queen and Wilhelmina. Apart from everything else, what really angered Frederick William was the discovery that not only had the English agreed to pay his son's significant debts, but that Frederick had exaggerated his indebtedness by more than double. To the self-righteous and miserly king, this was almost as bad as Frederick's attempted flight. Throughout the questioning, Frederick proved very adept saying what his inquisitors wanted to hear while still not completely knuckling under. This of course only further infuriated his father. In the course of the questioning the existence of Frederick's substantial library was revealed. The king ordered it sold for the best price possible. Duhan, Frederick's old tutor who had been instrumental in acquiring the library, was exiled to far-off Memel (now in Lithuania) along with the librarian.[107]

The long list of questions concluded with a series specifically written by the king himself, and which made Mylius very uncomfortable, as they went well beyond the realm of normal legal procedure. At the interrogators' insistence, an unusual preamble was inserted into the record:

> Here at His Royal Highness's command follow the questions, formulated by His Majesty himself, which were put to the Crown Prince:
>
> Question 179: What does he [Frederick] deserve and what punishment does he expect?
>
> Answer: I submit myself to the will and mercy of the King
>
> Question 180: What does a man who soils his honor and plots a desertion deserve?
>
> Answer: I do not consider that I have been lacking in honor.
>
> Question 181: Were there not enough good examples [of desertion and its punishment] before his eyes in his regiment?
>
> Answer: Yes.
>
> Question 182: Does he still deserve to spend his days with men of honor?
>
> Answer: I regret what I have done, but I have never looked at things in that light.
>
> Question 183: Does he still deserve to be king?
>
> Answer: I cannot be my own judge.
>
> Question 184: Does he wish to be given his life, yes or no?
>
> Answer: I submit myself to the will and mercy of the King.
>
> Question 185: As he has by a breach of honor made himself incapable of succeeding to the throne, does he wish, to save his life, to abjure and renounce his succession in such a way that the renunciation will be confirmed by the whole [Holy] Roman Empire?

---

[107] When Frederick became king in 1740, he recalled his old tutor from exile. The two men remained close until Duhan's death in 1746.

Answer: I am not so devoted to life as that, but His Majesty the King will not treat me with such severity.

As these questions indicate, Frederick William was seriously considering disinheriting his son, in favor of his younger son William, who was very much his favorite. (Parenthetically, we might suppose that had he done so, William would have been subjected to the same sort of treatment as his brother.) It was also certainly not impossible that the king was considering the death penalty for his son, just as any other deserter would have been executed.

At the same time, Katte was being questioned, and he freely confessed to everything he had done to aid his friend. He averred that he had done whatever he could to restrain Frederick, and that he thought Frederick would never go through with it, and even if he did, he would return shortly of his own free will. He had never plotted or conspired against the king; his only motivation was to help his friend escape his father's anger. He was asked, "Does he [Katte] agree that, if he had been able, he would have escaped?" to which he answered, "If the Prince had left, I would have followed him, but I was always sure he would not go."

Due to the severity of the charges and their political implications, a special tribunal was convened for the court-martial made up of three generals, three colonels, three lieutenant-colonels, three majors, and three captains. Each rank had one vote collectively, and the chairman, another general, had a sixth vote. In their verdicts, delivered on October 27 and 28, there was almost complete unanimity concerning the underlings. Ingersleben was let off with a slap on the wrist, as his only "crime" had been to act as a go-between for Frederick and Doris Ritter. Spaen's offense was more serious — he had assisted Frederick in an earlier attempt to flee — and he was drummed out his regiment and sentenced to up to six years in prison. Peter Keith deserved death, and he was hanged in effigy as he had already fled the country. On Katte's punishment, however, there was significant disagreement. The majors, colonels, and lieutenant-colonels voted for death, while the captains and generals wanted life imprisonment. The chairman cast the deciding vote for life imprisonment, as the desertion had never actually occurred. The king was, however, not happy with this. He instructed the chairman to meet again and deliver another verdict. When they came back with the same verdict, Frederick William overruled them. In fact, he argued, according to the law, Katte should have his tongue ripped out with red hot tongs and be hanged, but instead he would be beheaded out of consideration for his family, as his father was a general and his grandfather a field marshal. He justified his decision:

While His Majesty is not in the habit of increasing sentences as a rule, but rather, usually reduces such whenever possible, this Katte is not only an officer of my army, but an officer of the *Garde Gens d'Armes*, therefore owing me an especial, personal loyalty over and above the ordinary. Since, however, this Katte had been in conspiracy with the rising sun [ie. Frederick], and intrigued with foreign ministers and ambassadors in the matter of desertion, and since it was not his job to plot with the Crown Prince, but on the contrary, he should have informed His Majesty. . . . His Majesty cannot see on what possible basis the Court Martial can have failed to pronounce the sentence of death. . . .His Royal Majesty also received a little schooling in his youth, and he learned the Latin tag: *fiat justicia et pereat mundus!* [Let justice be done though the world perish] . . . When the court martial has published this sentence on Katte, let him be told that His Majesty is sorry, but that it is better that he should die than justice be denied the world.

When he was informed that the sentence was attracting unfavorable comment in England, the king responded "If there were 100,000 Kattes, I would place them all on the rack." Frederick William did confirm the sentences of Spaen and Keith and pardoned Ingersleben.

When it came to judging Frederick, the court-martial was in a very tricky situation. They felt that they were not competent to judge the king's son and heir. The chairman of the court wrote in his sentence that they could not interfere in this matter, "especially since Your Majesty is better placed to punish Your son, both as father and as King." We may also surmise that the members of the court-martial felt trapped in a very dangerous predicament. If they pronounced a harsh sentence, who could predict what the king's attitude might be in the future? Might the mercurial and paranoid Frederick William eventually hold them responsible for meting out the punishment that he himself had pressed for? Moreover, what might happen to them if and when Frederick became king? How large a grudge would he bear? Indeed, Frederick William himself perceived this motive behind the court's prevarication:

I thought I had chosen men of honor who would not forget their duty, who would not worship the rising sun [ie. Frederick], and would only rely upon their consciences and the honor of their King. . . .They would have liked to gloss over the plan of the Prince and his toadies as a childish game which did not deserve such a punishment.

With Frederick's punishment still to be determined, preparations proceeded for Katte's execution at Küstrin. Katte's father, a general, pleaded for his life. The king wrote back to him: "Your son is a scoundrel and so is mine. What can we fathers do about it?" Katte's grandfather, a field marshal, also begged for his grandson's life, with like results. On November 4 the prisoner was transported from Berlin to Küstrin for execution. Throughout the journey, Katte impressed his escort with his composure and dignity, singing hymns and praying.

Meanwhile, in his cell, Frederick was oblivious to all this. Frederick William had taken personal charge of the details of the execution, including orders that his son was to witness it, that a soldier was to hold his head to make sure he saw everything. The scaffold was erected in the courtyard beneath Frederick's window. Early on the morning of November 6, an older officer entered Frederick's cell, and began to weep: "Oh my prince, my poor prince." Frederick believed that he himself was about to be executed: "So, speak, must I die then?" "No, my poor prince, no, you will not die, but you must allow the grenadier to take you to the window and keep you there." Years later, Frederick would reminisce: "That hateful citadel, no one spoke to me, dared speak to me, they left me alone with my sad reflections on my friend Katte." As Katte was led past Frederick's window, the prince cried out, "I beg of you a thousand pardons." "Monseigneur," replied Katte, "you owe me nothing." Katte was surrounded by officers of his regiment and the sentence was read aloud. He refused the customary blindfold, took off his wig and shirt, knelt on the sand and began to pray. The axeman severed Katte's neck with one stroke, an act which Frederick avoided witnessing only by passing out in a dead faint. The king had given instructions that the body and head were to be left lying on the sand until 2:00 in the afternoon, then removed and buried in a paupers' cemetery. The body was left as instructed, but someone at least covered it with a black cloth.

When he came to, Frederick was obviously distraught and did not eat or sleep for a period of days. His fate was still uncertain, and would remain so for some time. His execution was still not out of the question, but it does appear that Katte's had the effect of assuaging the king's wrath. It was also not inconceivable that Frederick would be disinherited in favor of his younger brother William, very much his father's favorite. Both courses of action would have posed considerable difficulties. Frederick's imprisonment and Katte's death were the talk of Europe, and most of it was unflattering to the king. While he did not care about public opinion, executing his own son and heir would have made his political situation much trickier. Depriving him of the succession while permitting him to live also posed grave complications.

What guarantee was there that when the old king died, Frederick would not retract his renunciation, thus plunging the kingdom into civil war? These complications, combined with his assuaged anger and Frederick's remorse would eventually result in an incremental rehabilitation of the Crown Prince in his father's eyes.

Frederick would remain at Küstrin for a period of eighteen months, until late February of 1732. At first, the restrictions on his freedom and activities were very strict. Weekdays, he was to rise at five o'clock in the summer and six in the winter. He was to put in a twelve-hour workday as a lowly clerk in the War and Estates Department (*Kriegs-und Domänenkammer*), the provincial administrative body, where he was to learn the practical business of finance and administration under the supervision of the director of the department. At 7:00 PM he had supper with his teachers, and lights out came at nine. Sundays he was to rise at four o'clock, and attend three church services during the day, with time for meditation and prayer in between. He was permitted a walk around the castle walls in the afternoon. Supper was at seven and he was to be in bed by eight or nine. His chaplain was instructed to dissuade him from his belief in predestination, but he and the prince's other teachers soon discovered that any attempt to force him was futile. The only way to achieve at least the appearance of the desired results was to work with Frederick, rather than against him. By the same token, Frederick was learning that in order to continue pursuing the interests dearest to his heart, such as the literature and philosophy of the Enlightenment, he needed to at least pretend to engage in those pursuits prescribed by his father.

Over time, as seemingly favorable reports of the prince's rehabilitation reached the king, the restrictions on Frederick's activities and freedoms were relaxed somewhat. In May of 1731, he received his first letter from his father, and in August, the king travelled to Küstrin for their first face-to-face meeting since their confrontation in Wesel in August of 1730. Frederick threw himself at his father's feet and was subjected to yet more reprimands. Finally, the king raised Frederick to his feet and embraced him. This was a kind of turning point in their relationship: Frederick seemed convinced that his father did indeed love him, in his own way, and the king was persuaded that his son's rehabilitation was sincere, if still incomplete. Frederick finally revealed to his father the full extent of his dealings with the British, and that the attempted desertion had been his idea and not Katte's. Frederick William outlined the likely consequences of a successful escape:

> Your mother would have suffered enormously, because I would naturally have suspected her of having knowledge of the affair; your sister [Wilhelmina] I would have locked up for life in a place where

neither sun nor moon would have shone; I would have marched into Hanover with my army and put everything to the torch and sword. . . . See, that would have been the fruit of your Godless and unthinking behavior.

The restrictions on Frederick's freedom were subsequently relaxed quite substantially. He was now permitted to go for walks outside the fortress and could go boating and shoot ducks. He could have two guests at dinner twice a week. Nevertheless, he was permitted no female company, and someone had to sleep in the same room with him.

The final test of Frederick's "re-education" was his willingness to submit to his father's choice of a marriage partner. While a British/Hanoverian marriage was still a theoretical possibility, Grumbkow and Seckendorff were still actively working against it. And the king needed little persuasion to deny his son that which he had long desired. In the end, Frederick William chose Elisabeth Christine of Brunswick-Bevern, a niece of the Holy Roman Empress. Frederick at this point had no inclination to marry but recognized very clearly that this was the price of his freedom. So, he submitted, but wrote of his reservations to Grumbkow, who had by now ingratiated himself with the heir to the throne:

> If I am forced to marry her, I will reject her away as soon as I am master, and I don't believe the empress will be too happy about that. I don't want a goose for a wife. Much more so, I want to be able to talk sense with her, or I shan't talk to her at all. So that is what is going to happen if I am forced, and no man can blame me for it, knowing that I was made to do something that was totally against my inclinations. . .

Descriptions of the princess's appearance and intelligence vary, but no one claimed that she was a great beauty or possessed anything more than average intelligence. To Wilhelmina, Frederick would write, "She is a decent sort and I wish her no ill, but I can never love her." And in another letter to Grumbkow: "I am sorry for the poor soul, for with all this, there will be one more unhappy princess in the world."

Frederick's reluctant agreement to marry the princess of Bevern was followed very closely by freedom from Küstrin in February 1732. Frederick had his commission in the army restored and spent the next several years garrisoned in the small town of Neuruppin. He and Elisabeth Christine were married in June of 1733, and true to his word, he tried to have as little to do with his wife as possible. For most of his time in Neuruppin, his wife resided in Berlin, and although they apparently did sleep together, no children were forthcoming. Despite some of his more extreme statements, Frederick did not hate his wife: "I should be the most contemptible of men if I did not sincerely respect my wife; for she is the gentlest creature and is always seeking how to please me." She clearly idolized him; she would write to her grandmother that "he is the greatest prince of our time."[108]

In 1736 Frederick and his wife relocated to a small castle in Rheinsberg, northeast of Berlin, where they lived for the next four years. Here Frederick was happier than at any other time in his life. He lived the life of a country gentleman and gathered around himself a group of close friends with similar interests: art, music, literature and philosophy. He began to correspond with many of the leading writers and intellects of the time, including Voltaire, the greatest of them all.

It would certainly be an exaggeration to say that relations between Frederick and his father were harmonious or that they came to see eye to eye. Nevertheless, in the years following Frederick's attempted flight and his imprisonment at Küstrin, they each came, perhaps grudgingly, to the realization that the other was not entirely in the wrong. The aging and increasingly sick king came to entrust more and more responsibility to his heir, and even came to express some pride in him:

> I am not that worried about living, for I leave behind me a son who possesses all the gifts for a good ruler. I should not have said that five years ago; he was still too young then; but, thanks be to God, he has changed and I am satisfied. He has promised me to maintain the army and I am reassured that he'll keep his word. I know he loves the soldiers, he has understanding and everything will go well.

For his part, Frederick's relations with his father were correct and obedient, even if he could express considerable bitterness towards him, especially to Wilhelmina.

Although only fifty-one, Frederick William I had been worn out by years of overindulgence in food, tobacco, and alcohol, not to mention the detrimental effects of his frequent bouts of rage. On his deathbed, he gave Frederick his last bits of political advice before telling him, "Was God not gracious to send me such a splendid and worthy son? My God, I die in peace, that I have such a worthy son and successor." Frederick was touched and flattered. No doubt the old king saw in his son's development the justification of rigorous discipline, his "tough love," so to speak. There may, indeed, be something to this point of view, if one is to judge by Frederick's career as king.

---

[108] Once Frederick became king in 1740, the two lived completely separate lives. The Queen had her own palace and court at Schönhausen palace. They saw each other very infrequently and only when necessary. In 1763, when Frederick saw his wife for the first time in six years, he remarked, "Madame has grown quite fat."

Frederick the Great remains one of the most enigmatic European rulers of the early modern period. He remained devoted to the arts and culture for his whole life, and was an enthusiastic and knowledgeable patron, as well as accomplished amateur musician and composer. He corresponded with and debated with the leading writers and intellects of his time. He was a prolific writer, in both verse and prose, although critics are virtually unanimous in their dismissal of his verse. At the same time, he proved to be utterly ruthless and opportunistic in his dealings with other rulers. Shortly after his accession, he invaded the wealthy and prosperous Habsburg province of Silesia, with absolutely no legal justification whatsoever, and despite treaty obligations that guaranteed the integrity of the Habsburg empire. The young prince who condemned the *Realpolitik* of Machiavelli in his first published work, *Antimachiavel* (written in the Rheinsburg years) would prove one of its most adept practitioners. The philosopher-king who proclaimed himself the "first servant of the state," had no compunction in sacrificing the lives of thousands in war. The British ambassador would note the "motley composition of barbarity and humanity that so strongly marks [his] character:"

> I have seen the King weep at a tragedy—as an individual he often appears and really is humane, benevolent, and friendly, yet the instant he acts in his Royal capacity these attributes forsake him, and he carries with him desolation, misery, and persecution wherever he goes.

What was the impact of his miserable childhood and youth? Did the abuse at the hands of his father make Crown Prince Frederick into King Frederick the Great? In the end, these questions are unanswerable, but there is one thing we can say with a fair degree of certainty. The experiences of his youth and childhood, the discord between his mother and father, his abuse at the hands of his father, the trauma of Katte's execution, and his eventual rehabilitation all taught him the essential importance of concealing his true self. He had very few close friends, and even those could be discarded when convenient.

Katte's execution likely showed him how dangerous it was, how vulnerable he became, when he became too emotionally invested in a relationship. It may well be that his father made him into a better general and ruler than he might otherwise have been. It is, however, absolutely certain that he made him into an unhappy and emotionally crippled man. Then again, it may be that being a good and happy man and being an effective ruler are mutually exclusive propositions, or at least so mutually incompatible that very few were able to be both.

Conclusion

In the previous chapters, we have examined five case studies in which relations between kings and their son were particularly toxic. In three of these cases (Charles VII and Louis XI, George I and George II, and Frederick William I and Frederick II), the son did eventually succeed his father as king. In the other two (Philip II and Don Carlos, and Peter the Great and Alexei), the son predeceased his father and thus never reigned. What can these case studies tell us about early modern Europe, about royal dynasties, and about family dynamics?

Academic historians are rightly very reluctant to draw "lessons" from the past. For one thing, the data of history are so vast and varied that one can find a "lesson" for just about case one might want to make. In addition, historical circumstances are always changing; no two situations are ever exactly the same, and thus what might be an appropriate conclusion to draw at one time would be exactly the wrong conclusion at another. So, if there are indeed general conclusions to be drawn from these case studies, they should not be seen as ironclad laws, or as guides to what to do or not to do in the future. With these caveats in mind, I think we can indeed draw some tentative conclusions from the cases we have examined.

The most obvious is that power and family harmony are extremely problematic bedfellows. It is certainly no accident that succession planning is the single most prominent topic in the literature on family business. As we have seen, only a third of family businesses survive through the second generation, and only ten per cent survive the third. When the power in question is in the form of hereditary monarchy, it places additional strains on family harmony, as the son may have to wait decades to assume the role for which he was born and for which he has been trained since birth.

As mentioned previously, the family practices of these early modern ruling dynasties also intensified this conflict. Early marriage to complete strangers, pressure to produce as many heirs as possible as soon as possible, and the subordination of personal desire and inclination and family harmony to the dictates of the "firm" all combined to magnify the stresses inherent in the king–heir, father–son relationship. It surely did not help that child rearing practices in these royal families meant that affective ties between parents and children were distant at best, and that in many cases, surely, lack of secure attachment produced emotionally stunted adults such as Louis XI or Frederick the Great. Animosity between mother and father, and the use of children as pawns in a power struggle, also reacted with these dynamics to further poison family harmony.

Developmental psychology also helps us to understand these conflicts. It is all too easy to forget that we are dealing with adolescent boys. As we know, brain development in the prefrontal cortex, which controls higher level executive functions, continues through adolescence. This explains in part risk-taking behavior among adolescent boys, which today might consist of excessive drinking or promiscuous sex, but in the cases examined here resulted in flight from and/or opposition to the king. At the same time, the heir, as a maturing adolescent, is confronted with the challenges of identity exploration.

One of the ways that this identity exploration could emerge was in deliberate opposition to the father. In several of the cases we have examined, heirs deliberately decided to do exactly the opposite of what their fathers had done. This was certainly the case with Louis XI and Charles VII, Frederick I and Frederick William I, Peter and Alexei, and to a lesser extent with George I and George II.

In Chapter 1, we noted research that indicated that the very qualities that make for a successful founder of a family business are milder forms of traits that might otherwise be considered psychopathic. This was certainly true of Peter the Great and Frederick William I. Even among those rulers whom we could not consider charismatic "founder" figures, the business of government clearly came before family harmony. If as we noted in Chapter 1, "The attributes of a healthy business system are usually at complete odds with attributes of a healthy family system," then it is certainly even more the case that the attributes of a hereditary monarchy are at odds with the attributes of a healthy family system.

In the sixteenth century the Florentine diplomat, politician, and political theorist Niccolò Machiavelli asserted in *The Prince* that a successful ruler could not always adhere to morality and expect to keep power:

> . . . if a prince wants to maintain his rule, he must learn how not to be virtuous, and to make use of this or not according to need. . . . [H]e should not deviate from what is good, but he should know how to do evil, if that is necessary.

In other words, the practical business of governing and maintaining power sometimes requires those who rule to commit acts which otherwise transgress morality. By the same token, the dynamics of hereditary monarchy as it was practiced in early modern Europe practically foreordained intergenerational conflict. Indeed, the five cases we have examined are not unique; they are unusual only in the depth of bitterness between fathers and sons and the seriousness of their consequences. There are literally dozens of other cases where hostility between king and heir was present, but did not reach the headline-grabbing proportions of our cases. In these five cases we see the normal state of affairs gone to extremes; they are different in degree, not kind, from the normal relations between kings and heirs.

To approach Machiavelli's point from a somewhat different angle: it may well be that the dysfunctional family life of these early modern royal dynasties was important in producing effective rulers. In other words, the qualities inherent in a loving father and in a devoted son may be inimical to the qualities necessary for an effective king. The emotional detachment of Louis XI or Frederick the Great quite possibly made them better rulers, but worse men. Had they been raised in loving and supportive families, it is conceivable that they would have trouble making the ruthless and sometimes unscrupulous choices that helped to ensure the success of their reigns. It was extremely difficult (and rare) to be both an effective ruler and a good man.

Throughout the preceding chapters, I have made numerous comparisons between early modern monarchies and contemporary family businesses. These comparisons are real and important, but imperfect. And indeed, the major differences between them help to explain in part why relations in royal families could become so toxic. In the realm of family business, a variety of options exist to smooth intergenerational tensions. Outside managers can be brought in, phased-in retirement can be executed, family members can be given decorative and lucrative, but essentially powerless positions, and so on. Even so, more family businesses fail in managing the transition from father to child than succeed at it. These options were not available to early modern rulers, at least not without grave risk. Should the worst come to pass, a family business can be sold or liquidated, and this, as we have seen, is quite a frequent occurrence. A kingdom, however, cannot be sold or placed into receivership. The very system which has produced these dysfunctional families persisted from generation to generation, and these tensions and hostilities continued to fester and intensify, with no solution in sight.

Tolstoy was wrong — these unhappy families were all unhappy in the same ways. Above all, what these episodes tell us is families can be happy, or they can be powerful, but it is exceedingly difficult to be both.

Selected Bibliography

What follows is not a comprehensive bibliography, but rather a selection of works that will allow the reader to pursue various topics further, if she or he so wishes, as well as to indicate some of the major works that I have used in my research.

Chapter 1

Ariès, Philippe. *Centuries of Childhood: a Social History of Family Life.* Trans. Robert Baldick. New York: Knopf, 1962.

Board, Belinda Jane and Fritzon, Katarina, "Disordered personalities at work," *Psychology, Crime and Law,* 11, 2004, 17–35.

Fritz, Roger. *Wars of Succession: The Blessings, Curses and Lessons that Family-Owned Firms Offer Anyone in Business.* Santa Monica, CA: Merritt Publishing, 1997.

Fleming, Quentin J. *Keep the Family Baggage out of the Family Business: Avoiding the Seven Deadly Sins that Destroy Family Businesses.* New York: Fireside, 2000.

Gordon, Grant and Nicholson, Nigel. *Family Wars: Classic Conflicts in Family Business and How to Deal with Them.* London: Kogan Page, 2008.

Handler, Wendy C. "Succession in family business: A review of the literature." *Family Business Review* 7 (2), 1994:133-56.

Hunt, David. *Parents and Children in History: The Psychology of Family Life in Early Modern France.* New York: Harper Torchbooks, 1970.

Kertzer, David I. and Barbagli, Mario, eds. *Family Life in Early Modern Times*, vol. 1. New Haven: Yale University Press, 2001.

Kets de Vries, Manfred F.R. *Family Business : Human Dilemmas In The Family Firm : Text And Cases.* London: International Thomson Business Press, 1996.

Kolb, Bryan, Ian Q. Whishaw, and G. Campbell Teskey. *An Introduction to Brain and Behavior.* 5th ed. New York: Worth Publishing, 2016.

Pollock, Linda. *Forgotten Children: Parent–Child Relations from 1500 to 1900.* Cambridge: Cambridge University Press, 1983.

Siegler, Robert S., Judy S. Deloache, Nancy Eisenberg, and Susan Graham. *How Children Develop.* 4th Canadian Edition. New York: Worth Publishers, 2014.

Steinberg, Lawrence D. *Adolescence.* 11th ed. New York: McGraw-Hill, 2017.

Chapter 2

Barbé, Louis A. *Margaret of Scotland and the Dauphin Louis.* London: Blackie and Son, 1917.

Basin, Thomas. *Histoire de Charles VII*, 6 vols. Paris: 188191.

Basin, Thomas. *Histoire des règnes de Charles VII et de Louis XI*, 4 vols. Ed. J. Quicherat. Paris: 185559.

Bernus, P. *Louis XI et Pierre de Brézé.* Angers: G. Grassin, 1912.

Champion, Pierre. *Louis XI.* Trans. W.S. Whale. London: Cassell, 1929.

Cleugh, James, *Chant Royal: The Life of King Louis XI of France (1423–1483).* New York: Doubleday, 1970.

Colville, A. "Jeunesse et vie privée de Louis XI." *Journal des Savants*, May–June 1908.

Commynes, Philippe de. *The Memoirs of Philippe de Commynes*, 2 vols. Ed. Samuel Kinser, Trans. Isabelle Cazeaux. Columbia, S.C.: University of South Carolina Press, 1969–73.

Kendall, Paul Murray. *Louis XI.* New York: Norton, 1971.

Legeay, U. *Histoire de Louis XI*, 2 vols. Paris: 1874.

Vale, M.G.A. *Charles VII.* London: Eyre Methuen, 1974.

Chapter 3

Bratli, C. *Philippe II, Roi d'Espagne: Ètude sur sa vie et son caractère*. Paris: H. Champion, 1912.

Cloulas, Ivan. *Philippe II*. Paris: Fayard, 1992.

Douais, C., ed. *Dépêches de M de Fourquevaux, ambassadeur du roi Charles IX en Espagne, 1565–72*, 3 vols. Paris: 1896–1904.

Forneron, Henri. *Histoire de Philippe II*, 4 vols. Paris: 1881.

Gachard, L.P. *Don Carlos et Philippe II*. Paris: 1867.

Grierson, Edward. *King of Two Worlds: Philip II of Spain*. London: Collins, 1974.

Kamen, Henry. *Philip of Spain*. New Haven: Yale University Press, 1997.

Parker, Geoffrey. *Philip II*, 3rd ed. Chicago: Open Court, 1995.

Pierson, Peter. *Philip II of Spain*. London: 1975.

Williams, Patrick. *Philip II*. New York: Palgrave, 2001.

Chapter 4

"The Tryal of the Czarewitz Alexis Petrovich, who was Condemn'd at Petersbourg, on the 25th of June, 1718." London: 1715.

"The Prerogative of Primogeniture . . . Written on the Occasion of the Czar of Muscovy's Reasons in His Late Manifesto for the Disinheritance of the Eldest Son from the Succession to the Crown." London: 1718.

Bushkovitch, P. "Power and the Historian: the Case of Tsarevich Aleksei 1716–1718 and N.G. Ustrialov 1845–1859." *Proceedings of the American Philosophical Society* 141 (1997):177-212.

Bushkovitch, P. *Peter the Great: the struggle for power, 1671–1725*. New York: Cambridge University Press, 2001.

Dmytryshyn, B. *Imperial Russia: A Sourcebook: 1700–1917*. New York: Holt, Rinehart and Winston, 1967.

Hughes, Lindsey. "A Note on the Children of Peter the Great." *Study Group on 18th-Century Russia Newsletter* 21 (1993): 10-16.

Hughes, Lindsey. *Peter the Great: A Biography*. New Haven: Yale University Press, 2002.

Klein, J., et al., eds., *Reflections on Russia in the Eighteenth Century*. Cologne, Weimar, Vienna, Bölau Verlag: 2001.

Korb, J.G. *Diary of an Austrian Secretary of Legation at the Court of Czar Peter the Great*, 2 vols. Trans. Count MacDonnell. London: 1863/1968.

McLeod Gilchrist, M. "Aleksei Petrovich and Afrosin'ia Fedorovna." *Slavonica* 1 (1994): 4766.

Oliva, L.J. *Russia in the Era of Peter the Great.* Englewood Cliffs NJ: PrenticeHall, 1969.

Oliva, L.J. *Peter the Great. Great Lives Observed.* Englewood Cliffs NJ: Prentice-Hall, 1970.

Perry, John. *The State of Russia under the Present Czar.* London: Cass, 1967.

Putnam, Peter, ed. *Seven Britons in Imperial Russia.* Princeton: Princeton University Press, 1952.

Vernadsky, G. *A Sourcebook for Russian History*, vol. 2. New Haven: Yale University Press, 1972.

Chapter 5

Arkell, Ruby L. *Caroline of Ansbach, George II's Queen.* Oxford: Oxford University Press, 1939.

Black, Jeremy. *George II: Puppet of the Politicians?* Exeter: University of Exeter Press, 2007.

Edwards, Averyl. *Frederick Louis, Prince of Wales 1707–1751.* London: Staples Press, 1947.

Hatton, Ragnhild. *George I: Elector and King.* London: Thames and Hudson, 1978.

Jordan, Ruth. *Sophia Dorothea.* New York: George Braziller, 1971.

Benjamin, Lewis. *The First George in Hanover and England*, 2 vols. London: Pitman and Sons, 1908.

Plumb, J.H. *The First Four Georges.* London: Batsford, 1957.

Quennell, Peter, *Caroline of England.* London: Collins, 1939.

Redman, Alvin. *The House of Hanover.* Toronto: Longman, Green, 1960.

Trench, Charles T. *George II.* London: Allen Lane, 1973.

Van Der Kiste, John. *King George II and Queen Caroline.* Stroud, Gloucestershire: The History Press, 1997.

Walters, John. *The Royal Griffin, Frederick, Prince of Wales 1707–51.* London: Jarrolds, 1972.

Young, Sir George. *Poor Fred, the People's Prince.* London: Oxford University Press. 1937.

Chapter 6

Frey, Linda and Frey, Marsha. *Frederick I: The Man and his Times*. New York: Columbia University Press, 1984.

Gaxotte, Pierre. *Frederick the Great*. Trans. R.A. Bell. New Haven: Yale University Press, 1942.

Gooch, G.P. *Frederick the Great: The Ruler, The Writer, The Man*. London: Longmans, Green, 1947.

Koser, Reinhold. *Friedrich der Grosse als Kronprinz*. Stuttgart: 1886.

Lavisse, Ernest. *The Youth of Frederick the Great*. Trans. Mary Bushnell Coleman. New York: AMS Press, 1972.

MacDonough, Giles. *Frederick the Great: A Life in Deed and Letters*. New York: St. Martin's, 2000.

Paret, Peter, ed. *Frederick the Great: A Profile*. London: Macmillan, 1972.

Ranke, Leopold von. *Memoirs of the House of Brandenburg and History of Prussia during the Seventeenth and Eighteenth Centuries*, 3 vols. Trans. Sir Alexander and Lady Duff Gordon. New York: Greenwood Press, 1968.

Ritter, Gerhard. *Frederick the Great: A Historical Profile*. Trans. Peter Paret. Berkeley and Los Angeles: University of California Press, 1968.

Rosental, Norman, ed. *The Misfortunate Margravine: The Early Memoirs of Wilhelmina, Margravine of Bayreuth, Sister of Frederick the Great*. London: Macmillan, 1970.

Schieder, Theodor. *Frederick the Great*. Trans. Sabina Berkeley and H.M. Scott. London: Longman, 2000.

Simon, Edith. *The Making of Frederick the Great*. London: Cassell, 1963.

Printed in the United States
By Bookmasters